1970

University of St. Francis
GEN 829.3 I73r
W9-ADI-549
3 0301 00032940 5

A READING OF *BEOWULF*

A READING OF
BEOWULF

EDWARD B. IRVING, JR.

Yale University Press New Haven and London 1968

Designed by Elizabeth Hacker,
set in Fairfield type,
and printed in the United States of America by
The Colonial Press Inc., Clinton, Massachusetts.
Distributed in Canada by McGill University Press.

Library of Congress catalog card number: 68–13911

For

Andrew, Edward, Alison the small one—
hu ða æþelingas ellen fremedon!

PREFACE

Just as an epic hero's identity (or a monster's) often becomes more clearly defined when we focus our attention on what he is not, the scope and intention of this book may become more apparent to the reader by way of some negative definitions. This book is not a compendium and critical analysis of previous commentary on *Beowulf,* even though a study of that kind would be of great usefulness. It is certainly not a close textual study of the poem, in the editor's sense of textual. For the sake of convenience I have accepted many traditional readings that I might have challenged in another context. The book does not attempt to provide a systematic and coherent metaphysic or esthetic for the poem that would satisfy the theorist.

My intention here was to lighten ship as much as possible in order to move unimpeded toward examining *Beowulf* closely, in its own terms as nearly as I could conceive them, and from several different angles of approach. The use of several approaches (they are reflected in the several chapters) has caused a certain unavoidable amount of overlapping, for which I should apologize; at the same time, I must admit that I was often pleased enough to find myself arriving at the same destination by different paths.

I have tried to keep in mind an audience composed not exclusively of professional students of Old English literature, but also of those interested in the epic genre, those attracted by our growing understanding of early medieval culture, or perhaps even a few members of that large body of professors of English who once "did" *Beowulf,* usually under duress, if there are any whose spark of interest in the poem has not been wholly extinguished.

It is chiefly for the benefit of the nonspecialist that I have furnished translations for the quoted passages, but the scholars may find commentary in capsule form in these translations and will enjoy watching me get into trouble. I could scarcely hide from them the fact that these translations are often pragmatic and tendentious; while I never knowingly gave up all responsibility for accuracy, I chose without scruple whatever best supported my argument of the moment wherever I could select from a range of connotations. I should confess the fact that I often, when in doubt as to the exact sense of a passage, stole a look at William Alfred's interesting translation of the poem (in the Modern Library volume, *Medieval Epics*) and sometimes received illumination. Whether my own translations reflect this I am not sure.

More than one idea in this book has been borrowed, sometimes unwittingly, from my old friend John C. Pope of Yale, but I had little choice. He was simply dead right about some things in the poem, and that was that. I am grateful to him for offering a number of suggestions for improving the manuscript. James L. Rosier, my colleague at Pennsylvania, has also been generous with useful comments on portions of the manuscript, as has my former student Gayle Byerly. Wayland Schmitt of the Yale University Press has furnished just the kind of supportive therapy an editor should provide. None of these kind people is to be held accountable for any remaining inadequacies, to which I myself must gloomily claim title.

A Summer Research Fellowship from the University of Pennsylvania was of great assistance while I was writing this book.

I should like finally to direct a special word of thanks to my wife for never dreaming of checking references, typing the manuscript, or preparing the index. She undertook instead to keep the author cheerful enough to do such chores for himself.

EDWARD B. IRVING, JR.

CONTENTS

CHAPTER ONE

The Text of Fate

> Everything, however, is what it is, and in the moral world leans for its existence on its contrary, as courage upon the possibility of cowardice, magnanimity on that of meanness.[1]

In one very important sense the Old English poem *Beowulf* is the product of centuries. Much of its meaning is directly traceable to the traditional style itself, especially to those rhetorical patterns inherited by the poet and used by him almost unconsciously. Such patterns tend to give shape to the events he describes and largely determine the nature of his comments on those events—largely but of course not entirely, for it would be unwise to deny originality to the *Beowulf* poet or to see him as merely a mechanical producer of verses. Yet before we move on to the evidence for his individual genius in later chapters it would be advisable to look first at some of the habitual constructions that in themselves create so much of the atmosphere of the poem. A great deal of what we see here in miniature will be exemplified on a larger scale in the poem as a whole.

Since a study of all the rhetorical patterns would be a book in itself, we must limit ourselves to examining a few impor-

1. W. Macneile Dixon, *Tragedy* (2d ed. London, C. Arnold & Co., 1925), pp. 110–11.

tant patterns. Most of this chapter will be concerned with negative constructions, since they have always been recognized as a striking feature of Germanic rhetoric. They surely play a major role in creating the impression of a persistent tone of irony and understatement that modern readers receive from this poetry, and they also have much to do with the usual representation of behavior in extreme terms. Particular attention will be given to that form of rhetorical heightening which is provided by the frequent combination of a negative clause or phrase with the adversative conjunction *ac* or with other words such as *hwæðre* or *swa þeah,* with the general meaning usually something like: "It is by no means A; on the contrary it is B." [2]

Defining the Ideal Hero

The poet may use negative terms to state or amplify his conception of what a true hero should be in two different ways. He may mention what a true hero is not or does not do (namely, bad things), or he may mention what a nonhero is not or does not do (namely, good things).

Let us begin by looking at some examples of the second kind of statement, in which characters or behavior more or less sharply defined as being the opposite of heroic are typi-

2. Some remarks by Randolph Quirk in the introduction to his book, *The Concessive Relation in Old English Poetry* (New Haven, Yale University Press, 1954), probably suggested this general subject to me originally. I should make clear that the study here means to be suggestive rather than statistically exhaustive. Not all negatives in the poem are included, for example, although those negatives that are made more emphatic by the addition of some intensifier (e.g. *nealles, no, ne . . . wiht*) have all been examined. Enough examples will be cited to point to a pattern, but examples that are of no special rhetorical interest will sometimes be omitted.

cally described. Two such examples occur in the passage in Hrothgar's sermon where the wicked king Heremod is described. Heremod is, to be sure, an antitype of the ideal king rather than of the ideal hero, but the passage illustrates the principle of the construction especially well.

> Ne wearð Heremod swa
> eaforum Ecgwelan, Arscyldingum;
> ne geweox he him to willan, ac to wælfealle
> ond to deaðcwalum Deniga leodum.[3]
> (1709b–12)

> Heremod was not so [helpful] to the descendants of Ecgwela, to the honorable Scyldings; he did not grow up to be what they wished—far from it, he grew into the slaughter and violent death of the Danish people.

In such a passage we can sense the full rhetorical effect of this adversative form of statement. Here we have the energetic clash of powerful opposites: growth, potentiality for good, and the people's will on one hand; murder and destructiveness on the other. On one side of the *ac* fulcrum is stated (in negative terms) one ideal of true kingship: that the king grow into what his people wish him to be, or that he grow to become loved by his people. On the other side of the *ac* the two tautological compounds *wælfealle* and *deaðcwalum* put particularly heavy stress on the anarchic violence we actually find in this king. Heremod's brutality leads to alienation from humanity, as we see in the following lines:

3. The text quoted here and throughout (unless otherwise indicated) is basically that of E. V. K. Dobbie, *Beowulf and Judith*, Anglo-Saxon Poetic Records, 4 (New York, Columbia University Press, 1953). Dobbie's text has been somewhat simplified for the purposes of this book by the omission of his brackets and italics in those cases where he is indicating readings from the Thorkelin transcripts. I do use brackets and italics in the customary way to indicate emendations of the manuscript, however, and I occasionally modify Dobbie's punctuation.

> breat bolgenmod beodgeneatas,
> eaxlgesteallan, oþþæt he ana hwearf,
> mære þeoden, mondreamum from.
> (1713–15)

> In furious anger he cut down his table-companions and comrades in arms, until at last he went off alone, that famous prince, away from men's joys.

Keeping two opposites alive simultaneously in the hearer's mind (in this instance, attributes of good and bad kings) may be the most important function of this form of rhetoric.

What we find here, and in many similar passages, is a form of statement in terms of extremes, where poetic energy may originate in the violent oscillation of sense from one extreme to another. Our second example, from the passage immediately following the lines we have quoted, shows just such an effect.

> Ðeah þe hine mihtig god mægenes wynnum,
> eafeþum stepte, ofer ealle men
> forð gefremede, hwæþere him on ferhþe greow
> breosthord blodreow. Nallas beagas geaf
> Denum æfter dome; dreamleas gebad
> þæt he þæs gewinnes weorc þrowade,
> leodbealo longsum. (1716–22a)

> Even though mighty God had favored him and exalted him beyond all men in joys of might and strength—still a bloodlust grew in his secret heart. He gave no rings to any Danes to gain glory; no, he lived to be joyless and to suffer pain for his violence, and longlasting affliction.

Here *hwæþere* serves as the rhetorical fulcrum. We are told that, on the one hand, God, by giving Heremod the same gift of heroic strength he has given Beowulf, has encouraged him and raised him above other men. But Heremod suddenly turns to evil, and to a particular form of evil (stinginess, not giving rings) that is peculiarly ironic in view of God's generosity toward him. The very willfulness of his behavior is signaled by the abrupt adversative transitions *hwæþere* and *nallas*. The expression "not giving rings" is in fact here a notable understatement, since Heremod apparently murders his subjects. We see the same expression later in Hrothgar's sermon, in the exemplum of the man corrupted by pride and the devil's arrows, a man much resembling Heremod:

> Þinceð him to lytel   þæt he lange heold,
> gytsað gromhydig,   nallas on gylp seleð
> fædde beagas,   ond he þa forðgesceaft
> forgyteð ond forgymeð,   þæs þe him ær god sealde,
> wuldres waldend,   weorðmynda dæl.   (1748–52)
>
> What he has held for so long now seems to him too little; he covets fiercely—never any longer does he proudly bestow ornamented rings; and he then ignores and scorns the created world, the great share of honors which God, Ruler of glory, had given him.

Even if we leave murder out of the picture, avarice itself is always something more serious than mere stinginess in Germanic heroic poetry; it represents the immoral violation of a personal relationship that happens to be symbolized by the exchange of material wealth. In this light we may with some justice regard avarice as a form of extreme behavior.

Unferth, the Dane who insultingly challenges Beowulf when he arrives at the great Danish hall of Heorot, is in some respects another antitype of the hero. One negative phrase of the type we are examining is applied to him:

> Gehwylc hiora his ferhþe treowde,
> þæt he hæfde mod micel,   þeah þe he his magum nære
> arfæst æt ecga gelacum.   (1166b–68a)
>
> Each of them trusted his spirit, that he had a great

> heart, even though he had not been honorable to his kinsmen in the play of sword-edges.

The past history of Unferth and his position at Hrothgar's court are by no means clear and may never be, but this remark by the poet, couched as it is in the habitual ironic mode of understatement, can hardly mean anything other than that Unferth has murdered his kinsmen.[4]

Again, the cowardly retainers who retreat from the dragon's attack and hide in the forest are certainly pictured as non-heroes:

> Næs ða lang to ðon
> þæt ða hildlatan holt ofgefan,
> tydre treowlogan tyne ætsomne.
> Ða ne dorston ær dareðum lacan
> on hyra mandryhtnes miclan þearfe,
> ac hy scamiende scyldas bæran,
> guðgewædu, þær se gomela læg,
> wlitan on Wilaf. (2845b–52a)

> It was not long before those slow in battle came out of the forest, ten cowardly faith-breakers together; they had not dared to make play with their spears in their lord's moment of great need; on the contrary, in shame they bore shields and armor to where the old man lay, and they looked at Wiglaf.

Now that the dragon is dead and the danger over, they come forward quickly, although when they were needed they did not come at all.[5] But the negative clause here (2848–49) serves to define very plainly their primary obligation as re-

4. The reader will find in Chapter Four a more extensive discussion of the larger context of this scene, the Great Banquet in Heorot.

5. The phrase *næs ða lang to ðon* or its equivalent seems at times to be a half-ironic way of describing a noticeably rapid sequence of events, as, for example, in *Beowulf* 2591 or *Guthlac* 903 ff.

tainers: to come to their lord's help when he has need of them. The clause with *ac* that follows presents a minor problem in interpretation, however. Precisely what is being opposed to what? If the emphasis in the preceding clause is on *scamiende,* is the chief contrast then between the retainers' previous shamelessness in flight and their present feelings of mortification? More interesting is the possibility of an ironic contrast between the help they did not bring when it was so urgently needed and the useless shields and corselets they now officiously carry to the place where Beowulf lies dead.

Another passage in which the retainers' duty is stated flatly and unequivocally by means of a negative phrase is the following:

> Nealles him on heape h*a*ndgesteallan,
> æðelinga bearn, ymbe gestodon
> hildecystum, ac hy on holt bugon,
> ealdre burgan. (2596–99a)

> In no way did those war-comrades, those sons of noblemen, take their stand around him in formation as fighting-men should; no, they fell back into the forest and took care of their own lives.

This is again rhetorical statement in terms of the polarizing of possible behavior into two extreme kinds. The alliteration here of *hildecystum* and *holt* draws our attention to the alternatives: to stand in military formation or to go hide in a forest. As so often in Old English poetry, and in Germanic literature generally, this kind of statement vividly dramatizes a character's free choice of action, at the same time that a phrase like *aeðelinga bearn* reminds us of his hereditary aristocratic obligations. Heroic life is consistently presented as a series of such radical choices.

Another possible violation of heroic decorum, though in this instance certainly a venial one, may be the storm of emotion that overwhelms King Hrothgar when he says farewell to

Beowulf, as the hero takes leave of Denmark and returns home.

> Wæs him se man to þon leof
> þæt he þone breostwylm forberan ne mehte,
> ac him on hreþre hygebendum fæst
> æfter deorum men dyrne langað
> beorn wið blode. (1876b–80a)
>
> That man was so dear to him that he could not hold back the surge in his breast; on the contrary, a secret longing in his bosom for the dear man strained against rational restraints, burned in his blood.

Beowulf's feelings on this occasion are not described. Assuming that he too feels some measure of grief, one may perhaps see a contrast between his stoical behavior and Hrothgar's yielding to the expression of emotion (a moment before we were told of Hrothgar's tears). But the more important contrast here is between youth and age (often referred to in this part of the poem[6]) rather than between heroic self-restraint and emotionalism. Hrothgar's long experience in disappointment has taught him that they will probably never see each other again; Beowulf is still too young to see the world this way. The rhetorical structure of this sentence differs somewhat from the structure of the previous examples, in that here we have a parallel rather than the usual contrast, for the ideas of the dearness of the man, the fight for self-control, and the hot wave of emotion are really to be found here on both sides of the *ac* fulcrum. Possibly the *ac* construction in this instance may serve simply to emphasize in a general way the strength of Hrothgar's feelings, since such a construction ordinarily suggests some form of emotional tension.

Let us turn now to some examples of the more common

6. For example: *ealdum infrodum* 1874; *oþþæt hine yldo benam / mægenes wynnum* 1886b–87a.

way of defining the heroic ideal by negations, this time by negating or denying the nonheroic. It goes without saying that courage is the most important heroic attribute; consequently there are a number of negative expressions that allude to the hero's courage in terms of his "not fearing" or not showing other signs of cowardice.[7] Not only phrases but *un* compounds like *unforht* or (in *The Battle of Maldon*) *unearg* (uncowardly) fall into the same category.

In *Maldon,* as I have suggested elsewhere, constant reminders of the possibility of flight from battle do much to increase the dramatic tension of the poem.[8] There, of course, such verbal reminders operate in the context of a narrative that in fact describes mass flights. While the flight of the cowardly retainers does of course take place in *Beowulf,* it does not have as much relative importance in the poem; it is merely one dark background stroke in the tremendous heightening and brightening of the figure of Beowulf. Even though they are used less intensively than in *Maldon,* such formulas probably serve to keep alive at the edge of the audience's consciousness the thought that it is after all normal behavior to be frightened under such conditions.

From an assortment of negative phrases describing other nonheroic attributes, we might construct an interesting model of the Anglo-Saxon nonhero: a man who kills his companions over drinks and secretly weaves an ensnaring net of malice for others; who has a ferocious temper and the bad manners to find fault with gift swords.[9] Behavior like this may well have

7. For example: *nis þæt seldguma* 249 (that is no hanger-about in the hall [but a fighter]); not being frightened but . . . 2967b–69; not fleeing a step but . . . 2524b–27a; not dreading battle 2345–49a; not flinching from violence 1537; not caring about life 1442, 1536.

8. Edward B. Irving, Jr., "The Heroic Style in *The Battle of Maldon,*" *Studies in Philology,* 58 (1961), 457–67.

9. Respectively: *nealles druncne slog / heorðgeneatas* 2179b–80a; *nealles inwitnet oðrum bregdon / drynum cræfte* 2167–68a; *næs him hreoh sefa* 2180b; *nales wordum log / meces ecge* 1811b–12a.

been common in England in the seventh or eighth century, perhaps even common enough to be called a realistic norm. But, since such speculation takes us beyond the bounds of our poem, it would be more profitable to examine these expressions in context. Three of them happen to occur in the same scene.

The final lines (2101–62) of Beowulf's report to Hygelac after he has returned to Geatland project an image of Hrothgar as ideal king, stressing as they do the grief Hrothgar had to suffer under the oppression of Grendel, the warmth of his affection for Beowulf, and, above all, his great generosity. The speech comes to its climax when Beowulf orders Hrothgar's splendid gifts to be brought into the hall and presents them formally to his uncle Hygelac. Hrothgar's magnanimity is used here (as nearly everything in the poem is used sooner or later) to reveal to us Beowulf's own virtues: in this instance, his love, generosity, and loyalty.

The occurrence of three of our negative expressions in this triumphant scene is of interest partly because it reveals what comes into the poet's mind as he contemplates uncle and nephew. A central theme all through this passage is fidelity, symbolized as usual by the exchange of gifts, and, again as usual, we are urged to think both of the affection that inspires the gifts and the obligations they entail. It is entirely characteristic of Old English poetic style that fidelity must be defined or set off or deepened in meaning by strong hints of its opposite.

In his presentation speech to Hygelac, Beowulf mentions that the arms Hrothgar has given him once belonged to Heorogar, Hrothgar's older brother, and that Hrothgar had not wished to give them to Heorogar's son Heoroweard. We are not told what Hrothgar's reason for this last decision may have been, but later versions of the story in Saxo Grammaticus and in the saga of Rolf Kraki make it seem at least possible that Heoroweard, like his cousin Hrothulf, may also have been eying his uncle's throne.[10] In any event the reference to the Scylding royal family must at least have reminded the poet of some plotting nephew, whether Heoroweard or Hrothulf, for otherwise the ensuing description of Beowulf as a nephew loyal to Hygelac would have had little point.

Swa sceal mæg don,
nealles inwitnet oðrum bregdon
dyrnum cræfte, deað ren[ian]
hondgesteallan. Hygelace wæs,
niða heardum, nefa swyðe hold,
ond gehwæðer oðrum hroþra gemyndig.
(2166b–71)

> This is how a kinsman should behave—and not be secretly weaving a treacherous net for others or laying a deathtrap for a comrade. His nephew [Beowulf] was indeed very loyal to war-toughened Hygelac, and each of them was attentive to the happiness of the other.

This passage is a good example of the rhetorical effect we have been discussing. The semantic rhythm here is positive (*swa sceal mæg don*)—negative (the *nealles* clause)—positive (Beowulf's own loyalty). From a different point of view one could see it as constructed in another way: the first two parts are statements of ethical alternatives, while the third is a specific instance of choice. Beowulf has chosen one of the two possible modes of behavior.

What is done in miniature in this brief passage is done on a larger scale in the scene as a whole. Into this scene of absolute and dedicated fidelity in Hygelac's hall the poet introduces a flood of dark reminders of treachery in Heorot, chiefly

10. See R. W. Chambers, *Beowulf: An Introduction* (3d ed. with a supplement by C. L. Wrenn, Cambridge, The University Press, 1959), pp. 29–30.

through references to Hrothgar (2155), to Hrothgar's queen Wealhtheow and the marvelous necklace she gave Beowulf at the great banquet, and to an unnamed hypothetical non-hero who bears some resemblance both to Unferth and to the evil Danish king Heremod, as we can see in the following passage:

> Swa bealdode bearn Ecgðeowes,
> guma guðum cuð, godum dædum,
> dreah æfter dome, nealles druncne slog
> heorðgeneatas; næs him hreoh sefa,
> ac he mancynnes mæste cræfte
> ginfæstan gife, þe him god sealde,
> heold hildedeor. (2177–83a)

> Thus Ecgtheow's son [Beowulf], a man known in battles, showed his bravery in heroic deeds, lived to gain glory; never was he the one to strike comrades over drinks by the hearth; his temper was never savage. No, with the greatest strength of mankind this valorous man kept safe the abundant gifts which God had given him.

Strength and courage are essential to the hero but they are not enough. Heremod and Unferth, both fatally undisciplined, showed their aggressiveness in the violent disruption of social order; Beowulf, while assuredly a veteran warrior, a *guma guðum cuð,* saved his fighting for the battlefield. The negative image of the nonhero is needed here for clearer definition of the moral requirements of true heroism, as they are embodied in Beowulf.

Elsewhere and in somewhat different ways, negative phrases are used to differentiate Beowulf from other men. The Danish coastguard's awed reactions to his first sight of Beowulf, for example, are largely conveyed in a rapid series of expressions that define the nature of the hero by excluding the expected, the normal, the usual, by saying what he is not:

No her cuðlicor cuman ongunnon
lindhæbbende; ne ge leafnesword
guðfremmendra gearwe ne wisson,
maga gemedu. Næfre ic maran geseah
eorla ofer eorþan ðonne is eower sum,
secg on searwum; nis þæt seldguma,
wæpnum geweorðad, næf*ne* him his wlite leoge,
ænlic ansyn. (244–51a)

> Never have shield-bearers arrived here in a more open way, yet you were not sure of the permission of our fighting-men or the consent of our kinsmen. I never saw a bigger man on earth than one of you, that fighter in armor. He is certainly no hall-lounger, unless his looks belie him, his noble face.

How can the puzzled coastguard establish the identity of these strange visitors? He can do it only by excluding them from successive categories. Their behavior is entirely different from that of previous visitors to Denmark, who apparently have come either as deferential guests or as furtive spies. But these men come openly and confidently; they walk as if they already had the password. Indeed all the password they need walks among them in the person of Beowulf. And so at the end of this passage the coastguard singles out Beowulf from the rest of the band: he is bigger, braver, of a more resolute and heroic appearance. Yet it is interesting to see how such a luminous and compelling image is constructed out of negative expressions.

Later Wulfgar, who keeps the door of Hrothgar's hall, further distinguishes Beowulf and his men from other visitors. After a moment's inspection, he concludes that these men are not only brave men but that they are responsible and honorable volunteers rather than *wreccan,* that type so common in Germanic literature, roving professional adventurers or refugees from foreign vendettas.

Wen ic þæt ge for wlenco, nalles for wræcsiðum,
ac for higeþrymmum Hroðgar sohton. (338–39)

I believe that you have come to see Hrothgar out of sheer pride and greatness of spirit, certainly not as adventurers in exile.

Another negative construction (if we may take *forhicge* as expressing an essentially negative idea) sets Beowulf apart from ordinary warriors in respect to his method of fighting:

Ic þæt þonne forhicge . . .
þæt ic sweord bere oþðe sidne scyld,
geolorand to guþe, ac ic mid grape sceal
fon wið feonde ond ymb feorh sacan,
lað wið laþum. (435–40a)

I have no intention on that occasion . . . of carrying any sword or wide yellow-bordered shield to battle; on the contrary, I will be obliged to grapple with the fiend with my hands and fight for life, one enemy against another.

Other warriors in heroic poetry make much of the process of assembling their weapons for battle, but Beowulf is different. The difference is most clearly dramatized in the half-ironic "disarming of the hero" scene just before the fight with Grendel, in the course of which Beowulf methodically divests himself of all the traditional accouterments of the epic fighter in order to meet the monster with his bare hands.

Finally, as king, Beowulf differs from others in his response to Queen Hygd's offer to him of the throne of the Geats:

No ðy ær feasceafte findan meahton
æt ðam æðelinge ænige ðinga,
þæt he Heardrede hlaford wære
oððe þone cynedom ciosan wolde;
hwæðre he hi*ne* on folce freondlarum heold,

> estum mid are, oððæt he yldra wearð,
> Wedergeatum weold.[11] (2373–79a)

> None the sooner could the destitute Geats prevail on the prince in any way to become Heardred's lord or willingly to accept the kingdom; no, he [Beowulf] went on to maintain Heardred in his proper place in the nation by his friendly advice and respectful affection, until he [Heardred] grew up to rule over the Storm-Geats.

Placed in a situation of this kind, where the king is only a child, most men would yield readily to the reasonable pleas of their people to assume power. Many men would be only too glad to seize the royal authority. But Beowulf goes to the other extreme: far from plotting to seize power for himself, he devotes himself to keeping young Heardred in power by his friendly counsels. He will not accept a position that he thinks he does not deserve, even when it is freely (and probably legally) offered to him by a majority of the Geats and by their queen.

Defining the Monstrous

Just as the hero can be effectively defined by the use of negatives, so negatives can serve to describe the hero's chief antagonist Grendel, especially in his relation to some familiar human norm. In fact it may well be that the essential reality of Grendel is best understood in terms like these, for in many ways Grendel could be called an instance of Negative Man. As a fighter and as a "visitor" to the Danish hall that he

11. In line 2377 Dobbie reads *him,* most other editors *hine,* for MS *hī.*

devastates, he is often treated ironically as a peculiar kind of human warrior. But he is set off from ordinary warriors in one respect, for example, because, as Beowulf points out, for all his courage and ferocity he does not even know how to fight with a sword:

> Nat he þara goda þæt he me ongean slea,
> rand geheawe, þeah ðe he rof sie
> niþgeweorca; ac wit on niht sculon
> secge ofersittan. (681–84a)

> He has no knowledge of how to fight properly, to swing sword against me and hew at my shield, even though he is brave in his savage attacks; no, tonight we must do without swords, the two of us.

Not only is Grendel cut off from the normal concerns of a Germanic warrior by his ignorance of the use of weapons, but he is further excluded from the ranks of noblemen because he has no father, or at least his father's name is not known by men.

> þone on geardagum Grendel nemdo*n*
> foldbuende. No hie fæder cunnon,
> hwæþer him ænig wæs ær acenned
> dyrnra gasta. (1354–57a)

> People named him Grendel in the old days. They knew nothing of any father, whether any such mysterious spirit had ever been born for him.

Since, in all epic poetry, a patronymic is at least as necessary to a hero as a sword, Grendel's title to heroic identity is wholly obscured.

Unlike normal men, Grendel does not pay the Danish people the honor they surely deserve, but instead he obeys his own fierce impulses in disposing of them:

Nymeð nydbade, nænegum arað
leode Deniga, ac he lust wigeð,
swefeð ond sendeþ, secce ne weneþ
to Gardenum. Ac ic him Geata sceal
eafoð ond ellen ungeara nu,
guþe gebeodan. (598–603a)

He extorts toll, and honors no man of the Danish nation; quite the contrary, he does just as he pleases, butchers and sends to death (?), expecting no resistance from the Spear-Danes. But I am the one who will show him very soon now the strength and courage and fighting-power of Geatish men.

In this passage we see Grendel beyond the control of any of the Danes and equally beyond the control of any code of conduct that would be binding on noblemen.[12]

Grendel and his mother of course live somewhat beyond the pale, in a lake-bottom home which no human being has ever seen:

No þæs frod leofað
gumena bearna, þæt þone grund wite.
(1366b–67)

No one of the sons of men lives so old and wise that he knows the bottom [of that lake].

The range of human experience and wisdom cannot even reach the place where Grendel lives.

12. In the latter part of this passage we may note incidentally another use of the *ac* construction that *Beowulf* happens not to illustrate very impressively. Here the *ac* is an expression of the heroic response, signaling the deliberate placing of Beowulf's will (or Geatish will, since the alliteration in line 601 surely reinforces the contrast between Geats and Danes) against this wildly careering force of evil. Cf. also lines 1269–70. *Beowulf* has no other good examples, but this "heroic adversative" can be found in other poems; several of Juliana's speeches have this form (*Juliana* 105–16, 147–57, for example).

As was already suggested, several negative expressions of this kind are closely related to the poet's consistent and ironic presentation of Grendel as a mock thane, and serve to provide particularly compact and vivid statements of the irony. Grendel is first shown to us as a wretched exile from the human race, living in the darkness of social disgrace and spiritual isolation, perpetually bearing God's anger. Infuriated by the harmonious sounds of human joy in Heorot, he comes first as a "guest" to visit the hall; perhaps he is even viewed ironically as the good neighbor paying a social call on the new arrival (Heorot has just been completed and occupied). When the Danes abandon Heorot, Grendel "rules" there; it is in the context of a passage describing the wholesale evacuation of the hall by the terrified Danes that Grendel is called a "hall-thane" (142). But Grendel's authority in Heorot has limits.

Heorot eardode,
sincfage sel   sweartum nihtum;
no he þone gifstol   gretan moste,
maþðum for metode,   ne his myne wisse. (166b–69)

He lived in Heorot, that treasure-bright hall, in the black nights; but he was never permitted to draw near the gift-throne or the treasure because of the Lord, and did not know pleasure in it.[13]

Even though Grendel seems to be living in the hall, he cannot (perhaps has no wish to) approach the gift-throne—that is to say, make proper use like an ordinary retainer of the treasure for which Heorot is so famous. While the much-discussed

13. See the note in the second supplement of Fr. Klæber, *Beowulf and the Fight at Finnsburg* (3d ed. Boston, D. C. Heath, 1950), p. 465, and John C. Pope's remarks on this passage in his review of Arthur G. Brodeur's *The Art of Beowulf* (*Speculum,* 37 [1962], 415), where he paraphrases line 169b as "he feels no gratitude for gifts (or, as I prefer to think, no affection for treasure)."

phrase *for metode* might possibly mean "in the presence of a secular lord (who is distributing treasure to his men)," more likely it refers to God and hence suggests that a supernatural order in the world must finally set limits to the outrages of such creatures as Grendel.

In another well-known passage, the same kind of irony is used to bring out Grendel's distance from mankind. It is almost as if the Danes in the poem (or at least the audience listening to the poem) were being invited to try to bring Grendel into some meaningful and familiar pattern of reference, some relationship to the structure of human society. In this case the frame of reference is the Germanic wergild system of monetary compensation for wrongs done.

Sibbe ne wolde
wið manna hwone   mægenes Deniga,
feorhbealo feorran,   fea þingian,
ne þær nænig witena   wenan þorfte
beorhtre bote   to ban*an* folmum,
[ac se] æglæca   ehtende wæs,
deorc deaþscua,   duguþe ond geogoþe,
seomade ond syrede,   sinnihte heold
mistige moras;   men ne cunnon
hwyder helrunan   hwyrftum scriþað.
(154b–63)

He wished no peace-settlement with any man of the Danish force, and he refused to remove the deadly evil or to compound by making payment. No wise man had any cause to hope for the bright remedy from that butcher's hands! Far from it—that terrifying creature, the dark death-shadow, kept on plaguing them, young and old, tirelessly lying in wait and ambushing them, ruling the misty moors in endless night. Men do not know where such mysterious hellions go in their roamings.

The lines just preceding this passage have strongly emphasized the violence of Grendel's feud with Hrothgar (*heteniðas, fyrene, fæhðe, sæce*). But, as we see later in the poem in the story of Beowulf's own father Ecgtheow, human feuds can be resolved and peace can be restored, if the participants in feuds want peace. But *sibbe ne wolde*—Grendel does not want peace, nor indeed relationship of any sort with any human being, no matter how such relationship is (ironically) extended to him. Denied here emphatically is the (ironic) hope that he will abide by human laws and pay the fine for his murders, even though the idea is toyed with almost humorously for a few lines.

The verses that follow (here I assume that the *ac se* supplied by most recent editors in line 159 to replace letters lost from the manuscript is almost certain) move us abruptly, in the usual way of an *ac* construction, away from this temporary accommodation with mankind, this way of seeing Grendel as somehow human. A man as well as a monster could be called an *æglæca,* an inspirer of fear—Beowulf himself is called one in line 2592—but no man is a *deorc deaþscua,* a dark shadow of death. And then we move out quickly even further from the human center into perpetual night, the misty moors, all those areas beyond any ordering powers of the human imagination. As we cannot know his motives, so we cannot know Grendel's dwelling-places: *men ne cunnon.*

An ironic transaction of a somewhat similar kind is described by Beowulf in his report to Hrothgar on the fight with Grendel. In order to save his life, Grendel had left his arm behind when he fled. The act of leaving his arm seems to be represented as some kind of involuntary offering (and, if we take *feasceaft* literally, all he could pay) but this down payment nets him nothing.

No þær ænige swa þeah
feasceaft guma frofre gebohte;

no þy leng leofað laðgeteona,
synnum geswenced, ac hyne sar hafað
mid *ny*dgripe nearwe befongen,
balwon bendum. Ðær abidan sceal
maga mane fah miclan domes,
hu him scir metod scrifan wille.
(972b–79)

But the destitute man did not purchase any comfort by this action; the horrible plunderer, crippled by sin, lived none the longer for it; on the contrary, pain had seized him tight in an inescapable grip, in the bonds of death. And in that place he must wait, that man branded with crimes, to see how bright God will wish to judge him at the Great Judgment.

Perhaps it is significant that the words *guma* and *maga,* common words for man, are applied to Grendel in this passage, for what is stressed here is Grendel's sinfulness (*synnum geswenced, mane fah*) and his ultimate responsibility for his actions in the face of the Last Judgment. However badly Grendel may seem to fit the usual patterns of human society and behavior, he is not an animal; in some higher scheme of order he is seen as human and therefore responsible. Yet, just as the sacrifice of his arm gains him no respite, his suffering and death gain him no pity. A total failure as hero, he wins no glory or reputation in the eyes of others; he does not even win their momentary sympathy:

No his lifgedal
sarlic þuhte secga ænegum
þara þe tirleases trode sceawode.
(841b–43)

His parting from life did not seem pitiable in any way to any of the men who looked at the trail of one devoid of glory.

These curious ironic expressions, constantly bringing as they do the possibility of Grendel's humanity into the periphery of our consciousness even in the act of emphatically denying it, have considerable importance in the meaning of the poem, as we shall see when we look more closely at Grendel in Chapter Three. For, despite all his inhuman and monstrous attributes, it is ultimately Grendel's human ancestry that makes him the kind of monster he is—the renegade who has deserted humanity to live in the wilds of exile, the frantic destroyer of the society he was once symbolically driven from in his ancestor Cain, the bearer always of the mark of murderer, and the bearer too of the mark of man.

The Defeat of Expectation

The emphatic negative or negative-plus-adversative is often used in the poem to express a conflict of wish, hope, or intention with actuality, a conflict, that is, where what someone expects to happen does not happen.[14] In *Beowulf*

14. The formula survives into early Middle English literature. Two examples from Laʒamon:

> He wænde mid his crucche us adun þrucche.
> Ah tomærʒe, wæne hit dæi buð, duʒeðe scal arisen
> and oppenien ure castel-ʒæten; . . .
> Þus him ispac Octa wið his iuere Ebissa,
> ah al hit iwrað oðer þene heo iwenden.

(Quoted from *Selections from Laʒamon's Brut,* ed. G. L. Brook [Oxford, Clarendon Press, 1963, pp. 58–59].)

I had completed this chapter before reading Richard N. Ringler, "*Him Seo Wen Geleah:* The Design for Irony in Grendel's Last Visit to Heorot," *Speculum, 41* (1966), 49–67, which parallels my own arguments in this section at an extraordinary number of points and which goes into this particular device of rhetorical irony at even greater length. I have chosen to leave my own version unrevised on the grounds that an important point is even more effectively established by our two independent approaches.

the expectations of the evil characters are most often frustrated. Since Grendel is the only evil character whose mental processes we are told much about, it is not surprising that we are frequently told of his intentions and what happens to them. R. E. Kaske has already called attention to this pattern in speaking of Grendel's lack of *sapientia:* "There is a continual contrast between what Grendel hopes or expects and what actually happens, a sort of ὕβρις in him that contributes to poetic effect even if, logically, he could not be expected to foresee the outcome." [15] In a footnote to this passage Kaske adds a list of six passages of this type. Three of them contain the word *mynte* (intended):

1. mynte se manscaða manna cynnes
sumne besyrwan in sele þam hean.
(712–13)

> The evil attacker intended to entrap some human being in that high hall [but he soon meets a rough reception from Beowulf, lines 718–19].

2. mynte þæt he gedælde, ærþon dæg cwome,
atol aglæca, anra gehwylces
lif wið lice, þa him alumpen wæs
wistfylle wen. (731–34a)

> The atrocious demon intended, before day came, to separate the life from the body of each one of them, when his hope of eating his fill came true.

But here the poet immediately denies Grendel any possibility of the fulfillment of his expectation:

> Ne wæs þæt wyrd þa gen
þæt he ma moste manna cynnes
ðicgean ofer þa niht. (734b–36a)

15. "*Sapientia et Fortitudo* as the Controlling Theme of *Beowulf*," *Studies in Philology,* 55 (1958), 439.

It was not then destined that he be allowed to devour more human beings after that night.

3. Mynte se mæra, [þ]ær he meahte swa,
widre gewindan ond on weg þanon
fleon on fenhopu. (762–64a)

The renowned creature intended, if he could, to get farther away and flee from there into the depths of the fen.

Grendel wants to make his escape from Beowulf's crushing grip but is prevented from doing so by the hero until he finally breaks away mortally wounded. Lines 791–94a, describing Beowulf's unwillingness to let Grendel escape alive, seem to me to be the appropriate second element in this pattern of defeated expectation, although Kaske suggests lines 805a–08, a more general statement of destiny.

While these *mynte* formulas are quite remarkable in their similarity, other rhetorical patterns of the same kind appear in the account of Grendel's attack on Heorot. The passage, for example, that describes Grendel first reaching toward Beowulf after he has entered the hall is not free from difficulties of interpretation, but what is perfectly clear is that Grendel expects to find another succulent meal in the man he is about to pick up and that instead he encounters the wholly unexpected:

Forð near ætstop,
nam þa mid handa higeþihtigne
rinc on ræste, ræhte ongean
feond mid folme; he onfeng hraþe
inwitþancum ond wið earm gesæt.
Sona þæt onfunde fyrena hyrde
þæt he ne mette middangeardes,
eorþan sceata, on elran men
mundgripe maran.[16] (745b–53a)

16. This puzzling passage may very well demand emendation, but here I have tried to make some sense of the text as it stands.

* BEOWULF'S DEFEATING THE MONSTERS COULD BE A WAY OF SHOWING READERS THAT NO MATTER HOW STRONG THE ANTAGONIST MAYBE, MAN SHALL PREVAIL *

> He stepped up closer, seized then with his hand the brave man in his bed, the enemy reached toward [him] with his hand; he [Beowulf] quickly seized [him] hostilely and sat up against his arm. At once the shepherd of crimes discovered that he had never met on earth, anywhere in the world, a greater hand-grip.

Frustrated in his attack, Grendel instantly formulates a new intention—to run.

> He on mode wearð
> forht on ferhðe; no þy ær fram meahte.
> (753b–54)

> He became terrified in his heart; he could not get out of there any the sooner for that.

In spite of the extra strength his terror has presumably given him, even his hope of escape is blocked by Beowulf's strength.

The rhetoric of another sentence in this same scene is of interest:

> Ða þæt onfunde se þe fela æror
> modes myrðe manna cynne,
> fyrene gefremede (he [wæs] fag wið god),
> þæt him se lichoma læstan nolde,
> ac hine se modega mæg Hygelaces
> hæfde be honda; wæs gehwæþer oðrum
> lifigende lað. (809–15a)

> Then he suddenly realized—he who in the past, murderous [or: joyous?] in heart, had committed many crimes against mankind, being in a state of feud with God—that his body would simply not hold up any longer; but the bold kinsman of Hygelac had him by the hand. While alive each was the deadly enemy of the other.

The long five-verse relative clause between the verb *onfunde* and its object clause describes the past history of Grendel's malevolent will and the crimes to which it has driven him, or the successes it has had. By delaying mention of what it is that Grendel discovers, the syntactical construction delays for the audience, as well as for Grendel, the shocking realization of his antagonist's power. Grendel discovers that his own body fails him. It is almost as if his body were some trusted retainer, half-personified here, now no longer willing (*nolde*) to stand by him in crisis. Physical strength collapses in the face of the adversary's adversative: *ac* Beowulf had him by the hand, naked will against will, as the final phrase of the quoted passage suggests in its balancing of hatred against hatred.

Expressions juxtaposing Grendel's expectations with the actual event occur several times in Beowulf's own later accounts of the fight with Grendel. We are told, for example, that Grendel had no intention of leaving *idelhende,* empty-handed, when he came to Heorot (the temptation to see irony in the word *idelhende* in view of the murderous handclasp that is to follow is hard to resist); he hoped to put Beowulf in his *glof,* his food-container. But *hyt ne mihte swa,* things couldn't turn out that way, as Beowulf laconically puts it, *syððan ic on yrre uppriht astod,* after I stood up in anger.[17]

Mention was made earlier of Grendel's final desperate hope of surviving by leaving his hand and arm behind, as some kind of payment or sacrifice that would save the rest of his body. This hope is quickly frustrated; he lives none the longer for his sacrifice but is locked inexorably in a prison of pain, death, and damnation, as the emphatic negatives point out:

no þy leng leofað   laðgeteona
synnum geswenced,   ac hyne sar hafað

17. The passage referred to here is 2081–92, in Beowulf's long speech to Hygelac.

mid *ny*dgripe nearwe befongen,
balwon bendum. (974–77a)

The horrible plunderer, crippled by sin, lived none the longer for it; on the contrary, pain had seized him tight in an inescapable grip, in the bonds of death.

Later Grendel is described as having a brief moment of life's joys, but the very hand that was left behind to ensure him such a respite is soon the cause of his miserable death:

He on weg losade,
lytle hwile lifwynna bre[a]c;
hwæþre him sio swiðre swaðe weardade
hand on Hiorte, ond he hean ðonan
modes geomor meregrund gefeoll.
(2096b–2100)

He got away, enjoyed life's pleasures for a short time; but his right hand remained behind him in Heorot, and from that place, humiliated and grieving in heart, he fell to the bottom of the mere.

The phrase *swaðe weardade* cannot be easily translated into modern English but literally, of course, it means "guarded [his] track" and I think it possible here that Grendel's right hand is represented as serving as a rear guard to cover his retreat.

Taken as a group, these passages amply illustrate one aspect of Grendel's lack of *sapientia:* all his guesses about the future are wrong. In this he is certainly in contrast to Beowulf, who never makes guesses about the future in this way. Instead he is likely to sketch out the possible alternatives and then cheerfully commit the issue to God.[18]

More important may be the impression that the audience

18. See Beowulf's various formal vows: 442–55; 632–38; 677–87; 1474–91; 2529–37.

receives through these formulaic expressions of intention first of the tremendous and indefatigable will—properly called demonic—which drives this rough beast onward and then of the successive forcible, even brutal, defeats inflicted on his expectations. One effect of such an emphasis on intention is to cast the whole struggle of Beowulf and Grendel into clear-cut terms of the direct conflict of willpower. Grendel's will (if we may indeed apply such a term to an animal drive) is furious, tremendous, terrifying, yet we see it ultimately blocked, deflected, and finally destroyed by the only force capable of meeting it, a will even stronger and more determined. When the struggle is seen in such terms, the actual physical encounter can be reduced to an almost symbolic minimum, a touching of hands, in order to make clear the moral nature of this conflict.

There are other evil creatures in the poem besides Grendel who meet frustrations. Grendel's ancestor Cain was looking forward to enjoying the pleasures stemming from the murder of his brother Abel but found himself suddenly exiled far from mankind by God's power.[19] Grendel's mother was confident that she could pierce Beowulf's armor when she seized him under the water, but his ring-mail protected him.[20] The

19. Ne gefeah he þære fæhðe, ac he hine feor forwræc,
metod for þy mane, mancynne fram. (109–10)

He [Cain] gained no enjoyment from that violent act; on the contrary the Lord hurled him off into exile for that crime, far from mankind.

20. Grap þa togeanes, guðrinc gefeng
atolan clommum. No þy ær in gescod
halan lice: hring utan ymbbearh,
þæt heo þone fyrdhom ðurhfon ne mihte,
locene leoðosyrcan laþan fingrum.
(1501–05)

Then she reached for him and gripped the warrior in her frightful claws. But none the sooner did she manage to pierce that uninjured body. Rings formed a barrier on the outside so that she could not penetrate that war-covering, the metal-linked shirt which guarded his limbs, with her cruel fingers.

sea-monsters Beowulf encountered after he was separated from Breca in the great swim had made elaborate plans for enjoying dinner on the sea-bottom, but in the morning they lay dead instead.[21] While the dragon's peculiar mentality is scarcely explored in the poem, it is logical to assume that he had the intention of deriving some advantage from the gold he was guarding; if so, he was not a bit the better for it.[22] In any event it is indisputable that the dragon expected his barrow to protect him when he returned to it after ravaging the land of the Geats, but this expectation is not fulfilled:

> Hæfde landwara lige befangen
> bæle ond bronde, beorges getruwode,
> wiges ond wealles; him seo wen geleah.
> (2321–23)

> He had enveloped the inhabitants in flame, fire, and burning; he trusted in his barrow, in his fight-

21. Næs hie ðære fylle gefean hæfdon,
manfordædlan, þæt hie me þegon,
symbel ymbsæton sægrunde neah;
ac on mergenne mecum wunde
be yðlafe uppe lægon,
sweo[r]dum answefede, þæt syðþan na
ymb brontne ford brimliðende
lade ne letton. (562–69a)

Those wicked destroyers did not have the joy of eating their fill, of partaking of me as they sat about their sea-bottom banquet; no, in the morning, gashed and pacified by swords, they lay stranded on the beach, and never afterwards kept any sailors from their voyages on the high seas.

For a discussion in another context of the lively irony involved here, see James L. Rosier, "The Uses of Association: Hands and Feasts in *Beowulf*," *PMLA*, 78 (1963), 9–10.

22. He gesecean sceall
[ho]r[d on] hrusan, þær he haeðen gold
warað wintrum frod, ne byð him wihte ðy sel.
(2275b–77)

He is obliged to seek out a hoard in the earth, where, ancient in years, he will guard heathen gold; he will profit by it in no way.

> ing-power and his wall; that expectation deceived him.

The reader may notice that several of these passages contain marked elements of humor at the expense of the evil characters and the disappointments they suffer.

Finally one special instance of the double negation of expectation, something like a one-two punch, ought to be recorded. Beowulf tells his men how he killed Dæghrefn, the Frankish warrior who had slain King Hygelac.

> Nalles he ða frætwe Frescyning[e],
> breostweorðunge, bringan moste,
> ac in c*o*mp*e* gecrong cumbles hyrde,
> æþeling on elne; ne wæs ecg bona,
> ac him hildegrap heortan wylmas,
> banhus gebræc. (2503–08a)
>
> Never was he allowed to bring those valuables, that breast-ornament, back to the Frisian king; on the contrary, the guardian of the standard, brave and noble, fell in battle. And the sword did not kill him; no, my fighting grasp crushed his bone-house and the surges of his heart.

Since the Geatish landing force has been defeated, Dæghrefn certainly expects to carry loot to his king, but he has not counted on the power and opposing will of Beowulf. Dæghrefn falls in battle, as perhaps any warrior might expect to fall some day; but his presumable expectation that the sword will be the cause of his death is not fulfilled, for Beowulf simply crushes him in a bear-hug. To put this another way: that the great hero Dæghrefn is killed is remarkable; that he is killed in this way is incredible. Again, Beowulf's unique and "unexpectable" powers are set off.

Other examples of this same rhetorical pattern of defeated expectation appear throughout the poem, although most of them are of less interest in themselves. Still they add to the almost incessant reinforcement of certain themes important in the poem as a whole. Taken together such patterns, by their stress on intention and determination, keep before us the typical preoccupation of epic poetry with the will. Usually they offer a perspective on "fate" as being fundamentally a will-blocking force indifferent to the wishes of the characters, and often they bring out the complex role of the hero in cooperating with fate or serving as fate's agent.

The Pattern of "Until"

That Tolkien's famous essay on *Beowulf* ends with the phrase "—until the dragon comes" is appropriate, for the phrase reminds us of many such expressions with "until" that constitute a major theme pattern in the poem.[23] These expressions are generally similar in their implications to the negative phrases in the preceding section. Both rhetorical constructions place one kind or quality of human experience (usually success or the hope of success) in sharp and dramatic contrast with another kind of experience (usually failure or disaster). Here only those sentences that actually contain the words *oð* or *oððæt* (until) will be studied.[24]

There are thirty-six instances of these words in *Beowulf*. For purposes of this study we can discard some thirteen as being "neutral," that is, carrying no specific emotional charge, serving merely to describe journeys or movements in space or

23. J. R. R. Tolkien, "*Beowulf:* the Monsters and the Critics," *Proceedings of the British Academy,* 22 (1936), 295.

24. A great many other sentences of course express the same concept without using words for "until." See, for example, the well-known description of how Heorot towers high when first built, awaiting the fire that will destroy it (81b–85).

the passage of time.[25] It should be added immediately, however, that some of these are much less neutral than others; the term is quite relative. In a sentence like this, which describes the Geats' arrival at Heorot, the construction seems straightforward:

> Guman onetton,
> sigon ætsomne, oþþæt hy [s]æl timbred,
> geatolic ond goldfah, ongyton mihton.
> (306b–08)
>
> The men hastened on, marching together, until they could see the well-constructed hall, stately and gold-bright.

But the following sentence, on the other hand, contains a perceptible suggestion of suspended terror:

> Hordweard onbad
> earfoðlice oððæt æfen cwom.
> (2302b–03)
>
> The guardian of the hoard [the dragon] waited in impatient misery until evening came.

The more interesting rhetorical uses of the construction, however, can be broken down into simple descriptive categories. For our purposes we may use the naïve terms "good" and "bad" to describe events or situations that, in their context, are either desirable or undesirable from the point of view of the poet or his human characters. The pairs of events described in an "until" phrase may then be roughly classified as follows in these terms:

25. Under the heading of "spatial" are included the occurrences of the word in lines 219, 307, 622, 1414, 1640; under "temporal" the occurrences in lines 296, 1801, 2303, 2782, 2791, 3069, 3083, 3147. One can see how this division reflects the greater concentration on time in Part II of the poem and on "space" (i.e. action) in Part I.

good follows good—4
good follows bad —3
bad follows bad —6
bad follows good —10

In the first category, good follows good, three of the four passages are concerned with some form of hereditary succession. The Danish king Beow rules well in Denmark until Healfdene is born to succeed him (53–57a); Hrothgar prospers in war until a new generation of warriors grows to maturity (64–67a); Weohstan keeps the arms given him by Onela until his son Wiglaf is old enough to use them (2620–22). The fourth passage is similar in that it describes Beowulf's friendly protection of young Heardred until he is old enough to rule the Geats (2377–79b). The theme here is obvious: in the heroic world, strong rulers are the sole source of order. Social stability and continuity consists in the orderly succession of strong rulers.

In two of the three instances of "good follows bad," we can see that the change is the result of heroic character and initiative. Scyld is at first a destitute child in Denmark, but he lives to see consolation for that suffering and to exact obedience from all his neighbors (6b–11). Grendel rules Heorot until at last death comes to him at Beowulf's hands (1253–55a). In the third passage spring follows winter, melting the fetters of ice, as Hengest sits unhappily in Finn's hall (1131b–36a); Hengest and the Danes are then free to carry out their delayed vengeance against Finn.[26]

Few generalizations can be ventured about the category of "bad follows bad." Persistence in a course of violence is sometimes stressed. In the Ingeld episode, this passage occurs:

26. In reality the effect and implications of this image are too complex to fit our simple-minded categories here; see the discussion of the Finn Episode in Chapter Four, pp. 169–74.

> Manað swa ond myndgað mæla gehwylce
> sarum wordum, oððæt sæl cymeð
> þæt se fæmnan þegn fore fæder dædum
> æfter billes bite blodfag swefeð,
> ealdres scyldig. (2057–61a)
>
> In this way he will remind and admonish him on every occasion with words of pain, until the time comes that the woman's retainer will sleep blood-stained from the sword's bite, forfeiting his life for the deeds of his father.

The old retainer's rekindling of hatred in the young man is seen almost as the normal fulfillment of natural process. So, in Germanic literature generally, feuds once set in motion tend to grind on to their conclusion. Other events in a career of violence are connected with *oððæt* constructions: Grendel kills some of the Danes and rules until Heorot stands unusable for Hrothgar and his men (144–46a); Heremod slaughters his subordinates in fury until at last he goes away into "exile" (1713–15); Ongentheow attacks the Geats and then pursues them into a trap at Ravenswood (2928–35).[27]

We come now to the largest of these categories. That most of these "until" constructions should be "bad follows good" is in perfect keeping with the grim tone of the poem as a whole, its emphasis on tragic unawareness and unpreparedness, and its long perspective over several generations of men.

The passage in this category that happens to occur first in the poem may be taken as representative of this pattern; it deserves attention besides because it is one of the most elaborate rhetorical structures of the poem. The *oððæt* con-

27. If it is of any real importance to classify all these passages, I include tentatively under this heading two more examples. The Last Survivor wanders in misery over the grave of his nation until death's wave touches his heart (is death "good" or "bad" for him?) (2267–70a); the waves in the Grendel mere move up out of their proper place until the air becomes wet (1373–76a).

struction is at its very center, but the context should be quoted at some length.

> Ða se ell*org*æst[28]   earfoðlice
> þrage geþolode,   se þe in þystrum bad,
> þæt he dogora gehwam   dream gehyrde
> hludne in healle;   þær wæs hearpan sweg,
> swutol sang scopes.   (86–90a)
>
> Then that alien spirit suffered longlasting misery,
> the one who lurked in darkness, because every day
> he heard joy loud in the hall, there where the harp's
> song was, and the clear voice of the minstrel.

Then, after the scop's song of the creation of the world, which offers its own brief and memorable impressions of light and vitality, the poet continues:

> Swa ða drihtguman   dreamum lifdon
> eadiglice,   oððæt an ongan
> fyrene fre[m]man   feond on helle.
> Wæs se grimma gæst   Grendel haten,
> mære mearcstapa,   se þe moras heold,
> fen ond fæsten.   (99–104a)
>
> That was how those noble men lived in luck and joy—until one fiend from hell began to commit crime. That fearful creature's name was Grendel, a well-known prowler of the borders, ruling over moor, fen, and wild country.

Then there follows the account of Grendel's descent from Cain and the origin of the race of monsters. Finally Grendel comes to Heorot:

28. MS *ellengæst,* a jejune reading preserved by editors too ready to accede to scribal vagaries; the compound *ellorgæst* is used elsewhere four times of Grendel and his mother. Not that courage might not fairly be attributed to Grendel, but in this context what is poetically stressed is his alien, outsider aspect, his habitation *in þystrum,* away from the light.

Gewat ða neosian, syþðan niht becom,
hean huses, hu hit Hringdene
æfter beorþege gebun hæfdon.
(115–17)

He came then, after night fell, to visit that lofty house, to see how the Ring-Danes had settled into it after the pouring of beer.

Note first the paralleling, for purposes of strictest contrast, of *earfoðlice* 86 with *eadiglice* 100, and of *þrage geþolode* 87 with *dreamum lifdon* 99. The formal antithesis suggested on a small scale by such verbal patterns extends of course to much larger contrasts. The explanation in the scop's song of how the universe was created, following as it does upon the description of the building of Heorot and the establishment of the great Danish civilization it represents (its light gleams over many lands), has its complement in the explanation of Grendel's origin—how dark evil came into being in the midst of a universe of sunlight and green leaves. On one side of this great opposition we have human society in harmony with the divine plan, dazzling in images of light, song, and joy; on the other side we have Grendel-Cain, the individual who has freely chosen to rebel against human society and who is now outcast in a world of darkness, misery, and violence. We will examine this mythic pattern at greater length in Chapter Three.

At the very center of this opposition is the *oððæt* phrase, which, by introducing the element of time into the static opposition, sets the active conflict of the poem in motion. They lived in joy until . . . . The construction here (perhaps partly because of its semi-formulaic use in similar contexts) points both to human capacities for happy unawareness of the darkness outside and to the nature of a world that sooner or later always brings in on us its merciless "until," where time, change, and disaster operate outside man's powers of control.

The particular "good" broken in on by such ominous untils

is, as this Heorot-Grendel contrast implies, most often a social good. Social order is to be succeeded by social chaos. At one extreme, the social good may take the form of a friendly, if rivalrous, community of two: Breca and Beowulf stay together in their swim (partly for mutual protection) until a storm drives them apart.[29] At the other end of the range, it may take the form of the peace and order of an entire nation over a long period of time: Beowulf ruled the Geats well for fifty years, until a dragon began to gain power on dark nights.[30]

The reference to dark nights suggests that most primitive, durable, and effective of all poetic dichotomies, the opposition of light and dark, and images of light and dark are often associated with these constructions.[31] We see this contrast used to good effect, for example, in this sentence from Beowulf's report to Hygelac:

> Swa we þær inne ondlangne dæg
> niode naman, oððæt niht becwom
> oðer to yldum. (2115–17a)

In this way we enjoyed ourselves indoors the whole long day, until another night arrived for men.

29.
> Ða wit ætsomne on sæ wæron
> fif nihta fyrst, oþþæt unc flod todraf,
> wado weallende, wedera cealdost, . . .
> (544–46)

Then the two of us were together in the sea for five nights, until the waters, swelling waves, the coldest of storms, drove us apart.

30.
> He geheold tela
> fiftig wintra (wæs ða frod cyning,
> eald eþelweard), oððæt an ongan
> deorcum nihtum draca rics[i]an, . . .
> (2208b–11)

31. These images are examined further in Chapter Three. For an extended discussion of them see Herbert G. Wright, "Good and Evil; Light and Darkness; Joy and Sorrow in *Beowulf*," *Review of English Studies* (n.s.), 8 (1957), 1–11.

The poet combines the idea of being *inne*—inside, warm, and secure—with what seems to be suggested by *ondlangne dæg,* namely, the possession of a long space of time for relaxed enjoyment free from interruption, and thrusts against this combination the contrasting image of night (both darkness and time itself) arriving among men as an assailant or intruder.

Attention to such patterns of imagery may even provide some help in reaching satisfactory interpretations of such passages as the following, taken from the poet's account of the first night in Heorot, when Hrothgar decides to retire to sleep. Beowulf has just made his resolute vow to Queen Wealhtheow and the hall resounds with joy and new confidence.

> Þa wæs eft swa ær inne on healle
> þryðword sprecen, ðeod on sælum,
> sigefolca sweg, oþþæt semninga
> sunu Healfdenes secean wolde
> æfenræste; wiste þæm ahlæcan
> to þæm heahsele hilde geþinged,
> siððan hie sunnan leoht geseon meahton,[32]
> oþ ðe nipende niht ofer ealle,
> scaduhelma gesceapu scriðan cwoman,
> wan under wolcnum. Werod eall aras.
> (642–51)

Then once more as before powerful words were spoken inside the hall. The people were happy, and a sound went up from both victorious nations, until suddenly Healfdene's son [Hrothgar] decided to go to his bed for the night. He knew well that the monster had determined on attack on the high hall from

32. This is the MS text of line 648. Most editors, including Dobbie, insert *ne* after *geseon,* so as to make the line refer to the coming of night, and hence they usually read *oþ ðe as oþðe,* "or" rather than "until."

> the time they could make out the sun's light until
> gathering darkness and shapes of shadow raced up,
> dim under the clouds. The company stood up.

Like many others, this passage reveals the heavy emphasis that the poem places on the cyclic rhythms of joy and sorrow in human experience. The feast here is really a great outburst of joy and hope, which follows twelve long years of anxiety and despair for the Danes. But the sound of merriment is no sooner heard than a change is signaled, within the very space of a single alliterative line: *sigefolca sweg, opþæt semninga* . . . . Hrothgar's sudden decision to retire is not in itself occasion for alarm except insofar as it marks the end of communal joy, but the poet seems to touch here, as often, on such simple but profound primitive fears as the child's reluctance at bedtime to leave the warm safe circle. The next few lines are not clear beyond dispute, but we seem to be told that Hrothgar knew that Grendel had been waiting all day (or possibly all evening, from the beginning of sunset until total darkness) to make his assault on Heorot. Perhaps this knowledge on Hrothgar's part is offered as a kind of reason for his retirement from the scene; at night it is now Grendel's hall, as it has been for twelve years—or else it may now be Beowulf's hall, for Hrothgar's last act before leaving Heorot is to deed over the hall to Beowulf: *hafa nu ond geheald husa selest* (658).

In a more strictly poetic way, several effective contrasts are made here. In the final lines of the passage, through the channel of Hrothgar's imagination, the outside world of darkness is permitted to come into our consciousness; it comes rushing in—*scriðan cwoman*—on the heels of the *oþ* phrase, after having been staved off and held at a distance for those brief moments of light. The similarity in the language here to that used to describe Grendel when he actually comes (*com on wanre niht / scriðan sceadugenga* 702b–03a) points to the close identification of Grendel, who indeed is later described as *æfengrom* (2074) (evening-ferocious), with darkness itself. Yet he is no more than a conspicuously energetic pseudopod of that darkness. Here and throughout the poem we are to think of the ultimate darkness of chaos and nonbeing which hangs first over this proud and splendid civilization of Denmark (if only because we are so often reminded of the destructive feuds in prospect) and which, beyond that, hangs over all human institutions and all men. Against a background of this immensity the hall becomes a crucial symbol, and the defender of the hall the embodiment of a profound kind of courage even beyond ordinary heroism.

Old age and death figure in two instances of the "until" construction. Beowulf survives many battles until that one day when he is obliged to face the dragon.[33] And great Hrothgar was always blameless, especially in his generosity, until age took the joy of his strength from him, as it has often injured many a man.[34] These are the universal untils that come to all.

Weapons that outlast their owners are used as symbols of the pathos of human existence more than once in the poem, as we shall see in our examination in Chapter Five of the second part of the poem. One "until" phrase gives expression to this idea. The weapons and armor worn by the Danes in the Ingeld episode were once the property of the Heathobeards, who (it is implied) had rejoiced in the excellent quali-

33. Swa he niða gehwane genesen hæfde,
sliðra geslyhta, sunu Ecgðiowes,
ellenweorca, oð ðone anne dæg
þe he wið þam wyrme gewegan sceolde.
(2397–2400)

In this way he had survived every battle, violent conflict, act of courage, until that one day when he was obliged to fight against the dragon.

34. Þæt wæs an cyning,
æghwæs orleahtre, oþþæt hine yldo benam
mægenes wynnum, se þe oft manegum scod.
(1885b–87)

ties of these arms until they lost their comrades in battle, and afterwards lost their own lives.[35]

Finally, in the partially Christianized sermon that Hrothgar preaches to Beowulf, there is a passage containing both the kind of negative we examined earlier and an *oððæt* construction. Hrothgar is speaking of the fortunate man who can see no end to his prosperity.

> Wunað he on wiste; no hine wiht dweleð
> adl ne yldo, ne him inwitsorh
> on sefa*n* sweorceð, ne gesacu ohwær
> ecghete eoweð, ac him eal worold
> wendeð on willan (he þæt wyrse ne con),
> oðþæt him on innan oferhygda dæl
> weaxeð ond wridað. (1735–41a)
>
> Life for him is a feast. Disease and old age never block his path; evil sorrow never darkens his mind; no quarrels bring the savage attack of swords. No, for him the whole world goes as he wishes—he has no knowledge of something worse—until within him an enormous pride grows and puts forth shoots.

In its allusions to the common lot of human suffering from which this man thinks himself exempt, the rhetorical series of negative phrases leads us toward the "until" climax of unrealistic pride. But it is worth observing that the "until" construction here suggests something different from what is

35. On him gladiað gomelra lafe,
heard ond hringmæl Heaðabear[d]na gestreon
þenden hie ðam wæpnum wealdan moston,
oððæt hie forlæddan to ðam lindplegan
swæse gesiðas ond hyra sylfra feorh.
(2036–40)

On them will gleam the heirlooms of old fighting-men, once the treasured arms, keen and ring-marked, of Heathobeards while they were still capable of using weapons, until that time that they led their much-loved comrades and themselves to destruction in the play of linden-shields.

suggested by other examples in the poem. There such external forces as death, old age, or attack by evil creatures, all aspects of what we call fate and all beyond human control, are seen as arriving from outside to disrupt or destroy human happiness. That the "until" here is clearly internalized and placed in a pattern of moral cause and effect significantly reflects the Christian thinking of this sermon. It is important to recognize, however, that such a pattern is exceptional in *Beowulf*.

In summary, the methodical scrutiny of items on such arbitrarily selected lists as these can direct our attention to important poetic habits that might otherwise have been overlooked. In the passages cited in this chapter, we have seen the persistent tendency to present character and behavior in terms of opposites and to set off a positive by a negative wherever possible, and we have noticed how such polarization of value keeps the idea of the constant heroic choice alive in our minds. On a larger scale, we see how the monsters that the hero must encounter are at the same time greatly distanced from normal humanity and yet related to it. In the sequence of events in time a similar clash of opposites often occurs, where the outcome shows an extreme divergence from the expectation.

Even from this brief glance at the inherited rhetoric of Germanic poetic style, the reader should be able to gain some sense of what this style does best and most expertly—or, to view it another way, what it can scarcely help doing, being what it is. Any story that such a style sets out to tell will be in very large measure cut to fit its capabilities and limitations. Unless we make some initial effort to see through these rhetorical lenses we will inevitably misunderstand much about the poem.[36]

36. Two recent general discussions of the poem touch (in different ways) on correspondences of style and meaning; see Stanley B. Greenfield, *A Critical History of Old English Literature* (New York, New York University Press, 1965), pp. 85–91, and E. G. Stanley, "*Beowulf*," in *Continuations and Beginnings: Studies in Old English Literature* (London, Nelson, 1966), especially pp. 120–26.

CHAPTER TWO

The Hero Comes

To write of the hero in *Beowulf* is to write of everything in the poem, for there is nothing that does not serve in some sense to illuminate the character of the protagonist.[1] This chapter then must select for discussion only a part of the material which might be taken up under this heading. The nature of Beowulf's monstrous opponents and of the fights he has with them, as well as much that might have been included here about the aged Beowulf, will be deferred for discussion in later chapters.

Begin at the beginning. If the last word of the poem is *lofgeornost,* most eager for praise, the first three lines of the poem explain what is meant by this praise and how it functions.

> Hwæt! We Gardena in geardagum,
> þeodcyninga, þrym gefrunon,
> hu ða æþelingas ellen fremedon. (1–3)

1. For one concise and lucid presentation of this point of view see Joan Blomfield, "The Style and Structure of *Beowulf,*" *Review of English Studies* (o.s.), *14* (1938), 396–403. In her words, "The subject is disposed as a circumscribed field in which the themes are drawn out by a centre of attraction—in this case, the character of the good warrior. Far-flung tales and allusions, apparently scattered material and disconnected events are grouped in a wide sweep around the hero's character. In fact, these *are* his character" (p. 396).

> Hear me. We have heard tell of the strength of Spear-Danes, great kings, in days long past, and of how those princes carried courage into action.

Those times have long gone by, but men's memories still grope into the mists of the ancient days and seize on the *þrym* and *ellen,* the strength and courage, of Danish kings and noblemen. Memorable strength and courage, then, is the announced subject of the poem, and we are presented at the outset with a paradigm of praiseworthy conduct in Scyld, the *god cyning.* This brief proem that tells of Scyld does what the poem as a whole does: it defines these terms, shows them in action, and perhaps even tests them.

Just as the Scyld role of savior prefigures the role Beowulf is to play, the Scyld proem prefigures the action of the poem as a whole. The first requirement of the hero is strength, exercised by Scyld in the establishment of political order by conquest. After a secure society is established, its continuity is assured by God's gift of a son and heir to Scyld, and its further continuity will depend on young Beow's generosity to his retainers; if he wins their loyalty they will stand by him when he grows old.

There is a modulation here from the energetic celebration of sheer power toward an acknowledgment that, while power is initially essential, it is not in itself enough either for the individual or for the society. The king must depend on the loyalty of his men, and this loyalty is not won by fighting power alone, but by good treatment. Even heroes live in a world with other men.

The description of Scyld's funeral offers a sudden and beautiful revelation of the depths of emotion associated with this bond between men. We have moved from the power of violence to the power of love and the expression of profound gratitude. The scene dramatizes a mutual relationship of love: Scyld has come to save them, but could have done little without their devoted loyalty, and their gratitude i dependence on him, the Shield of their nation.[2]

Most readers of *Beowulf,* I think, recognize intuitively t the Scyld proem is curiously appropriate to the rest of the poem, despite its apparent irrelevance to the main action. Its relationship is predictive and thematic. The poem as a whole shows the same progression from deeds of power (Beowulf in Denmark) to sonship (Beowulf first adopted by Hrothgar and then returning to Hygelac) to generosity (the themes that cluster around Beowulf, Wiglaf, and the cowardly retainers) to a funeral where an entire nation sacrifices its treasure as a gesture of affection. The poem moves from detailed scenes of social life—feasts, ceremonial speeches, the presentation of gifts—into the bare-stage close focus of the last thousand lines and the loneliness of an individual's death voyage, and this same movement is paralleled on a small scale in the Scyld proem.

The proem, then, provides both a role for Beowulf to play and a generalized, though profoundly powerful, emotional atmosphere that will be perceptible in the poem as a whole. The ensuing description of the building of Heorot and of Grendel's attacks on it begins the process of sketching out a specific role, an immediate need for the hero. From the first mention of Grendel in the poem (line 100) to the first mention of Beowulf (line 194), the poet is developing with care the different aspects of the situation into which Beowulf must come. All is part of it: Grendel's demonic and God-cursed origins, his insolent and unhindered depredations in Heorot, and the rapid disintegration of Danish morale to the point where, in pure despair (or so it might have seemed to a Christian audience), they are ready to sacrifice to heathen idols. The summary passage at the end of this section of the poem reads:

2. Scyld's funeral is discussed in more detail in Chapter Five, in conjunction with Beowulf's funeral.

maga Healfdenes
mihte snotor hæleð
wæs þæt gewin to swyð,
ı, þe on ða leode becom,
rim, nihtbealwa mæst.
(189–93)

ı of Healfdene [Hrothgar] brooded
ɔiled] the troubles of the time, [but]
could not turn away the affliction.
For the gle which visited that people was too unequal, too vicious and longlasting, a harsh fated torment, greatest of night's evils.

Almost all epic poems must devote much of their time to developing the "heroic niche"—the problem their hero must solve, the deteriorating situation no one else can deal with, the space only a hero is large enough to fill. Consider the amount of time the *Odyssey* gives to exploring the usurpation of power in Ithaca by the suitors. Indeed, the greater part of the *Iliad* is nothing but setting the immense scene for Achilles' climactic heroic action. Here in this passage mention of Healfdene may remind us of Denmark's great past and the word *snotor* of Hrothgar's indisputable wisdom; but the key phrase is *ne mihte,* could not. Hrothgar simmers in impotent rage and misery, unable to act in any way against an affliction the massive dimensions of which are suggested by the powerful sonority of that heavily burdened final line: *nydwracu niþgrim, nihtbealwa mæst.* The challenge is far too great; a great king and a great nation lie in paralysis before it.

The hero, on the other hand, is the man who is *eacen,* who has that extra portion of strength which enables him to do what others cannot. He can do it, and he does do it, at the moment he wills it.

Þæt fram ham gefrægn Higelaces þegn,
god mid Geatum, Grendles dæda;

se wæs moncynnes mægenes strengest
on þæm dæge þysses lifes,
æþele ond eacen. Het him yðlidan
godne gegyrwan, cwæð, he guðcyning
ofer swanrade secean wolde,
mærne þeoden, þa him wæs manna þearf.
(194–201)

A brave man of the Geats, Hygelac's thane, heard of Grendel's deeds from his home; he was the strongest of all mankind at that time of this life, noble and endowed with special power. He ordered a stout wave-traveler made ready, and said he intended to visit the king across the swan-road, because that famous prince needed men.

Beowulf hears of Grendel's deeds and he *acts*, instantly, even before he speaks. He first orders the boat to be prepared for the voyage and only then voices his intention of going to Denmark. Others discuss the trip, urge him on, examine the omens for the voyage; but Beowulf has already chosen his men and is walking away, out of these conversations, down to his ship. As L. L. Schücking once suggested, the laconic brevity of this passage seems intended by the poet to bring out the rapidity of the decision, the firmness of the will, the sureness of the action.[3]

All these qualities are brought out even more by the descriptions of the voyages Beowulf makes. Because these descriptions are as formulaic and conventional as any passages in the

3. "Die ganze Stelle (194 ff.) ist von einer Kürze, hinter der möglicherweise eine stilistische Absicht steckt. Gesagt soll werden: Von Grendel erfahren und sein Schiff zur Fahrt fertig machen lassen, war für Beowulf eins." Levin L. Schücking, "Heldenstolz und Würde im Angelsächsischen, mit einem Anhang: Zur Charakterisierungstechnik im Beowulfepos," *Abhandlungen der Philologisch-historischen Klasse der sächsischen Akademie der Wissenschaften,* 42, No. 5 (1933), 36. This monograph remains one of the best studies of the specifically heroic aspects of the poem.

poem and bear a strong resemblance to each other, they will here be discussed together.[4] From a structural point of view, the similarity between the two voyages emphasizes strongly their function as a frame surrounding the sojourn in Denmark. Exactly as he came, Beowulf returns; in between occur the events at the great Danish court.

This frame is in strong contrast to what it surrounds. Denmark is shown to us in the poem in all its greatness but also in all its vulnerability: the last picture we have of it is of old Hrothgar weeping uncontrollably at Beowulf's departure. Hrothgar's grief is of course part of the indirect characterization of the hero, but the scene also reminds us of Hrothgar's earlier helplessness against the attacks of Grendel and recalls the painful and violent tensions that pervade the Danish court beneath its gracious exterior, tensions focused in the figures of Hrothulf, the apprehensive Wealhtheow, and perhaps also in Unferth. Viewed from a certain angle, Heorot is a world of despair; it is doomed, and man's best efforts will not help its inhabitants in the long run.

In contrast to such disturbing suggestions, the two voyages present a direct and simple perfection of action. Here is the description of the first voyage:

Fyrst forð gewat. Flota wæs on yðum,
bat under beorge. Beornas gearwe
on stefn stigon; streamas wundon,
sund wið sande; secgas bæron
on bearm nacan beorhte frætwe,
guðsearo geatolic; guman ut scufon,
weras on wilsið, wudu bundenne.

4. The reader is referred to the statistics on the two passages assembled by Robert E. Diamond, "Theme as Ornament in Anglo-Saxon Poetry," *PMLA, 76* (1961), 461–68. Of the 47 verses devoted to the first voyage (lines 198b–200 and 208–28), he finds 27 to be formulaic; and of the 48 verses describing the second voyage (lines 1896–1919) he finds 38 to be formulaic.

Gewat þa ofer wægholm, winde gefysed,
flota famiheals fugle gelicost,
oðþæt ymb antid oþres dogores
wundenstefna gewaden hæfde
þæt ða liðende land gesawon,
brimclifu blican, beorgas steape,
side sænæssas; þa wæs sund liden,
eoletes æt ende. (210–24a)

Time passed. The boat floated in the waves below the shore. Men climbed eagerly onto the prow, as the currents swirled, whirled against sand, carrying their gleaming harness and fine wargear into the ship's embrace, and then shoved their well-lashed ship out on its longed-for journey. Then it traveled over deep sea, driven by the winds, floating foam-necked like a bird, until at the set time (?) of the second day the curved prow had covered the miles so that the sailors could sight land—flashing sea-cliffs, steep hills, a chain of headlands. The sea was crossed, at the end of the voyage (?).

The main purpose of these descriptions is to characterize the hero by dramatizing his habitual mode of action. What we are to marvel at, perhaps revel in, when we hear of both voyages is "the achieve of, the mastery of the thing," that sense of easy effortless power and total accomplishment. *Þa wæs sund liden,* the poet says at the end of the first voyage: then was the sea journeyed over—something was emphatically done to the sea, it was mastered by the hero as *lagucræftig mon,* the sea-skilled man. Yet, despite this sense of effortlessness, in the customary actions mentioned in both voyages—loading the boat, getting it under way, tying it up after landing—there is a feeling of strict control and discipline in the smart performance of necessary actions. For these seafarers are acutely conscious of danger: at the end of the first voyage they thank God for their easy journey (most sea voyages were not easy).

> Þanon up hraðe
> Wedera leode on wang stigon,
> sæwudu sældon (syrcan hrysedon,
> guðgewædo), gode þancedon
> þæs þe him yþlade eaðe wurdon.
> (224b–28)

> From there the Geat people quickly stepped up onto land, tied up the sea-wood (mailshirts clashed, war-clothing), thanked God that their voyage had been easy.

At the end of the second voyage, the boat is tied up carefully so as not to be damaged by waves.

> Hraþe wæs æt holme hyðweard geara,
> se þe ær lange tid leofra manna
> fus æt faroðe feor wlatode;
> sælde to sande sidfæþme scip,
> oncerbendum fæst, þy læs hym yþa ðrym
> wudu wynsuman forwrecan meahte.
> (1914–19)

> The harbor-guard was ready by the sea; he had been gazing far out over the water eager to see the dear men for a long time. He moored the roomy ship to the sand, secure with anchor-bonds, lest the power of waves wreck the lovely vessel.

And in both voyages the wind is favorable, making the trip rapid. Luck is with them; when Beowulf wills to go, the wind is right. Like the hero Brutus in Laȝamon's *Brut, he hafde wind he hafde weder after his wille.*[5] Heroes are not

5. MS Otho, line 639; quoted from *Laȝamon: Brut,* ed. G. L. Brook and R. F. Leslie, Early English Text Society, No. 250 (London, Oxford University Press, 1963), *1,* 33.

quite gods able to control winds entirely, but they take the fullest advantage of them.

In its full implications the image of the hero as sailor is a marvelously effective one, as the authors of the *Odyssey* and *Moby-Dick* knew well. The complex combination of many elements—the skill and prudent discipline of the sailor-warrior, his requisite wary attitude toward the uncontrollable and toward luck, his imperturbable courage, the favoring wind—somehow goes toward creating the image of the hero, who gives himself, commits himself, launches himself boldly (with a sharp weather eye astern) onto a sea that bears him to his destination. These voyages in *Beowulf*, in actuality, become resonant renderings of heroic power. The key word is *wilsið:* this is a voyage that is the very projection of disciplined will. The Geats' ship floats like a foamy-necked bird; they fly effortlessly to the desired shore.

To Denmark come these men of power and piety, to a Denmark whose present situation is a state of siege, suggested by the initial image of a guard by a wall, holding off enemies. In the challenging speech of the coastguard, we see immediately what Denmark is. The coastguard's sense of duty, his responsible dignity, the wall of formal language he interposes, all these things reveal a proud nation. But in the very course of this first sober challenge, the defensive wall is effectively breached.

Næfre ic maran geseah
eorla ofer eorþan ðonne is eower sum,
secg on searwum; nis þæt seldguma,
wæpnum geweorðad, næfne him his wlite leoge,
ænlic ansyn. Nu ic eower sceal
frumcyn witan, ær ge fyr heonan,
leassceaweras, on land Dena
furþur feran. Nu ge feorbuend,
mereliðende, min[n]e gehyrað
anfealdne geþoht: ofost is selest

to gecyðanne hwanan eowre cyme syndon.
(247b–57)

> I never saw a bigger man on earth than one of you, that fighter in armor; he is certainly no hall-lounger, unless his looks belie him, his noble face. Now I must know your origin, before you move on any farther into the land of the Danes as spies. Now, you foreign mariners, listen to my one thought: haste is best for making known where you have come from.

The coastguard falters in his ritual of dignified procedure when he looks closely at Beowulf. Who is that one man, greater than any on earth? Where did this band get their look of absolute assurance? Staggered, led off the track of his formal inquiries, he must force himself to come back to the present problem, as the series *nu . . . nu . . . ofost is selest* in the last sentences reminds us: steady there, back to the present, the job at hand.[6]

Beowulf is not only impressive in appearance, but he is himself responsible and dignified and answers precisely as he was told to answer, in the very same formal dialect, one might say: identifying his band by placing it in relationship to nation and to king, before offering the credentials of his own father's name, an act that is of course a way of placing himself in the aristocratic class.

Despite these similarities of manner, one aspect of Beowulf and his mission is brought out in the contrast between his speech and behavior and the attitude of the coastguard. It lies in the opposition between open and closed—if such usefully loose terms may be employed to point to something hard to describe but very apparent in the poem. On one side we see the defensive, formal, and cautious attitude appropriate to

6. See M. W. Pepperdene, "Beowulf and the Coast-Guard," *English Studies, 41* (1966), 409–19, esp. 416–17, for a somewhat similar interpretation of the coastguard's reaction.

the Danish coastguard standing by his wall, with his talk of spies, passwords, and invaders; on the other side we notice the conspicuous openness of Beowulf's arrival and of his reply itself. This openness can be seen in Beowulf's references to the public and unconcealable reputation of his father, who was well known, *folcum gecyþed* (262), and who is still remembered by a great many people all over the world, and in his explicit disavowal of any secrecy whatever in his mission:

> Habbað we to þæm mæran micel ærende,
> Deniga frean, ne sceal þær dyrne sum
> wesan, þæs ic wene. (270–72a)
>
> We have an important mission to the famous lord of the Danes; I do not think anything should be secret about it.

And indeed, by that kind of happy accident which sometimes helps distinguish good poetry from bad, the idea of openness even appears in the formulaic phrase the poet has selected here to introduce Beowulf's speech: *wordhord onleac* 259, he unlocked his hoard of words.

Openness is one part of the courtesy—more than courtesy, tact—which is evident in these early speeches of Beowulf. His appeal to the coastguard for advice; his admission that the rumors the Geats have heard about Grendel might very well not be true; his presenting himself at this point merely as a well-meaning adviser to Hrothgar who might be able to suggest a plan whereby Hrothgar could overcome Grendel—all illustrate this quality of tact. For, as a foreign champion whose very presence is potentially an insult to a humiliated people, Beowulf must not only disarm the Danes' hostility but he must gain acceptance from them, and gain it from each individual he encounters.

Although there is some difference of opinion as to their precise meaning, the concluding lines of Beowulf's first speech can be viewed as another instance of tact, if the last six lines (280–85) are understood as a long "if" clause that speculates about the uncertain future, rather than as something like a threatening ultimatum to Hrothgar.[7] Here is the passage:

> Ic þæs Hroðgar mæg
> þurh rumne sefan ræd gelæran,
> hu he frod ond god feond oferswyðeþ,
> gyf him edwendan æfre scolde
> bealuwa bisigu, bot eft cuman,
> ond þa cearwylmas colran wurðaþ,
> oððe a syðþan earfoðþrage,
> þreanyd þolað, þenden þær wunað
> on heahstede husa selest. (277b–85)

> I can furnish advice on this subject to Hrothgar in all generosity as to how that brave old man will overcome his enemy—if the torment of evils is ever to change for him, and relief to come back, and the hot surges of care to grow cooler, or [it may well be that] he will endure a time of suffering ever after and be oppressed by misery, as long as that best of houses stands there in its high place.

What my translation tries to bring out is this point: that Beowulf has a plan which may help Hrothgar, *if* any way out of his troubles is ever destined to be, and that Beowulf recognizes realistically the possibility that Hrothgar may be destined to misery permanently. Beowulf knows his own powers, that is to say; in knowing as well that he cannot change fate, he recognizes his limitations. What Beowulf is certainly not saying here, it seems to me, is that if Hrothgar

7. They are taken in the former sense by Anton Pirkhofer, *Figurengestaltung im Beowulf-Epos* (Heidelberg, C. Winter, 1940), p. 106. Both this study and Schücking's "Heldenstolz und Würde" seem to me to address themselves far more profitably to the central issues of the poem than does much recent criticism.

does not hurry to accept the "plan" he will never have another chance to get rid of Grendel.

Something about the way Beowulf has spoken has persuaded the Danish coastguard that the Geatish band offers no threat to his sovereign.

> Weard maþelode, ðær on wicge sæt,
> ombeht unforht: "Æghwæþres sceal
> scearp scyldwiga gescad witan,
> worda ond worca, se þe wel þenceð.
> Ic þæt gehyre, þæt þis is hold weorod
> frean Scyldinga." (286–91a)

> The guard, fearless officer, spoke from where he sat on his horse: "The intelligent shield-warrior, one who thinks properly, must make judgments on both words and deeds. This much I hear: that this is a band loyal to the lord of the Scyldings."

Not only the disarming openness of Beowulf's manner but his cautious way of offering assistance and his ready concessions to the potential power of fate may have struck a response in the coastguard, for he himself seems to show a similarly circumspect attitude toward the future in the last lines of his own speech:

> Swylce ic maguþegnas mine hate
> wið feonda gehwone flotan eowerne,
> niwtyrwydne nacan on sande
> arum healdan, oþðæt eft byreð
> ofer lagustreamas leofne mannan
> wudu wundenhals to Wedermearce,
> godfremmendra swylcum gifeþe bið
> þæt þone hilderæs hal gedigeð.
> (293–300)

> Furthermore I will tell my men to keep your ship safe against any enemy, to watch over the new-tarred

> boat on the beach until, with its curved prow, it will carry the dear man back to Geatland across the sea-currents, whichever of the brave men is fated to survive the onslaught unharmed.

While he seems quite confident that Beowulf will return to his boat, the last clause of this speech has a way of cautiously knocking on wood: Beowulf will come back, or whichever of them is lucky enough to come back alive. But it should be added that there are other ways in which this passage has been taken.[8]

Close study of this part of the poem increases a reader's respect for the poet's artistry. His economy of means is remarkable: each speech, each gesture is part of a slow-developing epiphany that is meant to be savored by an intent audience. The ways of presenting and characterizing the hero are constantly varied, almost in the rhythm of speech—action—speech—action.

After the Geats leave the coastguard and proceed toward Heorot, an important passage describes their appearance as they walk up to the hall.

> Stræt wæs stanfah, stig wisode
> gumum ætgædere. Guðbyrne scan
> heard hondlocen, hringiren scir
> song in searwum, þa hie to sele furðum
> in hyra gryregeatwum gangan cwomon.
> Setton sæmeþe side scyldas,
> rondas regnhearde, wið þæs recedes weal,
> bugon þa to bence. Byrnan hringdon,

8. My translation follows Klæber and Dobbie in the interpretation of the last clause. The translations by Clark Hall and William Alfred, however, both take the last two lines here quoted as an independent sentence and hence as virtually a flat statement that Beowulf will be the survivor.

guðsearo gumena; garas stodon,
sæmanna searo, samod ætgædere,
æscholt ufan græg; wæs se irenþreat
wæpnum gewurþad. (320–31a)

The highway was well-paved with stones, and the path guided the men together. Each mailshirt shone, hard and hand-linked; the bright iron-rings in their armor shrilled as they came walking up to the hall in their menacing wargear. Weary from the voyage, they placed their wide shields with the hardened rims against the wall of the building and sank down on the bench, as their mailshirts clashed, woven by cunning for war. The spears stood all together, the seamen's equipment, an ash-forest [iron-]grey on top. That iron troop was fitted out with good weapons.

This passage has great richness of sensuous detail, of a kind ordinarily more typical of Homeric epic poetry than of Germanic.[9] Appeal is made to sight (*scan, scir, æscholt ufan græg*), to sound (*song, hringdon,* and the distinctly onomatopoeic effect in *hringiren scir*), and to touch (*heard hondlocen, regnhearde*). But details like this only contribute a certain added vividness to the dominant impression that the passage gives: a sense of disciplined power. No individual is singled out from this group which marches toward the Danish hall, moving in a community of will. They have the weapons to use, we are repeatedly reminded, but none are to be put to use on this occasion. The wide shields are placed against the wall; the spears are stacked together; the heavily armored men peaceably take seats on the bench. The impression of

9. See also Arthur G. Brodeur's discussion of this passage in *The Art of Beowulf* (Berkeley and Los Angeles, University of California Press, 1959), pp. 41–44; he especially emphasizes the patterns of variation.

power so finely suggested by gleam of polished steel and clash of mail is, paradoxically, brought out all the more strongly by the intense self-control that accompanies its display here. The final image of the forest of spears[10] standing *samod ætgædere,* all together like a company of men[11] beside the group of seated men, is like the image of a ghost-band, the image of potential power still vibrant in the scene.

We should note that it is to this total impression of the approaching Geats that Wulfgar, Hrothgar's majordomo, responds directly in his speech of challenge.

> Hwanon ferigeað ge fætte scyldas,
> græge syrcan ond grimhelmas,
> heresceafta heap? Ic eom Hroðgares
> ar ond ombiht. Ne seah ic elþeodige
> þus manige men modiglicran.
> Wen ic þæt ge for wlenco, nalles for wræcsiðum,
> ac for higeþrymmum Hroðgar sohton. (333–39)

> From what place do you bring these plated shields, grey mailshirts, mask-helmets, this army of spear-shafts? I am Hrothgar's herald and officer. I have never seen so many foreigners so courageous. I believe that you have come to see Hrothgar out of sheer pride and greatness of spirit, certainly not as adventurers in exile.

Their weapons, symbols of raw power, meet his eye first. But what kind of power and how used? It is his office to read these symbols and by them to judge men and their motives. One manifestation of power can be ruled out: they are clearly not piratical adventurers or refugee exiles on the prowl. The same air of self-assuredness that impressed the coastguard

10. So I would interpret *æscholt ufan græg*: a forest of ash trees iron-grey at the top rather than their normal green. This reading was suggested by Brodeur, *The Art of Beowulf*, p. 30.

11. As in *sibbegedriht samod ætgædere* 387, 729.

impresses Wulfgar; he knows intuitively that it is the purest heroic energy which has brought them there.[12]

It is also part of Wulfgar's office, so far as we can tell, to uphold *duguðe þeaw,* decorous courtly behavior and the proper observance of ritual, and consequently one may think of him as challenging Beowulf to measure up to his standards in this respect. We have very little courtly conversation in Old English poetry outside of *Beowulf* to judge by, but surely Beowulf's speech here is a flawless specimen of courteous rhetoric.

> Him þa ellenrof andswarode,
> wlanc Wedera leod, word æfter spræc,
> heard under helme: "We synt Higelaces
> beodgeneatas; Beowulf is min nama.
> Wille ic asecgan sunu Healfdenes,
> mærum þeodne, min ærende,
> aldre þinum, gif he us geunnan wile
> þæt we hine swa godne gretan moton."
> (340–47)

> Then, famous for his daring, the proud lord of Geats answered, speaking his words as he stood grim in his helmet: "We are sharers of Hygelac's table. My name is Beowulf. I wish to explain my errand to that famous prince your lord, Healfdene's son, if he is willing to grant us permission to see him, great man that he is."

12. Motivation is contained in the key phrase *for wlenco,* which is hard to translate. Small wonder, if the quality of being *wlonc* really includes all that Schücking ("Heldenstolz und Würde," 20 n.) attributes to it: "Treue, ein Begriff, der oft fast mit 'Ehre' identisch gebraucht wird, weil er der Kern des Pflichtensystems ist, Aktivität, Entschlossenheit, Zuverlässigkeit im Halten von Versprechungen . . . , Klugheit, Überlegenheit, Freigebigkeit, wie auch Beherrschung der gesellschaftlichen Form." Pirkhofer (*Figurengestaltung,* pp. 106–07) calls attention to the occurrence of *wlonc hæleð* 331, describing Wulfgar, and *for wlenco* 338 and *wlanc Wedera leod* 341, describing Beowulf.

There are noteworthy contrasts here: the introductory sentence emphasizes Beowulf's strength and tough soldierly appearance (*heard under helme*); the speech itself opens with Beowulf's quiet self-identification and continues in the soft and deferential tones of his modest request to see Hrothgar. Courtesy and power coexist here; it is essentially the same contrast expressed earlier in the description of the Geats' arrival at the hall, a contrast only when analyzed, of course, for then we can see the two parts of the inseparable paradox in the figure of Beowulf: absolute strength, absolutely controlled and guided.

Wulfgar's use of some of the words of Beowulf's speech in his own reply is perhaps in itself evidence that the hero has passed this particular test.[13] More importantly, Wulfgar when he speaks to Hrothgar seems to have been as impressed by Beowulf as the coastguard was earlier. Like the coastguard, he seems to come close to forgetting his official speech in his excitement and to move beyond the mere routine transmission of a message to personal praise of the hero:

> Her syndon geferede, feorran cumene
> ofer geofenes begang Geata leode;
> þone yldestan oretmecgas
> Beowulf nemnað. Hy benan synt
> þæt hie, þeoden min, wið þe moton
> wordum wrixlan. No ðu him wearne geteoh
> ðinra gegncwida, glædman Hroðgar!
> Hy on wiggetawum wyrðe þinceað
> eorla geæhtlan; huru se aldor deah,
> se þæm heaðorincum hider wisade. (361–70)

Geatish people, come from far away, have been carried here over the ocean's circuit. The one in

13. B. *wille ic* / W. *ic . . . wille;* B. *mærum þeodne* / W. *þeoden mærne;* B. *hine swa godne* / W. *se goda.* Cf. Wulfgar's later recasting of Hrothgar's speech (371 ff.) in lines 391–98.

command the warriors call Beowulf. They are petitioning to be allowed to exchange words with you, my lord. Be sure not to refuse them your conversation, gracious Hrothgar! In their wargear they seem quite worthy of the respect of noblemen; at any rate, their leader is a good man, the one who led the warriors here.

Also worth noting in this speech is the shifting back and forth from singular to plural, individual to group, Beowulf to his band of Geats. Such shifting is evident also in the way the coastguard sees first the group and then singles out Beowulf within it, and indeed it runs all through this part of the poem. In this speech Wulfgar moves from group (*Geata leode*) to individual (*þone yldestan . . . Beowulf*) and again from group (*hy benan synt . . . hy wyrðe þinceað*) to individual (*huru se aldor deah*). Significantly the speech ends with the focus on Beowulf.

In the impression it gives of powerful unified movement and purpose, as we have seen in the voyage and in the march to Heorot, the group of men surrounding Beowulf serves partly to characterize him. At the same time it serves also as a foil or contrasting background to set him apart. To take a simple example:

Aras þa se rica, ymb hine rinc manig,
þryðlic þegna heap; sume þær bidon,
heaðoreaf heoldon, swa him se hearda bebead.
(399–401)

Then the mighty one rose, many a warrior around him, a powerful band of thanes; some of them waited there and guarded the arms as the brave man commanded.

While Beowulf clearly rises above the many warriors who surround him, in such passages they seem also to be in part reflections of his power and sounding boards for his heroic qualities. The hero is extended and amplified by surrounding mirrors. These descriptions also remind us that the hero exists as one man among men, that he moves among them, that he works in (and, in Beowulf's case, for) a social world. Even though Hrothgar speaks almost exclusively of Beowulf as an individual, known already by reputation and believed already to be the rescuer sent by God to save Denmark, Wulfgar remains severely plural in his language when he invites the Geats to enter the hall. Such a form of address maintains the emphasis on the group, and the hero now moves with his men (*snyredon ætsonne,* they hastened together) under the roof of Heorot.

But now, in his third speech, the climactic address to Hrothgar (lines 407–55), Beowulf must step forward from the group, alone at last, and assert himself as an individual in the frankest terms. He does so in a speech that is resoundingly first-person-singular throughout: in the 49 lines of the speech there are no fewer than 27 instances of forms of the first person pronoun, and only one reference to his men ([*ond*] *minra eorla gedryht* 431). We can now see that the focus on the group which was so evident before this speech serves as a device of dramatic contrast to bring out the glorious burst of heroic egotism that follows. It is now high time for the hero to lay aside modesty and stand out from the crowd.

The speech begins with Beowulf's statement of who he is —and here, as almost always, he begins to define his own identity by stating his relationship to his lord Hygelac—and what he has done (*mærða fela*), and then it moves on to a brief account of how it happened that he heard of Grendel and how he was urged by his people to undertake the voyage to Denmark. The Geats back at home are summoned only as witnesses to his strength, forming a kind of objective validation for his claims.[14] So far things are calm, and the heroic

14. Pirkhofer, *Figurengestaltung,* pp. 108–09.

power has been kept pretty much under wraps, but now it breaks out as he begins to describe, in flashing rapid movements, his monster-slaying of the past.

> Selfe ofersawon, ða ic of searwum cwom,
> fah from feondum; þær ic fife geband,
> yðde eotena cyn ond on yðum slog
> niceras nihtes, nearoþearfe dreah,
> wræc Wedera nið (wean ahsodon),
> forgrand gramum, ond nu wið Grendel sceal,
> wið þam aglæcan, ana gehegan
> ðing wið þyrse. (419–26a)

> They themselves [the Geats] looked on when I came back covered with blood from the enemies' ambushes. That was where I bound five of them, wiped out a race of giants, and killed water-monsters in the waves by night; I had hell's own time of it, but I got even with them for their attack on the Geats—they were asking for trouble. I obliterated those devils. And now it's with that terrible monster Grendel that I have a lawsuit to settle, all by myself.

A series of forceful verbs—*cwom, geband, yðde, slog, dreah, wræc, forgrand*—builds up an exultant momentum; without pause we are carried on to Grendel (*ond nu wið Grendel sceal*) as the next logical object of violence. (That the fight with Grendel is described in lawyer's terms, after all this violence, is typical of Anglo-Saxon irony.) Indeed the impetus of this burst of heroic energy is so great that it carries Beowulf a little beyond good manners, for he has not yet asked Hrothgar for permission to undertake the fight. So now the style changes, and in formal terms Beowulf requests leave to cleanse Heorot. Control has been clamped on again, as we can see in the leisurely respectful mode of address, the four honorific vocatives, the shift from active verbs to nouns. This is Wulfgar's courtly dialect again.

Ic þe nu ða,
brego Beorhtdena, biddan wille,
eodor Scyldinga, anre bene,
þæt ðu me ne forwyrne, wigendra hleo,
freowine folca, nu ic þus feorran com,
þæt ic mote ana [ond] minra eorla gedryht,
þes hearda heap, Heorot fælsian. (426b–32)

Prince of the bright Danes, protector of Scyldings, I wish to ask you now for one favor: that you not refuse, keeper of warriors, noble friend of peoples, now that I have come this far, permission for me alone and my troop of men, this rugged band, to cleanse Heorot.

The alternation of styles continues. When Beowulf mentions Grendel's scorn of weapons and resolves to fight him barehanded, what begins as calm and earnest discussion concludes with the grim visualization of conflict in terms of absolute opposition:

Ac ic mid grape sceal
fon wið feonde ond ymb feorh sacan,
lað wið laþum; ðær gelyfan sceal
dryhtnes dome se þe hine deað nimeð.
(438b–41)

On the contrary I will be obliged to grapple with the enemy with my hands and fight for life, one enemy against another. Whichever one death takes will have to submit to the Lord's judgment.

And the mention of death leads to Beowulf's cool and detached guess at what will undoubtedly happen to him if Grendel wins, a prospect he recounts with something like humorous gusto. The notion that he is merely an athletic simpleton with no idea of what is in store for him in this fight must be dispelled; he knows that Grendel scorns weapons, that Grendel will try to capture and devour Geats in the hall, that he may very well succeed in capturing and devouring Beowulf.[15]

> Na þu minne þearft
> hafalan hydan, ac he me habban wile
> d[r]eore fahne, gif mec deað nimeð.
> Byreð blodig wæl, byrgean þenceð,
> eteð angenga unmurnlice,
> mearcað morhopu; no ðu ymb mines ne þearft
> lices feorme leng sorgian. (445b–51)

> No need at all for you to cover up my head [in funeral rite; see Dobbie's note on the line]; no, *he* will want to have me bright with blood, if death takes me. He will carry off the bloody corpse, intending to taste (?) it; walking alone he will eat it without remorse and make marks on the moor's hiding-places. No, there will be no need for you to be concerned with the care of my body any longer!

Variants of the same formula ring like a refrain through the latter half of the speech: *se þe hine deað nimeð, gif mec deað nimeð, gif mec hild nime*. Death is a possibility that Beowulf is ready not only to concede but to examine with interest and practical realism: if I end up being killed in this affair, send this mailshirt back to Hygelac; it's very valuable. Things will happen as they will happen.[16]

15. Schücking ("Heldenstolz und Würde," pp. 37–38) points out that Beowulf's ability to picture clearly what might happen to him is what contributes most of the dominant tone of iron determination in this speech.

16. The reader may recall that the well-known statement of the heroic attitude in Tennyson's *Ulysses* contains a similar facing of the possibility of disaster:

> For my purpose holds
> To sail beyond the sunset, and the baths
> Of all the western stars, until I die.
> It may be that the gulfs will wash us down:
> It may be we will touch the Happy Isles,
> And see the great Achilles, whom we knew.

Yet the description of Grendel carrying off Beowulf's body has a kind of casual gaiety about it; it is a ghoulish situation totally controlled by humor. For there is evidence that Beowulf is playing on words throughout in most Hamlet-like fashion. Hrothgar will be relieved of the burden of funeral arrangements since Grendel has agreed to take care of them. He will "bear" the body, presumably like some grotesque pallbearer; he will take care to *byrgean* it (taste it? bury it? or—conceivably—a pun on both?[17]); he will walk alone, in a funeral procession of one, eating it *unmurnlice,* without much mourning; and then at last he will "mark" his moor hideouts (with a memorial inscription of some sort?). This hero Beowulf, with his eyes wide open, has the strength and control of the situation to joke in the face of death. The same boisterous kind of heroic humor comes out again in Beowulf's reply to Unferth, as we shall see shortly.

Hrothgar's reply (to treat it very briefly) draws for us the limits of his own effectiveness, any ordinary man's effectiveness. He once settled successfully the feud in which Beowulf's father had been involved, for that was a problem that it was possible for a man to deal with; but now he is faced with the feud with Grendel, something insoluble in such terms, a *feohleas gefeoht.* He confirms the gory picture Beowulf has just sketched; indeed, he says, men have often boasted in the past that they would wait for Grendel to come, but all that was left of them in the morning was blood on the floor and on the benches. But his gloomy attitude toward these facts is sharply differentiated from Beowulf's, here and elsewhere.

The exchange between Unferth and Beowulf that follows is the climax of the process of challenge and heroic response.[18]

17. Certainly not a very good pun in the original Anglian dialect we assume for the poem: the Anglian forms would be *byrga(n)* (bury) and *berga(n)* (taste). If we leave the pun aside as quite improbable, the single meaning "bury" here ought not to be entirely rejected as a possibility.

18. Only a few aspects of this complicated episode are relevant

By the time we reach the end of Beowulf's reply to Unferth, Hrothgar is wholly convinced that Beowulf will help him, as the poet tells us, and shortly thereafter Hrothgar turns the hall over to Beowulf, as he has never done to anyone before. Whatever may be Unferth's role in the court or in the traditional legend of Heorot, clearly his dramatic function in this part of the poem is to present this final challenge to Beowulf and by that challenge to bring out new aspects of the hero.

The literary problem here seems to me to be this, if we consider it from the poet's point of view: how to show your hero's more aggressive and ferocious qualities when he is among friends. Book VIII of the *Odyssey* offers a well-known parallel to the situation here, which is most illuminating. The hero comes by sea to a highly civilized country; he is put through some situations that test his tact and resourcefulness, and he is required to give evidence of civilized behavior; yet at a certain point it becomes necessary for him to manifest his *furor heroicus* without actually attacking his hosts directly.[19]

Odysseus, the amiable guest of the Phaeacians, is watching their athletic contests when he is deliberately insulted by Euryalus:

> I should never have taken you for an athlete such as one is accustomed to meet in the world. But rather for some skipper of a merchant crew, who spends his life on a hulking tramp, worrying about his outward

---

to the discussion here. Two recent articles on Unferth treat the problem of his role in some detail: see James L. Rosier, "Design for Treachery: the Unferth Intrigue," *PMLA*, 77 (1962), 1–7, and Norman E. Eliason, "The Þyle and Scop in Beowulf," *Speculum*, 38 (1963), 267–84.

19. This particular instance of parallels has been most recently examined (from the point of view of traditional narrative patterns) by Albert Bates Lord, "Beowulf and Odysseus," *Franciplegius: Medieval and Linguistic Studies in Honor of Francis Peabody Magoun, Jr.*, ed. Jess B. Bessinger, Jr., and Robert P. Creed (New York, New York University Press, 1965), pp. 86–91.

> freight, or keeping a sharp eye on the cargo when he comes home with the profits he has snatched. No; one can see you are no sportsman.[20]

Odysseus' answer is sharp indeed and couched in terms of counterinsult: "That, sir, was an ugly speech, and you must be a fool to have made it. . . . You have the brains of a dolt. You have stirred me to anger with your inept remarks." After he has hurled the discus a tremendous distance, Odysseus launches into an open assertion of his powers:

> Philoctetes was the only one who used to beat me with the bow when we Achaeans practiced archery at Troy. Of all others now alive and eating their bread on the face of the earth, I claim to be by far the best.

But most interesting is the speech made by King Alcinous of the Phaeacians after Odysseus has ended his boast.

> 'My friend,' said the King, 'we can take no exception to what you say. Angered as you are at the way this fellow came up and insulted you in the lists, you naturally wish to prove your native mettle. No one who knew how to talk sense would thus have belittled your prowess.'

Here the literary device of what we might term the necessary insult is virtually explained to us. It becomes suddenly "natural" for the hero who has been attacked to reveal his powers; but his self-assertion does not really dispel the surrounding atmosphere of courtesy. The hero is granted the chance to play the roles of chivalrous Gawain and the rude and boisterous Green Knight at the same time.

In *Beowulf,* it is hard for a modern reader not to feel that

20. Homer, *The Odyssey,* trans. E. V. Rieu (Baltimore, Penguin Books, 1946), p. 126.

Unferth's rude speech gives expression to some of the unconscious tension and antagonism that one can assume must have existed among the Danes, humiliated as they were by their own failure. In any event, the speech abruptly shatters an artfully woven spell of peace and harmony:

> Scop hwilum sang
> hador on Heorote. Þær wæs hæleða dream,
> duguð unlytel Dena ond Wedera.
> *Un*ferð maþelode, Ecglafes bearn,
> þe æt fotum sæt frean Scyldinga,
> onband beadurune. (496b–501a)

> At times the minstrel sang, clear-voiced in Heorot. There was happiness among men, a great host of Danes and Geats. Unferth spoke up, son of Ecglaf, sitting at the feet of the Scyldings' lord; he unwound war-runes.

The two peoples sit together, Danes and Geats, formed by the power of song and drink and courtesy into a single *duguð*, but the potential *unfrið, unsib, discordia* latent in the scene is given voice by the figure of Unferth.[21]

Unferth's attack not only permits Beowulf to describe one of his own past exploits in full, it absolutely requires that he do so, and in sufficient detail to refute Unferth's charges. The details that Beowulf adds of course inform us of other qualifications for his forthcoming tasks: his swimming prowess, his experience in battling monsters of the deep, his present maturity seen now in relation to the time when he was an exuberant boy. Most importantly it gives him the chance to be rude and tough and aggressive, and perhaps also even

21. See Morton W. Bloomfield, "Beowulf and Christian Allegory: An Interpretation of Unferth," *Traditio,* 7 (1949–51), 410–15, for a discussion of the probable origins of Unferth as an allegorical figure. But there is no need to assume, as Bloomfield does, that this is allegory squarely in the tradition of Prudentius.

frankly patriotic in his boasting of Geatish power, and yet to be all these things without losing the keenly sardonic edge of wit that is in itself evidence of rational and detached control.

Unferth makes two charges against Beowulf. First he alleges that Beowulf is an irresponsible braggart who attempts rash and senseless exploits involving the risk of life *for dolgilpe,* for the sake of foolish boasting. In other words, to return to the terms we have been using here, he claims that Beowulf is beyond any rational control, whether self-control or the intelligent advice of others, whom Unferth here represents as trying to dissuade him from the swimming contest. Secondly, Unferth claims that Beowulf simply failed to accomplish what he bragged about doing: he was beaten in the contest with Breca. Considered in the light of what is demanded for the task at Heorot, these charges are serious enough. If Beowulf is only a conceited and incompetent fool, the Danes will lose dignity by even entertaining his claims or tolerating his presence. They should send him away at once.

The test involves, of course, not only proper answers to these specific charges but the proper attitude toward the insulting speech itself. Hence Beowulf's answer must be directed, in a sense, against two antagonists: first Breca and then Unferth. Beowulf addresses Unferth directly in his first sentence, ironically full of mock admiration for Unferth's beery eloquence, but returns to him again only some fifty lines later, after he has told the full story of Breca and the swim.

Unferth considers the swimming exploit silly and dangerous. That much Beowulf is quick to concede in his admission that they were merely foolish boys at the time:

Wit þæt gecwædon cnihtwesende
ond gebeotedon (wæron begen þa git
on geogoðfeore) þæt wit on garsecg ut

aldrum neðdon, ond þæt geæfndon swa.
(535–38)

We two vowed and swore when we were boys (both of us still very young) that we would risk our lives out on the open sea, and so we did.

Beowulf's very admission of the boyishness of the exploit in its initial stages reminds us of his openness at the time of his arrival in Denmark. Both the candor and the boyishness become points in his favor insofar as they suggest an attractively wild vitality and exuberance. But the account Beowulf gives of the swim introduces the element of responsibility almost at once:

Hæfdon swurd nacod, þa wit on sund reon,
heard on handa; wit unc wið hronfixas
werian þohton. No he wiht fram me
flodyþum feor fleotan meahte,
hraþor on holme; no ic fram him wolde.
(539–43)

We both had naked swords in our hands when we swam out to sea, all very resolute; we intended to defend ourselves against whales. But he could never swim any distance away from me in the waves or any faster. And I did not wish to leave him.

Beowulf stays close to Breca in the swim, he implies, in order to keep an eye on him. Breca is unable to swim off by himself; Beowulf is unwilling to leave his friend. The contrast is sufficiently underlined by the *no . . . no* parallel construction and by the placing of *meahte* and *wolde* at the ends of successive lines. The irresponsible boy, if there ever really was one, has grown up fast.

What began as an exploit soon turns into an ordeal. Unferth had not said anything of this. Breca and Beowulf are separated by a storm and must struggle for their lives.

Ða wit ætsomne on sæ wæron
fif nihta fyrst, oþþæt unc flod todraf,
wado weallende, wedera cealdost,
nipende niht, ond norþanwind
heaðogrim ondhwearf; hreo wæron yþa.
(544–48)

Then the two of us were together in the sea for five nights, until the waters, swelling waves, the coldest of storms, darkening night, all drove us apart, and the vindictive north-wind came up against us. The waves were rough.

A storm, and with it very probably the conventional poetic associations of a storm for the Anglo-Saxon audience: exile, loneliness, the dreaded isolation of the individual. In a society so solidly based in communal tradition, to be together, *ætsomne,* is in itself a kind of joy; to be separated and alone is to suffer and to feel cold and darkness. This much we can learn from the Old English elegies, but there the meditative exiles can only mourn. Beowulf is an epic hero; he acts, and angry sea-beasts instantly materialize for him to act upon. The intricate details of the struggle with the sea-monsters are meant to sound authentic. Beowulf is dragged beneath the surface by these creatures, who intend to feast on him at their banquet on the sea-bottom. Instead they themselves lie dead up on the shore after the fight. Beowulf's descent and rise from the depths put an end to the monsters and clear the sea-lanes. Light breaks over his successful achievement, and he is able to sight land. Finally the sea bears him to shore.

In the literal sense Unferth is answered. Breca and Beowulf were not having a serious contest; what boasting they may have done was the innocent boasting of children; Breca could never outswim Beowulf. But Beowulf's speech provides another more compelling kind of answer by its transcendence of such small facts. More aspects of Beowulf's attractive character are incidentally revealed: his sense of humor, his friendship with Breca, his adventurous youth, and the way he seems to perform acts of public service by casual instinct (here by clearing the sea of monsters so that ships can pass through unharmed).

But beyond this Beowulf's account of the swim is a brilliantly successful instance of a poetic statement of theme. The pattern of physical action in this scene has many parallels elsewhere in the poem: the rising and falling, the sharp and dramatic reversals of fortune, the upsetting without warning of confident expectations—all these are expressed by the usual rhetorical signals already discussed in Chapter One. In this scene, however, it is the image of the sea, on which and in which all this action takes place, that gives an unusual concreteness and vividness to the familiar patterns.

For the dominant image here is of the swimmer in the sea, resisting it, yielding to it, being carried along by it. It is the image of the perpetual interaction of an active participant with a medium that is buoyant and supporting but always potentially fatal.

We should note that in this passage Beowulf uses at least four expressions of a kind familiar enough in the poem, expressions that attribute his success to agents outside himself. Two of them appear in these lines:

Hwæþre me gyfeþe wearð
þæt ic aglæcan orde geræhte,
hildebille; heaþoræs fornam
mihtig meredeor þurh mine hand.
(555b–58)

But it was granted to me to pierce the monster with the point of my battle-sword. A violent onslaught did away with the mighty sea-beast, through my hand.

And two of them in these:

Wyrd oft nereð
unfægne eorl, þonne his ellen deah.
Hwæþere me gesælde þæt ic mid sweorde ofsloh
niceras nigene. (572b–75a)

> Fate often rescues a man who is not doomed, when his courage is good. Anyway it fell to my lot that I killed nine monsters with my sword.

On three other occasions he gives credit to specific outside agents: to his mailshirt (and the unknown human hands that wove it for him) for helping protect him in the initial attack; to light from the east, God's bright beacon, which enables him to see the sea-cliffs; to the sea, which finally bears him to *Finna land.*[22]

Much of the peculiar power of this episode arises from the implicit comparison of man's life in a largely inscrutable and fate-dominated world to the figure of a swimmer in the sea—the heroic life, that is, for the hero is always a swimmer; perhaps others merely drift or, like Unferth, stay ashore in fear of the sea. Beowulf risks being carried by the sea, knowing its power is surely far greater than his own. Such clear-eyed recognition is not the least source of his strength.

Viewed in this way, the account of the swim seems to suggest, in powerfully symbolic terms, that the significance of man's life is in the encounter, and in the courage to em-

22. "To the imagination of a seafaring people, the power of the sea would be connected with a force not under human control, yet interwoven completely with the pattern of their lives" (Peter F. Fisher, "The Trials of the Epic Hero in *Beowulf*," *PMLA*, 73 [1958], 176). A different view is that of G. L. Brook (*A History of the English Language* [London, Andre Deutsch, 1958], p. 156): "The frequent impersonal constructions in Old English are in keeping with a belief in the subordinate nature of purely human actions which caused the hero of the Old English poem *Beowulf* to describe in a strikingly detached way his slaying of a sea monster." Brook goes on to refer to lines 555b–58.

brace the destructive element and to give oneself wholly to the sea—with that attitude combining both élan and wariness (or *fortitudo* and *sapientia*) so typical of this hero, as we have seen. Beowulf is carried away from his friend by the storm and fights for survival with all his courage and skill. Light comes; fate rescues him; the very sea itself now carries him to safety on the shore. It is not said explicitly that these last events are in any sense a reward for the way he has acted (who knows that?), but it is plain enough that the only reward one is likely to get will come as the result of the immersion of the individual in the sea of experience as it is, ready to risk all in the meeting. *Wyrd oft nereð unfægne eorl, þonne his ellen deah.* Fate will often save, the sea will often buoy up, the lucky man, when he has the courage, and when he swims strongly.[23]

The whole heroic tone of this narrative forms part of Beowulf's answer to Unferth, when he at last turns to him again at the end of his speech. And the other part of his answer consists in his deft and devastating use of verbal weapons. What deeds has Unferth ever done of this kind? If he had ever done any, Beowulf would certainly have heard of them, for Beowulf is well enough informed to know that Unferth has been involved in the murder of his own brothers.

23. The image of swimming seems to be ancient, ubiquitous, and inevitable. Cf. the shipwreck scenes in the *Odyssey* and the *Æneid*. Lucretius' famous lines (*De Rerum Natura II.* 1–2) on the pleasure of watching from the shore a swimmer struggling in rough waters are often quoted by the theorists of tragedy. Critics themselves use a similar metaphor:

> Think of life or tragedy as a divine law court, in which the dooms are proportioned to the mistakes of head or heart, and we wholly deceive ourselves. Conceive it rather under a different figure—the tide setting against the wind, the seas leaping high when the current of character makes against the gale of circumstance. Not until resisted does the current show its strength, not until it meets the unfriendly facts is character revealed. (W. Macneile Dixon, *Tragedy* [2d ed. London, C. Arnold & Co., 1925], p. 138)

But perhaps Unferth is better at killing brothers than monsters. It is even hinted that Unferth has never been able to defend Heorot against Grendel because of a crucial lack of moral authority: no brother-slayer can defend the hall against a descendant of Cain.

The conclusion of Beowulf's speech is blunt, witty, brilliantly rhetorical with its series of clashing *ac* phrases and the final ironic sentence:

Gæþ eft se þe mot
to medo modig, siþþan morgenleoht
ofer ylda bearn oþres dogores,
sunne sweglwered suþan scineð.
(603b–06)

> He who is permitted will once again go bravely to the mead-drinking, after the morning light of a new day, the sun clothed in brightness, shines from the south upon the sons of men.

Even Unferth can be courageous in the bright morning sunlight, after the danger has been cleared away. We come full circle to the opening of the speech with its allusion to those who are brave over a few drinks.

To round out this examination of the way the hero is presented in the poem, we should look at a scene, much like the Breca episode in some ways, that contains several of the techniques and themes we have been discussing. This is the passage preceding Beowulf's descent into the evil mere in search of Grendel's mother.

Hrothgar's famous description of the haunted mere (lines 1345–82) is so often read as an isolated set piece that its real meaning in context is usually ignored. It must be taken together with the speech by Beowulf that follows and with the action that follows as well. The symbolic associations of the mere will be discussed in a more appropriate place in the next chapter. Here it is enough to summarize the emotional effect of Hrothgar's description: it succeeds in creating an intense fear of the unnatural aspects of the mere, a fear that is objectified in the fine image of the hunted stag that would rather die on the shore than take refuge in a place so repugnant to every normal instinct. Hrothgar concludes his appalling vision by challenging Beowulf to invade this region, one which he has never yet even seen: *sec gif þu dyrre,* seek if you dare. This passage, together with Beowulf's answer, will have to be quoted at some length:

"Nu is se ræd gelang
eft æt þe anum. Eard git ne const,
frecne stowe, ðær þu findan miht
felasinnigne secg; sec gif þu dyrre.
Ic þe þa fæhðe feo leanige,
ealdgestreonum, swa ic ær dyde,
wund*num* golde, gyf þu on weg cymest."
Beowulf maþelode, bearn Ecgþeowes:
"Ne sorga, snotor guma; selre bið æghwæm
þæt he his freond wrece, þonne he fela murne.
Ure æghwylc sceal ende gebidan
worolde lifes; wyrce se þe mote
domes ær deaþe; þæt bið drihtguman
unlifgendum æfter selest.
Aris, rices weard, uton *r*aþe feran
Grendles magan gang sceawigan.
Ic hit þe gehate, no he on helm losaþ,
ne on foldan fæþm, ne on fyrgenholt,
ne on gyfenes grund, ga þær he wille.
Ðys dogor þu geþyld hafa
weana gehwylces, swa ic þe wene to."
(1376b–96)

"Now it is up to you again, and you alone, to find a way to solve this. You do not know that region yet, that dangerous place where you can find that sinful

> creature; seek her if you dare. As I did before, I will reward you for engaging in this fight with wealth and ancient treasures, with twisted gold—if you get away." Beowulf spoke, the son of Ecgtheow: "Do not be sad, wise man that you are. It is better for everyone to avenge a friend than to mourn a great deal. Each one of us has to live until the end of life in this world. If we can, we should earn fame before death, for that is the best thing a warrior can have after he is dead. Stand up now, guardian of the kingdom, and let us go quickly and look at the track of Grendel's mother. I promise you this: she will never escape to safety, not in the embrace of earth, not in the mountain forest, not at the bottom of the sea, no matter where she may go."

It is important to see that Beowulf in his reply is not concerned with the mere or its nature, despite the terrifying description; he is concerned with Hrothgar's state of mind. And he proceeds at once to the chief point he must make if he is to enlighten Hrothgar: he must explain the difference between passively contemplating the mystery of evil and acting promptly in resistance to it, the difference between *murne* and *wrece*. Do not live in sorrow, he tells Hrothgar; act, do not mourn; work to gain glory rather than sit waiting for the end of life to come. Now arise and walk over to look at the track; stand on your feet, move, take the symbolic step. And only after these insistent calls to action have been uttered does Beowulf refer directly to what Hrothgar has been saying of the mere. But now, to men on their feet and in action, the nature of the mere has become something else.

Hrothgar's description of the mere is spellbinding in something more than a figurative sense; the cumulative enumeration of horrors summons up a vision of the enemy's power which paralyzes the will. That is why Beowulf's reply contains an enumeration which can be understood as a form of counterspell or as an exorcizing incantation:

> Ic hit þe gehate: no he on helm losaþ,
> ne on foldan fæþm, ne on fyrgenholt,
> ne on gyfenes grund, ga þær he wille!

The clear light of the heroic will is in these chanted negatives, directed with full force against the dark places of the world and somehow robbing them of fear. Small wonder that Hrothgar recovers from his trance state and leaps to his feet, thanking God for what Beowulf has said.

The passage that follows (1399–1424) maintains the same fundamental contrast between Beowulf as the one who acts and Hrothgar as the one who feels. For, while it is true that Hrothgar is here taking action by making the journey to the mere, the emphasis is on his state of mind. The journey is Hrothgar's own private expedition of vengeance, for we are reminded of the identity of the latest victim:

> Magoþegna bær
> þone selestan sawolleasne
> þara þe mid Hroðgare ham eahtode.
> (1405b–07)

> She bore lifeless the best retainer of those who ruled over the hall with Hrothgar.

At the end of the journey, in a sentence constructed rhetorically to convey the maximum shock, by the delayed naming of the object found, the Danes find Æschere's head on the bank of the mere.

> Denum eallum wæs,
> winum Scyldinga, weorce on mode
> to geþolianne, ðegne monegum,
> oncyð eorla gehwæm, syðþan Æscheres
> on þam holmclife hafelan metton.
> (1417b–21)

> For all the Danes, the Scylding companions, it was torment to suffer in heart, it was grief to many a thane and every warrior, when, on the sea-cliff, they happened upon Æschere's head.

The shock at the end of Hrothgar's journey is not only that of finding Æschere's head; it is the shock of finding the mere itself, not now a fantasy but an actual place that is full of evil.[24] The Danes had seen the mere once before when they followed Grendel's footsteps there and glanced briefly at its blood-roiled surface. What was wanted then was merely evidence of Grendel's death; having obtained it, the Danes went frolicking back to Heorot in triumph, racing horses and listening to songs. Now they stare in gloomy horror at its loathsome inhabitants, really looking at it for the first time.

What the Danes are there for, poetically speaking, is to look, and to react emotionally, and not to act. The passage is full of phrases containing the idea of looking.[25] To reinforce the idea of looking by showing us what they are looking at so intently, the poet provides us with a rather elaborate description of the water-monsters in the mere, a description which is not, after all, otherwise really essential to the plot. We might be at the crocodile pool of a zoo. The Danes peer at these strange creatures, while Beowulf (or possibly another of the Geats, if *Geata leod* 1432 can be taken that way) takes a potshot at one of them. But while the Danes who have hauled the victim ashore are examining it, we notice that Beowulf's mind is already on other things. The contrast in their interests is sharply made:

24. The Danes are clearly the focus of interest during this journey. Hence it seems preferable to take the phrase *æðelinga bearn* 1408 as referring to Hrothgar rather than to Beowulf, and similarly *he feara sum* 1412.

25. For example, *wide gesyne* 1403; *wong sceawian* 1413; *folc to sægon* 1422; *gesawon* 1425; *weras sceawedon* 1440.

Weras sceawedon
gryrelicne gist. Gyrede hine Beowulf
eorlgewædum, nalles for ealdre mearn.
(1440b–42)

The men looked at the horrible strange thing. Beowulf put on his war-harness; he did not shrink from risking his life.

What then follows is a long and loving description of Beowulf's armor, item by item, concluding with the mention of the sword Hrunting, which Unferth is lending him. Beowulf's courage and Unferth's cowardice are brought into sharp and explicit juxtaposition:

Selfa ne dorste
under yða gewin aldre geneþan,
drihtscype dreogan; þær he dome forleas,
ellenmærðum. Ne wæs þæm oðrum swa,
syðþan he hine to guðe gegyred hæfde.
(1468b–72)

He himself [Unferth] did not dare risk life under the tumult of waves, or act like a hero; that was where he lost glory and a reputation for courage. It was not like that with the other man, after he had dressed himself for the fight.

While Unferth may not be the typical Danish warrior, in this context he is unquestionably representative of Danish inaction generally.

In his speech just before he enters the mere, Beowulf does not refer to the mere nor to his antagonist there, nor is he apparently concerned with his emotions or with his reputation, as Hrothgar and Unferth in their way have been. His speech is in fact a plain unsentimental last will and testament, showing a practical and very proper concern for the welfare of his men and for the disposition of his own possessions. He is not really concerned with the things so much as with the relationships they stand for: Beowulf in his new role as Hrothgar's adopted son, as leader responsible to his followers, as Hygelac's thane, as guest and borrower, courteously acknowledging an obligation to Unferth. We will examine these relationships more fully in succeeding chapters; they are among the enduring realities of the poem. Beowulf's eyes are fixed on the right things.

So at last Beowulf plunges into the terrible mere and into a sustained narrative of nearly a hundred lines of sheer breathless action, climaxed by the final purifying ritual, the cutting off of Grendel's head. The mere, nature invaded and poisoned by evil, is cleansed and freed by his action. Nowhere in the poem are we more conscious that this is heroic poetry, that the focus is always steadily on the hero, and that the heart of it all is action.

For action here is defined for us over and over by contrast. By presenting the reactions of others together with those of Beowulf, the poet offers a full range of emotional possibilities, at the same time demonstrating again and again the superiority of Beowulf's behavior. In the course of the fight under the mere, we are in fact close to Beowulf's subjective feelings, but they are inseparable from the actions he takes. Action unites it all: the terrifying nature of the *ælwihta eard,* the home of alien creatures, which Hrothgar had so vividly described; the helpless horror of the Danes in their inability to confront what they see with any action of their own; the hard-hitting actuality of Grendel's mother as antagonist; the casual and absolute resolution of the hero; and the final gratifying total accomplishment.

A hole is to dig, runs the child's definition. A hero is to act. We can explore the further meaning of Beowulf's actions and his character only by shifting our attention now to the nature of his opponents in the heroic contest.

CHAPTER THREE

Shapes of Darkness

Cain begat the race of Grendel, and Grendel begat the race of scholars who speculate as to what his significance might be. It would be convenient to conclude that Grendel and his mother are nothing but predatory trolls, taken for granted in those days as the normal hazards of boggy regions and no more symbolic than a pair of man-eating tigers that have to be hunted down, but hardly anyone has ever been satisfied to believe this. Grendel and his mother loom too large for that. A great nation is brought to its knees by Grendel; mighty warriors are completely helpless against him. And he is earnestly and persistently associated by the poet with Cain, with evil demons and devils, with hell and damnation, and is represented again and again as the bearer of God's very specific wrath. Only a hero of fabulous strength and remarkable moral stature is able finally to defeat Grendel, and the hero succeeds in killing Grendel's mother only after an exhausting battle. It is natural to expect to find the same measure of moral significance in the hero's opponents that we find in the hero himself.

The plot, or plots, of *Beowulf* may be found elsewhere without this aura of significance. The Icelandic *Grettissaga,* for example, offers some rather close analogues.[1] The Glam

1. For a lucid discussion of the many problems connected with these analogues and their relation to *Beowulf,* see R. W. Chambers, *Beowulf: An Introduction,* 3d ed. with a supplement by C. L. Wrenn

episode (chapters 32–35) is a local ghost story attached to an isolated farm in Iceland. Glam, a walking corpse, attacks the farmhouse and wrestles with the outlaw-hero Grettir, who has volunteered to stay there overnight. But this story has a wholly different function in the *Grettissaga*. In the context of the saga as a whole, the main point of the episode seems to be the fatal curse that is inflicted on Grettir by the defeated Glam, something for which there is of course no parallel in *Beowulf*. The Sandhaugar episode (chapters 64–66), in which Grettir fights a giant female troll and then descends under a waterfall to kill another giant, also takes place on a farm. Neither encounter is given any national importance by being placed in a royal court, and neither encounter is universalized or cast into moral terms of such striking polarity as those we find in *Beowulf*. Grettir himself (a fascinating character in his own right) bears little resemblance to Beowulf the ideal hero, for he is sinister, perhaps even mad, a little reminiscent of Joe Christmas in Faulkner's novel *Light in August*.

It is true that the adventures of Bothvar Bjarki, in the saga of Rolf Kraki (*Hrólfs Saga Kraka*, chapter 23), take place at the royal court of Denmark as Beowulf's adventures do, but they seem to be largely lacking in symbolic meaning and even in epic dignity. Bothvar is the typical swashbuckling *wrecca* who seems more concerned with extorting admiration from King Rolf through his manipulations of the coward Hott than with anything else; certainly the actual killing of the winged monster that attacks the hall seems almost incidental.

While other analogues in saga and folklore have been identified and assembled, none of them contains more than a general similarity in plot. The all-important context of both epic dignity and expansiveness as well as controlled and conscious

(Cambridge, The University Press, 1959), pp. 451–85. The relevant portions from the *Grettissaga* and *Hrólfs Saga Kraka* are also printed there with translations.

symbolic suggestion, that we find in *Beowulf* does not appear elsewhere.

The problem then is not really whether symbolic meaning appears in *Beowulf* but rather how far we can go in endowing Beowulf's encounters with the Grendel race with mythic or symbolic significance and what kind of evidence we can find to support our conjectures. We may as well begin by plunging ourselves abruptly into the world of myth to see how it feels. Does this passage sound any notes familiar to readers of *Beowulf*?

> The chaos demon (or demons) represented not only primeval disorder, but all dreadful forces that remain in the world and periodically threaten the god-won order: hurricane, flood, fire, volcanic eruption, earthquake, eclipse, disease, famine, war, crime, winter, darkness, death. They imagined either that the demon himself came back to life and renewed the combat, or that his progeny continued the war against the cosmos, ever striving for disorder and a return to primeval inactivity. His death amounted to no more than banishment from the ordered world: he was cast into the outer darkness beneath the earth or beyond it, that is, he was thrown back into the primeval chaos from which he came, where he and his minions lived on, ever ready to invade the god-established order and undo the whole work of creation. For the cosmos has been won from the chaos that still surrounds it, as a cultivated plot from the encompassing wilderness.[2]

This may seem a stiff dose of cosmic significance to take all at once, but I would maintain that no one who has reflected

2. Joseph Fontenrose, *Python: A Study of Delphic Myth and Its Origins* (Berkeley, University of California Press, 1959), p. 219.

on the first part of *Beowulf* could very well deny that this narrative sounds very familiar, even though it is in fact a summary of some of the beliefs of the ancient peoples of the Near and Middle East. It sounds familiar, I believe, because it actually describes very clearly the basic opposition we find in *Beowulf*, a pattern already noted in our examination of one of the "until" passages in Chapter One. On the evil side in *Beowulf* there is chaos and disorder, associated with darkness and with the submarine depths, personified in the figure of *Godes andsaca,* God's antagonist, whose various avatars include the devil, Cain, the ancient giants, Grendel himself. On the good side there is the hero who performs the act of creation (or who maintains what has already been created by other men) by defeating the forces of chaos in actual combat and thus protecting the "cultivated plot" from the "encompassing wilderness."

Of course there are important differences. Myth is likely to deal more with gods than with heroes. Beowulf is not a god in any sense whatever, not even in the limited sense that Scyld is godlike because of his supernatural and mysterious origins. Beowulf does not himself create anything; he does not even take part in the building of Heorot, although his cleansing of the evil mere might be considered an act of creative reclamation. He does not create empires; in his later career as regent and king of the Geats, he maintains and defends the kingdom rather than expanding it. There is in *Beowulf*, generally speaking, no cyclic or recurring reenactment of significant events, so important in myth properly defined, with its invariable associations with actual regularly repeated rituals. The historical nature of the events and characters in itself takes the story out of any cyclic pattern. We happen to know that Hygelac really existed and we can make fairly safe assumptions about the historicity of some of the other events and characters. If it really happened, then it happened once and once only. To use current critical terms, much of the action in *Beowulf* is "linear" rather than "cyclic"; it emphasizes the irrevocable effects of individual choice.[3] This is predominantly true even though the poem may include certain cyclic aspects.[4]

In venturing on such large generalizations, however, we ourselves run the risk of falling victim to the chaos-demons, or at least of summoning more devilish problems than we can deal with effectively at one time. In order to guarantee some grounding of our speculations in the facts of the poem itself, it would be better to test some of these ideas by thinking of them in relation to specific passages in *Beowulf*.

Like almost everything else in the poem, Grendel is most clearly defined and outlined by contrast, by being placed in juxtaposition to his opposite. His first appearance in the poem follows the description of the building of the great hall Heorot.

> Þa wæs Hroðgare heresped gyfen,
> wiges weorðmynd, þæt him his winemagas
> georne hyrdon, oðð þæt seo geogoð geweox,
> magodriht micel. Him on mod bearn
> þæt healreced hatan wolde,
> medoærn micel, men gewyrcean,
> þon[n]e yldo bearn æfre gefrunon,
> ond þær on innan eall gedælan
> geongum ond ealdum, swylc him god sealde,
> buton folcscare ond feorum gumena.

3. Harold H. Watts, "Myth and Drama," in *Tragedy: Modern Essays in Criticism,* ed. Laurence Michel and Richard B. Sewall (Englewood Cliffs, N.J., Prentice-Hall, 1963), pp. 83–105.

4. Perhaps the implicit analogy between Scyld and Beowulf suggests a recurring appearance of savior-heroes. Until the end of the world, furthermore, there is always the general possibility that "chaos-demons"—devils, giants, trolls, dragons—may again attack mankind, even though Beowulf puts an end to the individuals we find in this poem. The poem does give us a picture of human history as an inescapable treadmill of feud and warfare that has something permanent, if not exactly cyclic, about it.

> Ða ic wide gefrægn   weorc gebannan
> manigre mægþe   geond þisne middangeard,
> folcstede frætwan.   Him on fyrste gelomp,
> ædre mid yldum,   þæt hit wearð ealgearo,
> healærna mæst;   scop him Heort naman
> se þe his wordes geweald   wide hæfde. (64–79)

> Then Hrothgar was granted success in battle and glory in war, so that his kinsmen obeyed him willingly, until the time that the young men all grew up to maturity, a great host of companions. Then it entered his mind to wish to order men to build a great mead-hall, larger than the sons of men had ever heard of, and inside it to lavish on young and old shares of whatever God had given him, except the public lands and the lives of men. Then I heard that commands to make the building went out to many a tribe over this earth, orders for them to make the meeting-place beautiful. In time, quickly as human affairs go, the greatest of halls was entirely finished; he whose word was law far and wide created a name for it: *Heorot.*

Continuing in the dynastic pattern of Scylding military success previously seen in Scyld and Healfdene, Hrothgar in his youth becomes a famous warrior. Yet it is not imperial conquest but what grows and flowers out of the security such conquest creates that is ultimately important. Because Hrothgar is successful, his retainers obey him willingly and a new generation of young warriors is given time to grow up. An idea too is growing in Hrothgar's mind: to build Heorot, that great symbol of successful social order, in which he plans to play the part of good ruler by dispensing justice and showing generosity. In its turn Heorot grows out of both the obedience of the builders and the vital will of the king; it is an organic growth, a birth. It towers high as a sign of the fulfillment of royal élan. Godlike in his power, Hrothgar creates a name for what he has made.

"In archaic and traditional societies," writes Mircea Eliade, "the surrounding world is conceived as a microcosm. At the limits of this closed world begins the domain of the unknown, the formless. On this side there is ordered—because inhabited and organized—space; on the other, outside this familiar space, there is the unknown and dangerous region of the demons, the ghosts, the dead and of foreigners—in a word, chaos or death or night." [5] And it is true in *Beowulf*, as one critic has remarked, that "the poet's Heorot is the myth's world." [6] That the first act undertaken in the newly constructed hall is the song by the scop about God's creation of the world is extraordinarily appropriate, especially in the light of some of the rites and feeling connected with "sacred places." Eliade has this to say on the subject:

> The creation of the world is the exemplar for all constructions. Every new town, every new house that is built, imitates afresh, and in a sense repeats, the creation of the world. Indeed, every town, every dwelling stands at the "centre of the world," so that its construction was only possible by means of abolishing profane space and time and establishing sacred space and time. Just as the town is always an *imago mundi*, the house is a microcosm. The threshold divides the two sorts of space; the home is equivalent to the centre of the world.[7]

The individual reader must decide how far he wishes to pursue such parallels, but there is little doubt that in *Beowulf*

5. *Images and Symbols*, trans. Philip Mairet (London, Harvill Press, and New York, Sheed and Ward, 1961), pp. 37–38.

6. Fontenrose, *Python*, p. 528 n.

7. Mircea Eliade, *Patterns in Comparative Religion*, trans. Rosemary Sheed (London and New York, Sheed and Ward, 1958), p. 379.

itself the Song of Creation serves to exalt the significance of the building of Heorot by associating divine creativity, the creation of light and life, with the purely human creativity of the Danish civilization. There are verbal parallels connecting the two creative acts. *Folcstede frætwan* (make beautiful the meeting-place) in line 76 is echoed by *gefrætwade foldan sceatas* (made beautiful the earth's surfaces) in line 96; *scop him Heort naman* 78 (created the name Heorot for it) is echoed by *lif eac gesceop* 97 (created also life). God adorns his universe with limbs and leaves, just as the Danes, when they later restore beauty and order to Heorot after Grendel's attacks, adorn its walls with tapestries:

> Ða wæs haten hreþe   Heort innanweard
> folmum gefrætwod.   Fela þæra wæs,
> wera ond wifa,   þe þæt winreced,
> gestsele gyredon.   (991–94a)
>
> Then it was quickly ordered that the interior of Heorot be adorned by hands. There were a great many, both men and women, who prepared that wine-hall, that building for feasting guests.[8]

It is important to emphasize the "goodness" of Heorot that is brought out by this poetic association with divine creation. Some recent interpretations of *Beowulf* tend to make much of the corruption of the heroic society of Denmark. R. E. Kaske, for example, suggests that Grendel comes as "the product of the present Danish situation," by which he means their lack of *fortitudo,* and that Grendel is "the mindless force

8. See James L. Rosier, "The Uses of Association: Hands and Feasts in *Beowulf,*" *PMLA,* 78 (1963), 8–14. The identification of the two creations is also pointed out by Paul Beekman Taylor, "Heorot, Earth, and Asgard: Christian Poetry and Pagan Myth," *Tennessee Studies in Literature, 11* (1966), 119–30, who suggests some interesting parallels between *Beowulf* and the Old Norse creation story in the *Völuspá.*

which in a sense it [Danish *sapientia* or culture] has invited into being." [9] But I fail to see this kind of moral causality in the poem. Far more extreme is Margaret E. Goldsmith with this statement: "The spiritual sons of Cain are all those who 'build their cities' in this world, like Hrothgar at Heorot, pinning all their hope on a false good." [10] The point is that Heorot is not a false good in the poem; it is not something like Pandemonium or the Tower of Babel in *Paradise Lost*, an assertion of Satanic pride and arrogance. One often-quoted passage that may perhaps lead readers to such a view of Heorot is the following:

> Sele hlifade,
> heah ond horngeap, heaðowylma bad,
> laðan liges; ne wæs hit lenge þa gen
> þæt se *ecg*hete aþumswe*orum*
> æfter wælniðe wæcnan scolde.
> (81b–85)

> The hall towered up, high and wide-gabled; it waited for surges of violence and hostile flame. It was not very long then until the conflict of son-in-law and father-in-law was to awaken after the murderous onslaught.

The allusion is to the future feud between Hrothgar and Ingeld, his daughter's husband. Mighty as it is, Heorot will one day perish. But the tone of this passage is far from the smug I-told-you-so of the Christian moralizer; it is rather a tone of deep regret for the instability of all human things, even the greatest. The sons of Cain in the poem are the Grendels, not the Hrothgars. In terms of the dominant heroic

9. "*Sapientia et Fortitudo* as the Controlling Theme of *Beowulf*," *Studies in Philology*, 55 (1958), 438–39.

10. "The Christian Perspective in *Beowulf*," in *Studies in Old English Literature in Honor of Arthur G. Brodeur*, ed. Stanley B. Greenfield (Eugene, Ore., University of Oregon Press, 1963), p. 75.

values of the poem, Hrothgar's Denmark is represented as very nearly the height of human achievement.[11]

Some aspects of the passage introducing Grendel have already been commented on in the first chapter, where the rhetorical framework for bringing out the opposition between creation and destruction was examined. Other aspects of some importance remain to be discussed. For one thing, this part of the poem has theological implications. The statement that God has created every living thing implies that he has also created the evil Grendel, and the relationship of Grendel to God must be explained, in terms of the freedom of Grendel's ancestor Cain to make the choice of life or death. God is here presented in two roles: as the loving and bounteous creator and bestower of good things (the *god cyning* as generous ruler) and as the harsh avenger (the *god cyning* as strong administrator) who exiles Cain and crushes the opposition of the giants. While the two roles are recognizably functions of Germanic kings, they correspond as well with the traditional divine attributes of Mercy and Justice.

The solution to the problem of evil that is suggested here is the traditional Christian solution. Evil stems from the free will God has given his creatures; evil is regarded as a form of nonbeing (the image for it in the poem is darkness) toward which sinners turn when they turn away from God. Evil increases (or grows darker) in proportion to the distance from the divine center. There is no doubt that Grendel is firmly embedded in this theological context, and that this fact must remove him from the ranks of any merely animal monsters whose actions are devoid of moral significance.

Yet there is some danger in committing ourselves too wholeheartedly to these theological terms. It is essential to remember that Grendel is just as firmly embedded in a secular Germanic

11. For a more moderate and plausible Christian view of the poem, see Charles Donahue, "*Beowulf* and Christian Tradition: A Reconstruction from a Celtic Stance," *Traditio, 21* (1965), 55–116.

context. We saw how much God resembles the Germanic king figure. Cain, in the same secular terms, is the banished kin-slayer who, having made his free choice to rebel against his lord, now inhabits the hell of exile, *manncynne fram,* far from mankind. Despite the overtones of theology, Grendel himself (Cain *redivivus*) is not the conventional medieval devil figure but specifically the devil figure of the heroic society we find in the poem and no other. *Beowulf* is fundamentally heroic poetry, not theology (*pace* the neo-Augustinian critics); only in a role that this kind of poetry finds familiar and acceptable can Grendel enter the poem and function in it. He is the rebellious exile, the *ymbsittend,* the neighbor who cannot be tamed, will not pay tribute, refuses to be brought within the frame of social order by force of arms or rule of law.

Yet to see Grendel exclusively as a sociological problem has in turn its own dangers. To some extent it is true that Grendel is a projection and objectification of those irreducible disruptive forces in heroic society—disloyalty, murder, feud, anarchy—to which the poem so often alludes. Important as it is, this aspect of Grendel does not exhaust his symbolic meaning, because he has dimensions of significance beyond this, whether we call these dimensions cosmic or universal or metaphysical. One student of myth points out that Grendel "first attacked the hall because he hated the sound of revelry, laughter, and music that echoed there at night. Nothing better illustrates his true nature: he is Thanatos, denying life and joy, eternally at war with Eros." [12] In his essay on the poem Tolkien suggested these larger dimensions in somewhat different terms:

> It is just because the main foes in *Beowulf* are inhuman that the story is larger and more significant than this imaginary poem of a great king's fall. It glimpses the cosmic and moves with the thought of

12. Fontenrose, *Python,* p. 528.

> all men concerning the fate of human life and efforts; it stands amid but above the petty wars of princes, and surpasses the dates and limits of historical periods, however important.[13]

But we have been too abstract for too long. Our safest guide to an understanding of Grendel is a close study of his actual behavior in the poem. After listening to the minstrel's song, Grendel pays his first visit to Heorot.

> Gewat ða neosian, syþðan niht becom,
> hean huses, hu hit Hringdene
> æfter beorþege gebun hæfdon.
> Fand þa ðær inne æþelinga gedriht
> swefan æfter symble; sorge ne cuðon,
> wonsceaft wera. (115–20a)
>
> After night fell, he came then to visit the lofty house, to see how the Ring-Danes had settled into it after the pouring of beer. He found a band of noble warriors inside, sleeping after the feast; they were aware of no sorrow, no doom of men.

The passage begins deceptively with these ironically mild phrases of etiquette, and then moves into a peaceful scene of happy slumbers and blissful unconsciousness before flaring out into abrupt violence with:

> Wiht unhælo,
> grim ond grædig, gearo sona wæs,
> reoc ond reþe, ond on ræste genam
> þritig þegna, þanon eft gewat
> huðe hremig to ham faran,
> mid þære wælfylle wica neosan.
> (120b–25)
>
> Creature of disaster (?), grim and greedy, cruel and

13. J. R. R. Tolkien, "*Beowulf:* the Monsters and the Critics," *Proceedings of the British Academy,* 22 (1936), 295.

> furious, he was instantly ready and took thirty thanes from their beds; and then went back home gloating over his loot, making his way to his house with his fill of corpses.

The envelope pattern of the verse paragraph (*gewat . . . neosian* 115 is balanced by *gewat . . . faran . . . neosan* 123–25) frames and sets apart prominently the middle section where Grendel's nature stands revealed, revealed both in the impact of the four sudden and violent adjectives in lines 121 and 122 and in the incredible and appalling action itself.

If there had been anything *dyrne,* hidden or mysterious, about what Grendel was like, the Danes have now been offered ample evidence on which to base their judgment; a great cry of helpless horror goes up.

> Đa wæs on uhtan   mid ærdæge
> Grendles guðcræft   gumum undyrne;
> þa wæs æfter wiste   wop up ahafen,
> micel morgensweg.   Mære þeoden,
> æþeling ærgod,   unbliðe sæt,
> þolode ðryðswyð,   þegnsorge dreah,
> syðþan hie þæs laðan   last sceawedon,
> wergan gastes;   wæs þæt gewin to strang,
> lað ond longsum.   (126–34a)

> Then at dawn, at earliest daybreak, Grendel's power in war was no secret to men; then after the feast a lament was raised, a great cry in the morning. The famous king, the noble man who had always been brave, sat unhappy and suffered sorrow for his lost thanes, strong as he was, after they had all examined the track of the enemy, that damned spirit. That struggle was too hard, hateful, and longlasting.

The tragic incongruity of the situation is as usual brought out strongly by contrast: contrast between alliterating pairs of words like *wiste* and *wop,* contrast between suggestions of bravery and action in the past (*mære, ærgod, ðryðswyð*) and the present reality of inaction, sitting and suffering (*sæt, þolode, dreah, sceawedon*). The very slowness with which the astounded Danes come to understand what has happened to them is dramatized in these lines:

> Þa wæs eaðfynde þe him elles hwær
> gerumlicor ræste [sohte],
> bed æfter burum, ða him gebeacnod wæs,
> gesægd soðlice sweotolan tacne
> healðegnes hete. (138–42a)

> Then it was not hard to find a man who was looking for a bed elsewhere, where there was more elbow-room in the direction of the outbuildings, after it was indicated to him and stated truly, with an unmistakable sign—that hall-thane's hatred.

Note the effective placing of *healðegnes hete* at the end of the sentence after three somewhat redundant phrases that delay its impact.

The word *healðegn* here reminds us of the attempt to bring Grendel into comprehensible terms by describing him as a thane or (a little further on) as one who functions in terms of the Germanic wergild system; we discussed this series of references in Chapter One. This attempt is the only activity, if it can be called that, which is going on at this stage in the poem. Otherwise the Danes are pictured as being entirely in a state of helpless inaction, a state conveyed through many images of sitting, suffering, enduring, looking, thinking. All initiative for real action has gone over to Grendel, who now rules, fights, carries on feuds, pursues, lies in ambush, traps men, and commits crimes (lines 144–66a).

Grendel's motives, like his dwelling-place and his travels in the marshes, are beyond their vision and comprehension. He is *other* than man, he is mankind's enemy. Yet at the same time, in spite of the feeling they have of his distance from humanity, he is certainly *there* and not at any physical distance from them. Whatever he is and for whatever reason he came, he lives *in* Heorot, he usurps or tries to usurp their own roles as king or retainers, he blots out the treasure-bright hall with the darkness of his night-being:

Heorot eardode,
sincfage sel swneartum nihtum.
(166b–67)

He lived in Heorot, that treasure-bright hall, in the black nights.

As so often in Old English poetry, here the alliteration of *sweartum* with *sincfage sel* serves to heighten an emotional or thematic contrast.[14]

The much-discussed passage that follows, describing the Danes' recourse to prayer to heathen idols, may be better understood than it usually is if it is seen as following in the same line of thought the poet has been pursuing. That the wise men of the Danes, in their search for something to *do* in a situation where both thought and act seem to be paralyzed, turn to these heathen practices may merely be one dramatic way of indicating their infinite despair. Probably the effect of the reference to heathen worship on the original Christian audience was one of deep horror, and the poet may have been willing to achieve this emotional nonce-effect at the price of consistency in the poem as a whole, for the Danes elsewhere in the poem are certainly not represented as engaging in heathen practices or even as thinking specifically heathen thoughts.[15]

14. For a good discussion of this aspect of poetic technique, see Randolph Quirk, "Poetic Language and Old English Metre," in *Early English and Norse Studies Presented to Hugh Smith*, ed. Arthur Brown and Peter Foote (London, Methuen, 1963), pp. 150–71.

15. I offer this interpretation as the most plausible defense of the passage on artistic grounds, but without very strong conviction. Since the rigidly conventional Christian tone of the passage, while very

How this part of the poem prepares for the entrance of Beowulf as the symbol of effective action we have already discussed. Earlier we also mentioned the simple association of darkness with Grendel, which we can find in the passage just quoted and which runs consistently through the poem. It is important to recall that Beowulf is just as consistently associated with light. His victory over the sea-monsters and his sighting of land in the Breca swim come at dawn, when God's bright *beacen* sends its light from the east (569–70a). His vehement reply to Unferth ends with a prediction of morning light and the coming of the radiant sun (604b–06). Morning joyousness pervades the celebration that takes place when Beowulf and the Danes ride back from the mere after Grendel's flight (837 ff.), and it is a bright morning when Beowulf voyages back to his home (1802 ff.). After the death of Grendel's mother, light like the sun blazes out in the hall beneath the mere (1570–72a). Indeed, while it is no longer possible for us to give serious attention to the theories of Müllenhoff and the other enthusiasts for the Solar myth, we should remember that they were after all giving their attention to a symbolic pattern that was clearly there in the poem, however distorted or narrow their final interpretation of it may have been.

Light and dark are used in the broadest way to suggest a general contrast in values, of course, but the images have a further important relevance to the respective intelligences of the two characters. Grendel's darkness is to a marked degree the blindness of intellectual and moral confusion. Grendel

---

common in other Old English poetry, is not apparent elsewhere in this poem, the easiest solution is to regard the passage as an interpolation. See Tolkien's remarks in Appendix C to his essay, "*Beowulf*: the Monsters and the Critics." On the other hand, it is only fair to add that inconsistency is frequent in Old English poetry. As Kenneth Sisam has pointed out, "The poet exaggerates a mood or argument in order to make a strong impression, and at another place, for the same immediate purpose, says something inconsistent" (*The Structure of Beowulf* [Oxford, Clarendon Press, 1965], p. 46).

fights against God; this is a way of saying that perception of the moral order of the universe (which is God) is denied to Grendel. In this, as in other respects, Grendel shows a resemblance to Milton's Satan. In the early books of *Paradise Lost* Milton uses the same images (e.g. "darkness visible") far more systematically but for much the same purpose. On the other hand Beowulf lives in a world lit by truth. He knows that both he and Grendel too are under God's rule, as all things must be.

The scene just before Grendel's first encounter with Beowulf contains a contrast apparently constructed in terms similar to these. Beowulf's final speech to his men (677–87) is largely an explanation of why, unlike most heroes, he is taking off his sword and armor before going into a fight. Even though Beowulf has not yet met Grendel, he seems to have a clear understanding of him. Indeed he shows a kind of empathy with the wretched creature; poor Grendel does not know how to fight properly with swords. As we saw earlier, Beowulf shows the same knowledge of Grendel's nature and potential power when he describes to Hrothgar just what will happen to him if he is defeated by Grendel (442–51). Yet, even though Beowulf knows the possibilities well, he does not predict; that is for God to do.

> Ond siþðan witig god
> on swa hwæþere hond, halig dryhten,
> mærðo deme, swa him gemet þince.
> (685b–87)

> And afterwards let the God who knows, the holy Lord, decide on which side glory is to be awarded, just as it seems right to him.

Grendel, in contrast, really understands almost nothing, yet his mind, as we have seen, is brimfull of intentions, predictions, and expectations.[16]

16. See Chapter One, pp. 22–27.

The entire scene, in fact, seems to be focused on the great problems of knowing and foreknowing.

> Nænig heora þohte   þæt he þanon scolde
> eft eardlufan   æfre gesecean,
> folc oþðe freoburh,   þær he afeded wæs;
> ac hie hæfdon gefrunen   þæt hie ær to fela micles
> in þæm winsele   wældeað fornam,
> Denigea leode.   Ac him dryhten forgeaf
> wigspeda gewiofu,   Wedera leodum,
> frofor ond fultum,   þæt hie feond heora
> ðurh anes cræft   ealle ofercomon,
> selfes mihtum.   Soð is gecyþed
> þæt mihtig god   manna cynnes
> weold wideferhð.   (691–702a)
>
> Not one of them thought that he would ever escape and see his beloved homeland again, his people and the noble town where he grew up. Instead they had heard that, in the past, murder had finished off far too many Danish people in that very wine-hall. Still the Lord granted the Geatish people fate's weaving of luck in war, and help and comfort, so that they all overcame their enemy through the strength and power of one man. It is a truth widely known that mighty God has always ruled mankind.

When they lie down in Heorot, the Geats have no expectation of ever seeing their homes again—not an unreasonable conclusion to draw from the available evidence. But still no man's knowledge can be complete; God knows more than they can know. In the syntax of this passage, if the first *ac* (694), by bringing in the brutal and undeniable facts of the preceding twelve years, cancels their hopes, the second *ac* (696), introducing God's higher foreknowledge, cancels (or should cancel) their despair. But Beowulf's attitude is superior to that of the other Geats; he makes no assumptions about the future. In the last sentence of the quoted passage, the poet assures us at this tense moment of the poem that God has always controlled mankind.[17] This final assurance immediately precedes Grendel's entrance; it is in urgent consoling contrast to the dark night shadows that enter with him.

> Com on wanre niht
> scriðan sceadugenga. Sceotend swæfon,
> þa þæt hornreced healdan scoldon,
> ealle buton anum. Þæt wæs yldum cuþ
> þæt hie ne moste, þa metod nolde,
> se s[c]ynscaþa under sceadu bregdan;
> ac he wæccende wraþum on andan
> bad bolgenmod beadwa geþinges.
> Ða com of more under misthleoþum
> Grendel gongan, godes yrre bær;
> mynte se manscaða manna cynnes
> sumne besyrwan in sele þam hean.
> (702b–13)

The walker in shadow came striding through the dark night. The bowmen who were to have held the gabled hall slept—all but one. It was known to men that the demon attacker would not be allowed to snatch them off into the darkness when the Lord did not wish it. But he [Beowulf] was there watching in order to frustrate the will of the enemies, waiting enraged for the outcome of the battle. Then Grendel came walking from the moor under the

17. Charles Donahue ("*Beowulf* and Christian Tradition," pp. 86 ff.) sees this scene as the crucial *hora gratiae* for Beowulf, the time when he realizes that his strength is a gift of God and thus comes to experience faith. While Donahue recognizes the superiority of Beowulf's attitude in this scene, his general hypothesis requires him to demonstrate a gradual process of religious development in the character of the hero, a process for which the poem offers little evidence.

> misty slopes, bearing God's anger. That evil raider intended to trap some one of mankind in that high hall.

It is anything but easy to follow the shifting point of view in this passage, for the poet seems to be playing different degrees of awareness against each other. Grendel comes in darkness, a darkness that stands not only for the evil he represents and the terror he causes but also for the ignorance and delusion in which he moves, not only habitually but here on this occasion, since he has no idea what is in store for him in Heorot. The Geats sleep in their own darkness; their sleep is simply a sign that they are unaware of Grendel's approach. But there is a puzzling phrase here. Who are the men to whom "it is known" that Grendel will not be allowed to carry off the Geats? Not the sleeping Geats certainly? Could it be Christian believers generally with their trust in God's goodness? Or those in the audience who have listened to this story before? Beowulf himself, or those inside or outside the poem who have faith in him? I frankly do not know; my tentative answer would be those who have heard this story before. In any event, it is plain enough that by his own greater awareness Beowulf is distinguished from both Grendel and the sleeping Geats.

But there is one more point of view in the scene. From his own vantage point, God presumably is able to see the whole picture: Grendel coming, the men sleeping, the hero watchful. God's will does intervene in this scene, but only as it is put into action by Beowulf. Lines 708–09, describing Beowulf's furious wakefulness, seem almost to be an amplification of *þa metod nolde* in the previous line: Beowulf's attitude of readiness is an instrumentation of God's will. Just as Grendel bears God's anger, Beowulf bears God's favor and in some way shares his vision.

Lurching up to the hall in shadow and by misty slopes

and under clouds, Grendel is fast coming toward a kind of light, a fatal moment of insight. He does see something when he looks toward Heorot, but it is only its exterior.

> Wod under wolcnum   to þæs þe he winreced,
> goldsele gumena,   gearwost wisse,
> fættum fahne.   (714–16a)
>
> He moved under the clouds to a point where he most certainly knew the wine-hall to be, the gold-hall of men, bright with works of art.

Something new waits for him inside the hall: the essential will of man (and behind it the will of God) that creates and defends such a hall and such a civilization.

As we saw in our study of "defeated expectations" in the first chapter, Grendel's thoughts and feelings are given great prominence all through the scene of his fight with Beowulf. Beowulf's thoughts are scarcely mentioned. But Grendel's intentions and predictions are so massively frustrated that the fight itself comes to have a distinctly comic quality. It is always the figure with the most elaborate and serious plans who makes the most comic character; even the prat-faller of farce must seem to be overflowing with intentions just before he tumbles. Grendel counts his warriors before they are snatched; he exults in the expectation of eating his fill, *wistfylle wen* 734, in the near future. In contrast, Beowulf is meanwhile alertly studying Grendel's behavior in the present, so that he may know how to proceed against his antagonist.

> Geseah he in recede   rinca manige,
> swefan sibbegedriht   samod ætgædere,
> magorinca heap.   Þa his mod ahlog;
> mynte þæt he gedælde,   ærþon dæg cwome,
> atol aglæca,   anra gehwylces
> lif wið lice,   þa him alumpen wæs
> wistfylle wen.   Ne wæs þæt wyrd þa gen

þæt he ma moste manna cynnes
ðicgean ofer þa niht. Þryðswyð beheold
mæg Higelaces, hu se manscaða
under færgripum gefaran wolde. (728–38)

He saw many warriors in the hall, a great company of them sleeping side by side, a band of fighting kinsmen. Then his heart laughed. The atrocious demon intended, before day came, to separate the life from the body of each one of them, when his hope of eating his fill came true. But it was not then fate that he be allowed to devour any more of mankind beyond that night. The powerful kinsman of Hygelac was watching to see how the evil demon was going to behave under sudden attacks.

Grendel laughs at the droll helplessness of the sleeping Geats, but God and fate laugh at him. Notice the sequence of thought here: first, Grendel's exultant hope of killing all the men; then the poet's quiet reference to fate, making the point that Grendel has reached the end of his murderous career; then, following hard on the mention of fate, the picture of fate's agent Beowulf, intently watching, awake and ready. The sequence we saw in the preceding passage is repeated.

At this point perhaps it seems important to the poet to stress again the simple physical reality of Grendel, to show us his genuine power and presence, after so much semi-philosophical commentary. After his long silent approach Grendel suddenly shatters the iron-bound door, wrenching open with his hands the *recedes muþan* 724, the hall's mouth (a beautifully cannibalistic metaphor) and, eyes blazing like fire, walks onto the bright floor. In the description of Grendel devouring the sleeping man, brute physical violence could hardly be carried further.

> Ne þæt se aglæca yldan þohte,
> ac he gefeng hraðe forman siðe
> slæpendne rinc, slat unwearnum,
> bat banlocan, blod edrum dranc,
> synsnædum swealh; sona hæfde
> unlyfigendes eal gefeormod,
> fet ond folma. (739–45a)

> The frightening creature had no intention of delaying; no, first of all he swiftly seized a sleeping man and incontinently tore and bit at what covered his bones, drank blood from his veins, gulped great chunks of flesh. In a flash he had eaten all of the dead man, down to his hands and feet.

Destruction of society and of the individual, tearing open the hall and tearing apart the man, become parallel destructive acts. This murdering demon not only paralyzes the functioning of society by occupying its vital center, he eats men.[18] We hear something like the crunch as his real teeth bite into their real bodies; the passage has an intricate pattern of sound and rhythm. We have no trouble recognizing this kind of evil as absolute in itself; it needs no explanation or theological buttressing. And the sharp immediacy of this description furnishes an impeccable motivation for the action of Beowulf that follows: he must at all costs stop the butchery which is going on before his eyes and rescue fellow human beings from mankind's plain enemy.

Grendel takes one more step, touches Beowulf's outstretched hand, and comes at last, as the old Quakers used to say, upon a knowing.

> Sona þæt onfunde fyrena hyrde
> þæt he ne mette middangeardes,

18. The behavior of the Cyclops Polyphemus offers some interesting parallels to this scene (*Odyssey* IX. 287 ff.).

eorþan sceata, on elran men
mundgripe maran. He on mode wearð
forht on ferhðe; no þy ær fram meahte.
Hyge wæs him hinfus, wolde on heolster fleon,
secan deofla gedræg; ne wæs his drohtoð þær
swylce he on ealderdagum ær gemette.
(750–57)

At once the shepherd of crimes discovered that he had never met in the world, all over earth, in any other man a greater hand-grip. He became terrified in his heart, but he could not get away any the sooner because of that. His whole being strained to get away, he wanted to flee into sheltering darkness and rejoin the brawling society of devils; his company there [at Heorot] was not like any he had ever met before in all the days of his life.

Grendel's fanatic and powerful will is now instantly reversed in its direction; it is now *hinfus, utweard,* bent on flight. A reaction of pure terror at the strength of Beowulf's hand now suffuses everything: fear, flight, flight, flight, like the panicky jangling of an alarm bell. Yet all this happens before Beowulf has even risen to his feet.

If we accept the poet's invitation to think of Grendel as a warrior, we see him here in a light that makes him seem perfectly ludicrous: from the instant he touches the hand of a man lying on his bed he is completely demoralized and capable of thinking only of flight. This view of Grendel is essentially comic and derisive. It prepares us for the tone of the passage that follows (the famous *ealuscerwen* passage), which describes the fight from the Danes' point of view in what are clearly ironic and even comic terms.[19]

19. Comic also is Beowulf's remark in his later report to Hrothgar that Grendel was *to foremihtig . . . on feþe* (969–70), too overwhelmingly powerful in running away, for Beowulf to prevent him

Not only is Grendel sometimes regarded as a warrior of sorts, he is also viewed ironically as a guest visiting Heorot. Indeed, in the passage just quoted, there is some irony of this kind playing on the concept of Grendel as a social being. He prefers the *deofla gedræg,* the noisy company of devils, to the *drohtoð,* the society or company he has found in Heorot. A few lines later we are told that his visit to Heorot is a *geocor sið,* a sad journey. And now he is a guest at a party. Perhaps because the fight at Heorot is no fight at all really, since, so far as we can tell, it consists of Grendel's smashing much of the furniture in his frantic attempts to pull his hand out of Beowulf's grasp (so frantic are they in the end that he rips off his own arm at the shoulder), it seems to be presented comically as a wild party in the hall.

> Dryhtsele dynede; Denum eallum wearð,
> ceasterbuendum, cenra gehwylcum,
> eorlum ealuscerwen. Yrre wæron begen,
> reþe renweardas. Reced hlynsode.
> Þa wæs wundor micel þæt se winsele
> wiðhæfde heaþodeorum, þæt he on hrusan ne feol,
> fæger foldbold; ac he þæs fæste wæs
> innan ond utan irenbendum
> searoþoncum besmiþod. Þær fram sylle abeag
> medubenc monig, mine gefræge,
> golde geregnad, þær þa graman wunnon.
> (767–77)

> There was an echoing noise in the noble hall; for all the Danes, each brave inhabitant of the stronghold, each warrior, it was a real pouring of ale! Both the fierce guardians of the hall were furious. The hall resounded with noise. It was a great miracle that the wine-hall held together against the brave fighters,

---

from escaping. The reader will find other traces of irony in Beowulf's account.

> that it did not collapse on the earth, that beautiful building. But it was too firmly constructed by clever smiths' work, with iron bands inside and out. I heard that many a mead-bench, decorated with gold, was torn loose from the floor where those angry ones fought.

The much-discussed *ealuscerwen* 769 I have here translated as "pouring of ale"; I take it simply to be a term for a drinking party. The closest analogue to this scene in other Old English poetry may well be the feast of the wicked Assyrian king Holofernes, which is described at the beginning of the poem *Judith*.[20] Sheer noise seems to dominate the account of that drunken brawl. In *Beowulf* the tremendous din made by Grendel, first in struggling with Beowulf and later in roaring with pain and fright, seems to have reminded the poet of the ordinary or conventional occasion for such loud noise in a hall—a drinking party. He makes use of the opportunity to continue his ironic presentation of Grendel as a guest or caller at Heorot. The Danes then seem to be pictured, somewhat ironically, as hosts at the party. We do find some irony at the expense of the Danes elsewhere, whenever the poet places their inactivity and lack of heroic spark in contrast to the actions of Beowulf. Is it suggested here that the Danes had never really comprehended what kind of party they had invited Grendel and Beowulf to, that they were incapable even of imagining the scale of the fight and of the necessary destruction?

Perhaps this ironic metaphor of the party is developed even further.

Sweg up astag
niwe geneahhe; Norðdenum stod

20. Especially *Judith* 15–27. For a more detailed explanation of the compound and its context, see my article, "*Ealuscerwen:* Wild Party at Heorot," *Tennessee Studies in Literature, 11* (1966), 161–68.

> atelic egesa, anra gehwylcum
> þara þe of wealle wop gehyrdon,
> gryreleoð galan godes andsacan,
> sigeleasne sang, sar wanigean
> helle hæfton. (782b–88a)

> Sound mounted up, over and over again. Chilling fear seized each of the North-Danes who heard that lament from the outer wall, heard God's enemy sing a lay of terror, a song without victory, heard hell's prisoner bewail his pain.

Song is always associated with feasting in Old English poetry. Is Grendel's blood-curdling rendition the climactic performance at this strange party?

Grendel has one last discovery to make, a discovery expressed in another *onfunde* construction that suggests a process of education (809–18a). He finds out that his body cannot hold up against Beowulf's strength; it fails him, his arm is torn off, and he flees mortally wounded to die in his joyless home in the fens. His flight is viewed sometimes as the burrowing for cover of some wounded animal, sometimes as a fated progress to death and damnation. These lines are typical:

> Deaðfæge deog; siððan dreama leas
> in fenfreoðo feorh alegde,
> hæþene sawle; þær him hel onfeng.
> (850–52)

> Fated to die, he hid (?); then, bereft of joys, he laid down his life and heathen soul in that hiding-place in the fens. There hell took him.

The images are of withdrawal, imprisonment, cessation. These lines are immediately followed by the vital exuberance of the convivial ride back to Heorot by the rejoicing Danes. Young and old race horses and improvise songs, and the *hwilum*

. . . *hwilum* parallel construction in lines 864–74a (sometimes they did one thing, sometimes the other) suggests that the same spontaneous impulse of energy and joy in social community (a race and a recited poem are both social events) lies in both activities.

As Kemp Malone once suggested, one purpose of these lines may well be to make a contrast between the lighthearted and prematurely exultant return of the Danes from the mere on this occasion and the Geats' sober march back to Heorot with Grendel's head the next day.[21] But in the immediate context a further important effect lies in the contrast of these social joys with Grendel's damned and joyless solitude. Here we can see clearly the antisocial nature of the evil Grendel stands for. Driven out of the hall of life, he moves into the narrow and fatal world of the exile; from there to death is only a short step.

Þa he hean gewat,
dreame bedæled, deaþwic seon,
mancynnes feond. (1274b–76a)

Then he went away humiliated and robbed of joy to
find a death-dwelling, mankind's enemy.

There is no single answer to the problem of what Grendel represents, which may be just as well. He is not entirely the cosmic chaos demon of the mythologists, not the usual devil of the conventional medieval story, not simply a muscular brute of a troll—even though he borrows attributes from each of them. He is most consistently and distinctly placed in opposition to the society that this poem honors and to its values: loyalty, community, and even something very close to chivalry. Perhaps this is to say only that Grendel is opposed to the hero of the poem, who defends and embodies these

21. "Coming Back from the Mere," *PMLA, 69* (1954), 1292–99. It is probable, however, that it will be the reader rather than the listener who will notice a contrast of such widely separated elements.

values, and that we will find Grendel to be nothing in the end but the negative image of Beowulf. Grendel seems to be representative at times of an evil and arrogant individualism that is wholly destructive in its effects on society and has some connection thematically with the feuds smoldering below the surface of the poem or with a figure like Heremod, type of the self-willed and wicked king.

Yet, because of his strong association with dark natural forces—night, moor, fen, sea-bottom—Grendel cannot be entirely understood in these sociological terms. He is also nonhuman and represents the disorder endemic in the nonhuman world; hence he is the enemy of life itself as well as the enemy of a particular social system. He is the Other, the Darkness; he is Death. This dimension of Grendel is less emphasized than his "social" dimension, but it is there and gives depth and power to the way Grendel is presented. Perhaps it also foreshadows the way that the dragon in the second part of the poem is presented.

In some way Grendel is also related to the concept of fate, perhaps rather as a blind victim of it than as an agent of it. In his attitude toward the future and toward "the fruits of action," he is set in contrast with Beowulf. Grendel's combination of passionate juggernaut will and dimmed intellect encounter Beowulf's even stronger will and enlightened mind —enlightened because, by knowing what he cannot control, he controls far more than Grendel. In this general sense, then, perhaps Grendel suggests the dark irrational in man, which exists outside that circle of light standing for a vision of cosmic order and which moves inexorably toward self-destruction.

Last and not, I think, least, we should take account of the poet's comic treatment of Grendel and his defeat. To expose the essential incongruity of Grendel, half bogey and half outlaw, by bringing him into the sunlit world of laughter is a powerful exorcism, perhaps the most powerful of all. The devil cannot endure to be mocked. And the exact opposite of

Grendel as envious thick-witted skulker and sulker is the Beowulf whose clear assured vision of things so often takes the form of ironic wit and a grave gaiety.

In part, the encounter with Grendel's mother represents a continuation of the symbolic conflict with Grendel; in part, it introduces new dimensions of this conflict with evil, or at least new expressive forms for rendering it. From the first point of view, Grendel's mother is merely Grendel brought back to life, or at least not yet entirely dead; it may even be significant that Grendel's mother dies almost at the same moment her son is beheaded. Grendel was defeated in Heorot but not cleanly killed; it is almost as if in his mother something of him still writhes and strikes back. One passage in particular seems to reinforce this impression; the first part of it was quoted a moment ago, but not together with what follows it.

Þa he hean gewat,
dreame bedæled, deaþwic seon,
mancynnes feond, ond his modor þa gyt,
gifre ond galgmod, gegan wolde
sorhfulne sið, sunu *deað* wrecan.
(1274b–78)

Then he [Grendel], robbed of joy, mankind's enemy, went away humiliated to find a death-place; and then his mother, voracious and driven by fury, still had the will to make that grievous trip to avenge her son's death.

My translation here succeeds only in being awkward. In the original text the phrase *ond his modor þa gyt,* taken with the following verb *wolde,* suggests something like a pattern of momentary withdrawal and return of will. As Grendel falls, his mother rises; but the phrase *þa gyt* implies that her action is fundamentally an extension of the same evil will that drove

Grendel. Grendel's mother after all belongs to the same race of Cain, as we are reminded in the résumé of origins and past action that follows her sudden introduction into the poem. She shares many of her son's attributes; a single term like *ellorgæstas* 1349 (alien spirits) can cover both of them.

In some respects, however, Grendel's mother differs from her son, notably in respect to her motivation. Whatever it is that impels Grendel to attack the Danes is not easy to define in a brief phrase, as we have seen, whether we tend to think of it as some Iago-like motiveless malignity or as a destructive drive with complex metaphysical or mythical implications. What makes Grendel's mother run is a far simpler thing: she is a *wrecend,* an avenger.[22] In order to gain satisfaction for her son's death, she must take one life from the enemy; when she has done so she scurries home to the mere. There is little indication that she takes the same pleasure in destruction that Grendel did, or even that she would continue to make raids on Heorot after this one necessary mission. (If Beowulf and the Danes had thought she would return, they might have waited for her in the hall as they waited for Grendel, instead of seeking her out in the mere.) When she does fight Beowulf, her motivation is equally simple: she is defending her home (and perhaps also her son's body) from an invader.

As a result of this, readers have been known to regard Grendel's mother as more "human" and sympathetic than her son, because her motives are more understandable and defensible. From such an assumption one may easily go on to argue that the greater difficulty and increased savagery of Beowulf's fight with the female monster are really indications of the greater moral complexities of the second conflict: here

22. Certainly this is the role the poet most emphasizes. She is called a *wrecend* in line 1256, and the same word appears in the following phrases: *wolde . . . sunu deað wrecan* 1278; *heo þa fæhðe wræc* 1333; *wolde hyre mæg wrecan* 1339; *wolde hire bearn wrecan* 1546; *wif unhyre / hyre bearn gewræc* 2120–21.

we no longer have whitest white against blackest black but something ethically greyer and less absolute.

Possibly this is one useful way of understanding the relationship between the two fights. But there is some danger of simplifying or distorting, in the interests of moral symmetry, what the poem really contains. However "human" the motives of Grendel's mother may be thought to be, she is certainly not endowed with human attributes in other ways—indeed, quite the opposite. We are never admitted into her secret thoughts and feelings as we are admitted so often into Grendel's. Clawing at Beowulf with her sharp nails or crouched on top of his chest, she behaves much more like an animal than Grendel ever does. During the scene in the mere, an animal epithet is twice applied to her: *brimwylf* (she-wolf of the sea 1506, 1599).

Yet it must be said that a critic who goes over the various epithets applied to her in search of some clue to the poet's view of Grendel's mother is likely to be struck most forcibly by the very lack of them; she simply is not very often dignified by epithet. She does not carry the same load of formulas with symbolic suggestions (*dreame bedæled, feond mancynnes,* and the like) under which poor Grendel labors at all times.

It is important, however, to note the fact that most of the few epithets she does receive make reference to her dwelling-place in the depths of the evil mere.[23] To associate her with this setting is in itself enough to endow her with great significance, for the image of the mere is developed in richly symbolic terms. Grendel's mother is the mere, in fact: that is where we see her in action, and her action is in defense of it. We can form little impression of her nature if we fail to

23. For example, the compound *brimwylf* mentioned above; *merewif mihtig* 1519 (mighty sea-woman); *grimne gryrelicne grundhyrde* 2136 (grim frightful protector of the depths); *grundwyrgenne* 1518 (accursed creature of the depths); [of the two monsters] *huses hyrdas* 1666 (guardians of the house).

recognize that it is where she lives that gives her most of her being.

In the context of our earlier study of Beowulf's heroic behavior, we looked briefly at the speech Hrothgar makes when he hears the news of the attack by Grendel's mother (lines 1321–82); now we return to it to see from a different angle how dramatically and effectively it shifts the audience's attention toward the important new scene of the mere. The speech begins "inside" with Hrothgar's lament for his old friend and counselor Æschere and his memories of their life together, and then moves "outside" in search of the murderer. But the search is difficult and vision is obscured: Hrothgar's ignorance of the attacker's nature is evident in the first part of the speech. His terms are vague: he calls Grendel's mother a *wælgæst wæfre* 1331, a slaughtering spirit in restless uneasy motion (perhaps "hard to see clearly" is even implied by *wæfre*), something which vanishes *ic ne wat hwæder,* I know not where. Hrothgar must draw on hearsay evidence; he has heard some of his people report the existence of two shadowy "alien spirits" (*ellorgæstas* 1349), but their information is also sketchy (they do not know if Grendel's father exists or has ever existed).

But the vagueness characteristic of the first part of the speech is in contrast with the specific and concrete details (however bizarre they may be) that we find in the actual description of the mere. Men may only have caught glimpses of Grendel and his mother as they drifted through the distant misty marshlands, but the mere is there, and clearly seen. It can give us essential information about the nature of the enemy. The place comes to seem all the clearer as we move toward it out of emotional shock, out of confusion and vagueness. Even though the first adjective applied to the mere reinforces the idea of vague mystery (*dygel*—secret, hidden), the key to all its secrets is quickly revealed, and the nature of Grendel's mother is exposed.

Hie dygel lond
warigeað, wulfhleoþu, windige næssas,
frecne fengelad, ðær fyrgenstream
under næssa genipu niþer gewiteð,
flod under foldan. Nis þæt feor heonon
milgemearces þæt se mere standeð:
ofer þæm hongiað hrinde bearwas,
wudu wyrtum fæst wæter oferhelmað.
Þær mæg nihta gehwæm niðwundor seon,
fyr on flode. No þæs frod leofað
gumena bearna, þæt þone grund wite;
ðeah þe hæðstapa hundum geswenced,
heorot hornum trum, holtwudu sece,
feorran geflymed, ær he feorh seleð,
aldor on ofre, ær he in wille
hafelan [beorgan].[24] Nis þæt heoru stow!
Þonon yðgeblond up astigeð
won to wolcnum, þonne wind styreþ,
lað gewidru, oðþæt lyft drysmaþ,
roderas reotað. (1357b–76a)

A hidden land they defend—wolf-slopes, windswept cliffs, a treacherous marsh, where a mountain stream goes down under the darkness of the cliffs, water vanishing under earth. That mere stands not far from here, as we measure miles. Frost-coated groves hang over it; a firm-rooted forest stands guard on the water. Every night there you can see a deadly wonder—fire on the water. No one of the sons of men lives so old and wise that he knows the bottom of it. Even if the stiff-horned hart, that pacer of the wilds, made for this forest long running with hounds at his heels, he would sooner give up his life on the shore than enter there to save his neck. That is no decent place!

24. *Beorgan* for a word missing in the MS. Klaeber and most editors supply *beorgan;* Dobbie supplies *hydan.*

> From it tumultuous waves boil up dark to the clouds, driven by wind and foul weather, until the air darkens (?) and the sky streams with tears.

Every detail of this description makes the same statement about the mere: that it repels. Like some magnetic force field, its power drives the invader back. Its details may grow clearer as we approach but it becomes more difficult of access. It is defended not only by the ferocious Grendel race but by the wolves roaming its hillsides, the wind howling in its cliffs, the icy forest which protectively overhangs (*oferhelmað*) its evil center. Wise men's intelligence can never fathom these depths; not even the fear of death can compel the hunted hart to draw any nearer. The listener himself is baffled by its elemental paradoxes: water under earth, fire under water, water falling from the air, frost on the trees in summer. Yet for all that it is hidden and mysterious, a *wundor* to men, men need be in no doubt that what burns in the mere's depths is malice. There is no moral ambiguity here. This *wundor* is specifically a *niðwundor*, a mystery unmistakably and implacably hostile to man and his natural world, hostile most of all to the world of the *heoru*, a word suggesting all those secure and pleasant feelings that man associates with home and family (if we can judge by the etymology of the word).[25] That it is the hart, totem animal of the Danish dynasty and very symbol of its hall, which is most dramatically placed in conflict with the mere's malice is interesting, to say the least.[26] And all the malice in the mere finds its active spearhead in that *wif unhyre* (i.e. *unheore*), Grendel's mother.

The nature of the evil force is further defined, as usual by

25. Holthausen (*Altenglisches Etymologisches Wörterbuch*) connects the word (*hiere* in his normalization) with *hiwan* (household, family), and *hiwan* in turn with *hid* (land for one family) and *ham* (home). In *Beowulf* the word *unheoru* is also applied to Grendel's claw (987) and to the dragon (2413).

26. See Paul Beekman Taylor, "Heorot, Earth, and Asgard: Christian Poetry and Pagan Myth," p. 127.

contrast, by the very way in which the hero confronts it, particularly by means of the images that cluster around him immediately before and after the fight itself. We pointed out earlier that Beowulf disarmed himself before the fight with Grendel; here, on the other hand, a relatively long passage (1441b–72) deals with the arming of the hero. In his proper role as hero, Beowulf of course must be essentially alone in this venture, but a consistent pattern of details in the description of his arms keeps hinting at some half-realized form of human community around him. Beowulf may leave one undependable (or at least unheroic) companion on the shore in the person of Unferth, who lacks the courage to go with him but who sends his sword instead, but he takes with him to the mere-bottom three half-personified comrades. Call them Byrnie, Helm, and the sword named Hrunting.[27]

These inanimate retainers are represented as being sensible of obligation and as having skills. Note the description of the byrnie, for instance:

> Scolde herebyrne hondum gebroden,
> sid ond searofah, sund cunnian,
> seo ðe bancofan beorgan cuþe . . .
> (1443–45)

> The mailshirt of battle, hand-fashioned, broad,
> glittering with ornament, was obliged to make trial
> of swimming [or: of the water], [that shirt] which
> knew how to protect the body . . . .

Ordinarily the phrases *scolde cunnian* and *beorgan cuþe* would certainly be applied to human beings. Again, the helmet is described:

> Ac se hwita helm hafelan werede,
> se þe meregrundas mengan scolde,

27. For an interesting discussion of the symbolic aspects of armor in the poem as a whole see George Clark, "Beowulf's Armor," *ELH*, 32 (1965), 409–41.

secan sundgebland   since geweorðad,
befongen freawrasnum,   swa hine fyrndagum
worhte wæpna smið,   wundrum teode,
besette swinlicum,   þæt hine syðþan no
brond ne beadomecas   bitan ne meahton.
(1448–54)

But the shining helmet guarded his head, [the helmet] that was obliged to stir up the depths of the mere and seek the swirling waters, [the helmet] adorned with treasure, clasped round by chains a lord might wear, just as some weapon-smith had fashioned it in bygone days, shaping it marvelously and studding it with boar-figures, so that no flashing blade or battle swords could ever bite it.

Here the actions of guarding and seeking attributed to the helmet are at least partly volitional ones. If we consider the helmet as object rather than as subject, we should take into account the fact that the form *hine* used here could be as easily translated "him" as "it." Germanic swords typically "bite," but the word *bitan* still carries the suggestion of flesh to bite into. Finally the sword has its own measure of personification: it has a name of its own, it has never let any man down, and it has in the past performed *ellenweorc,* a deed or deeds of courage. Later, when the sword fails in the fight, we are told that it has lost *dom,* reputation, just as warriors do.

Not only does the personification of his weapons surround Beowulf with "human" echoes, but the frequent references in these descriptions to the human hands that once linked together the rings of his byrnie or to the long-dead smiths who lovingly fashioned his helmet or tempered his sword blade emphasize repeatedly that these objects are above all human artifacts, and that Beowulf carries with him into the poisoned mere more hopes and hands than his own.

The past and future owners of such objects are also important to the poet and his hero. As we saw earlier, Beowulf devotes much of his final speech to Hrothgar (1473–91) to instructions for the disposal of his treasures and his own sword. Human relationships and human commitments wholly dominate this speech. Hrothgar is acknowledged as Beowulf's temporary lord and adoptive father; Beowulf, conscious as leader himself of his responsibility for his own men's welfare, asks Hrothgar to be their *mundbora,* legal protector, in the event of his death; as Hygelac's loyal retainer, Beowulf wants the gifts sent back to his lord; and, finally, he is scrupulous in repaying his debt to Unferth by bequeathing him his heirloom sword. All these involvements with other men cling to the hero like his armor before he enters the mere-world, for he makes his entrance into that world preeminently as a representative of the human race, *gumena sum,* who penetrates the *ælwihta eard,* the homeland of alien and nonhuman creatures (1499–1500).

As Beowulf swims toward the bottom, the inhabitants of the mere attack him, but his armor protects him first from the claws of Grendel's mother and then from the teeth of the sea-monsters who swarm around him. In the fight that takes place in Grendel's sea-bottom hall, not only does the sword fail to wound Grendel's mother but Beowulf is quickly overmatched in his own special skill of barehanded wrestling. Only his armor saves him, for the third time, from being stabbed to death by his assailant.

> Ofsæt þa þone selegyst   ond hyre seax geteah,
> brad [ond] brunecg,   wolde hire bearn wrecan,
> angan eaferan.   Him on eaxle læg
> breostnet broden;   þæt gebearh feore,
> wið ord ond wið ecge   ingang forstod.
> Hæfde ða forsiðod   sunu Ecgþeowes
> under gynne grund,   Geata cempa,
> nemne him heaðobyrne   helpe gefremede,

herenet hearde, ond halig god
geweold wigsigor; witig drihten,
rodera rædend, hit on ryht gesced
yðelice, syþðan he eft astod. (1545–56)

Then she sat with all her weight on that visitor to her hall and drew her shortsword, wide-bladed and bright-edged, intending to avenge her son and only child. From his shoulders hung the meshed breast-nets; that saved his life, staving off any entry of point or edge. The son of Ecgtheow, champion of the Geats, would have come to a sorry end there deep beneath the earth if the byrnie, that rugged war-net, had not given him its help and if holy God had not had control of victory; the wise Lord and Ruler of heaven decreed the event easily and justly, as soon as Beowulf stood up again.

In the fight we see Beowulf's armor repelling attack much in the same way that the mere itself repels invasion from outside. But a battle between two such impregnable defenses is likely to be a draw unless some new element can be introduced. In his armor Beowulf may be able to survive, but he cannot win. It is at this point that a complex new element is indeed introduced, although readers may not all agree on just what it is.

It is basically, I think, that vital extra margin of power which distinguishes the hero as individual and unique force from the hero as representative man. The armor has been essentially an image of this representative aspect of Beowulf; the giant-sword that Beowulf now seizes—or rather the very act of seizing that sword—stands in some way for that special blend of wild daring, restless strength, alert intelligence, luck, and divine favor that makes a hero. It does not really matter whether or not we identify the sources of that heroic power; no one knows these anyway, any more than anyone knows where heroes like Scyld come from. An assortment of possibilities is laid before us here. Is it the intervention of God's grace? That is what Beowulf tells Hrothgar later (1661–64). How much is due to Beowulf's own unaided efforts in rising to his feet? Does the hero bend the formidable power of the giant-sword back against its own owners and makers? Is the evil world essentially self-destructive, only to be attacked by its own dark energies? Yet could any other man but Beowulf have had the strength even to have lifted this sword from the wall where it hung?

The important thing is the action itself. In heroic poetry a dilemma is solved, a draw is broken, a theory is proved, by action and action alone. Over and above all else, the passage about the giant-sword is a joyous celebration of action.

> Geseah ða on searwum sigeeadig bil,
> eald sweord eotenisc, ecgum þyhtig,
> wigena weorðmynd; þæt [wæs] wæpna cyst,
> buton hit wæs mare ðonne ænig mon oðer
> to beadulace ætberan meahte,
> god ond geatolic, giganta geweorc.
> He gefeng þa fetelhilt, freca Scyldinga
> hreoh ond heorogrim hringmæl gebrægd,
> aldres orwena, yrringa sloh,
> þæt hire wið halse heard grapode,
> banhringas bræc. Bil eal ðurhwod
> fægne flæschoman; heo on flet gecrong.
> Sweord wæs swatig, secg weorce gefeh.
> (1557–69)

Then among the weapons he caught sight of a sword endowed with luck, an ancient sword of the giants, strong-edged, a warrior's prize; it was the most splendid of weapons, only it was bigger than any other man could carry to battle-play, a great and beautiful work of giants' forging. He laid his hands to the ringed hilt, that wild and deadly soldier of the

> Scyldings, drew out the patterned blade in full despair, then struck in fury; and the hard sword smashed against her neck, breaking the bone-rings. Clear through that doomed flesh-cover went the sword; to the floor she crashed. The sword was bloody; the man exulted in his deed.

The tense frustrations of helpless inaction are dramatically released. First we have to see the weapon itself: see it fully, examine, hover over it in a series of descriptive noun and adjective phrases. Then we seize it and act. The sword stroke is lovingly detailed in an exhilarating series of verbs, a little reminiscent of a series of stop-action photographs: *gefeng, gebrægd, sloh, grapode, bræc, þurhwod, gecrong*. This is a fully savored *weorc*, a deed, an act, and it is for a man to rejoice in. This sense of fulfilled joy seems to be expressed by the light image that follows:

> Lixte se leoma, leoht inne stod,
> efne swa of hefene hadre scineð
> rodores candel. He æfter recede wlat;
> hwearf þa be wealle, wæpen hafenade
> heard be hiltum Higelaces ðegn,
> yrre ond anræd. (1570–75a)

> The light gleamed, and a radiance blazed out in the interior, just as the candle of heaven shines bright from the sky. He looked around the hall and then turned quickly and moved along the wall, the weapon's hilt in his upraised hand, Hygelac's man, strong, angry, determined.

And action continues, now aided by the light that has appeared literally. Beowulf can now see his way to find the body of Grendel and deliver the ultimate exorcising blow.

> Hra wide sprong,
> syþðan he æfter deaðe drepe þrowade,

heorosweng heardne, ond hine þa heafde becearf.
Sona þæt gesawon snottre ceorlas,
þa ðe mid Hroðgare on holm wliton,
þæt wæs yðgeblond eal gemenged,
brim blode fah. (1588b–94a)

> [Grendel's] corpse bounced into the air after it suffered a blow after death, a solid deadly stroke, and Beowulf cut the head from it. At once the wise men who were looking at the mere with Hrothgar noticed that the turmoil of waves was all mingled and colored with blood.

The climactic action of the beheading is in contrast with the lack of activity up above on the shore, where the Danes are still looking.

The world above is the world of normality to which Beowulf and the audience must now return. In this normal world no one expects heroic miracles. After they see the blood the Danish elders persuade Hrothgar and the other Danes to give up their vigil and go back to Heorot. Beowulf's own Geats stay watching out of loyalty but without real hope. It is just at this point, before Beowulf returns to the surface, that the strange incident of the melting of the giant-sword is introduced.

Þa þæt sweord ongan
æfter heaþoswate hildegicelum,
wigbil wanian. Þæt wæs wundra sum,
þæt hit eal gemealt ise gelicost,
ðonne forstes bend fæder onlæteð,
onwindeð wælrapas, se geweald hafað
sæla ond mæla; þæt is soð metod.
(1605b–11)

Then, after [being covered with] the blood of the fight, that sword of war began to vanish in icicles of battle. It was a great miracle for it to melt entirely just as if it were ice melting, whenever the Father eases the frost-fetter and slackens the ropes that bind up the water, he who has power over all times and seasons. He is the true Measurer of things.

The melting of the sword is the last of the great unnatural miracles of the strange mere-world, and it shows the last perceptible waning effect of the evil power of the Grendel race: their still potent blood can dissolve the sword blade. But the simile of ice seems to be a modulation out of that mere-world into the world of normal and natural miracles, into a still wondrous but always orderly world controlled by a benevolent God. The simile itself pictures a process of change: as the sword melts, the mere-world fades out, spring returns, and the reality of God's true power grows once more clear. By being cleansed, the mere is restored to nature; Beowulf swims up through ordinary water, which has now subsided into its proper place *under wolcnum* (1631), under the clouds rather than among them as before.

Cleansing implies the restoration of normality in human society as well as in physical nature. Beowulf moved out of the very midst of a world of men, as we saw, when he descended into the mere; now in full triumph he returns to that same world.

Com þa to lande lidmanna helm
swiðmod swymman; sælace gefeah,
mægenbyrþenne þara þe he him mid hæfde.
Eodon him þa togeanes, gode þancodon,
ðryðlic þegna heap, þeodnes gefegon,
þæs þe hi hyne gesundne geseon moston.
Ða wæs of þæm hroran helm ond byrne
lungre alysed. Lagu drusade,
wæter under wolcnum, wældreore fag.
Ferdon forð þonon feþelastum

ferhþum fægne, foldweg mæton,
cuþe stræte. Cyningbalde men
from þæm holmclife hafelan bæron
earfoðlice heora æghwæþrum,
felamodigra; feower scoldon
on þæm wælstenge weorcum geferian
to þæm goldsele Grendles heafod,
oþðæt semninga to sele comon
frome fyrdhwate feowertyne
Geata gongan; gumdryhten mid
modig on gemonge meodowongas træd.
(1623–43)

The protector [lit. helmet] of the seamen then came swimming powerfully to land; he exulted in the sea's booty, that massive burden which he carried with him. Forward they went then to meet him, that mighty band of thanes, thanking God, exulting in their lord, rejoicing that they were permitted to see him safe. Then from that brave man helmet and byrnie were quickly loosened. The mere sank down, [became] water under the clouds, bright-stained with death-blood. Marching away from that place with joy in their hearts, they moved forward along the earth-way, the familiar road. Men bold as kings carried the head away from the sea-cliff, each of the gallant men staggering under the load; it took four men to bear with heavy labor Grendel's head on a spear to the gold-hall, until at last fourteen brave war-keen Geats came striding up to the hall; the lord of men walked brave in the midst of his men across the fields near the mead-hall.

Beowulf's reunion with his men is vividly presented here: he swims to land exulting, and exulting they move forward to greet him and minister to him. Now victory is complete:

armor can be removed, and the mere subsides. As Beowulf's men reform once again their community with their leader, the poet provides something like a heroic action of their own to give expression to their pride in him: the arduous carrying of Grendel's enormous head to Heorot. Beowulf's great act and his return have reconstituted and revitalized this human community, freeing it for such a creative action. All through the passage compounds and phrases remind us of the reestablished relationship: *lidmanna helm* (protector of seamen), *gumdryhten* (lord of men), *ealdor ðegna* 1644 (lord of thanes); and there is the massive impression of collective power that we get from the last four lines of the quoted passage. Even the unusual phrase *cyningbalde men* seems to strain the prefix *cyning-* a little beyond its recorded uses elsewhere, in order to stress the close relationship between leader (*cyning*) and followers.

Furthermore Beowulf's jovial speech to Hrothgar, as he presents him with Grendel's head and the giants' sword hilt, also reasserts and broadens the sense of human community, now extending it beyond the Geats' comitatus to the Danes. After he summarizes the fight, Beowulf concludes with a promise that echoes an earlier one:

> Ic hit þe þonne gehate, þæt þu on Heorote most
> sorhleas swefan mid þinra secga gedryht
> ond þegna gehwylc þinra leoda,
> duguðe ond iogoþe, þæt þu him ondrædan ne þearft,
> þeoden Scyldinga, on þa healfe,
> aldorbealu eorlum, swa þu ær dydest. (1671–76)
>
> I promise you this now: you will be able to sleep free from care in Heorot, together with your band of men, with every retainer of your people, the old and the young; you will have no need, lord of the Scyldings, to fear the evil loss of your men's lives from that direction, as you did before.

In their very redundancy, the four verses beginning with *mid þinra secga gedryht* linger over the significant reestablishment, at long last, of human community in Heorot. The monsters that threaten it have been defeated.

CHAPTER FOUR

Scenes of Heroical Life

Even though in important ways Beowulf is set apart from other men, he shares the traditional values of Germanic society. When we concentrate on examining his battles with the monsters, we are necessarily stressing his uniqueness; most men are not qualified even to meet monsters, let alone defeat them. But when we see him in the scenes at court, or with his uncle King Hygelac or his young kinsman Wiglaf, we are conscious of the ways in which he not only accepts but asserts to the fullest extent the values of the world he lives in. In the long run, of course, both his detachment from the ordinary activities and capabilities of men and his involvement in them are needed for the developing of that stereoscopic effect of reality which this poem (like all major poems) creates.

In this chapter then it goes without saying that we will be examining scenes of social interaction. Most epic poems move quickly from one concrete and rather formally composed scene to another.[1] *Beowulf* is not an exception. Looking at these major scenes should help us form a clear picture of the social world of which Beowulf is a part.

1. See the discussion of this point by Thomas Greene in "The Norms of Epic," *Comparative Literature,* 13 (1961), 202 ff., especially his useful division of such scenes into "ethical" and "pathetic" episodes.

The Great Banquet

Probably the most elaborate single scene in the poem is the Great Banquet in Heorot, which takes place after the victory over Grendel and immediately before the surprise attack of Grendel's mother on the hall. For purposes of analysis here, we may divide this scene roughly into three parts: the beginning of the feast, mostly taken up with the awarding of gifts by Hrothgar to Beowulf (lines 1008b–62); the minstrel's story of Finn and Hengest (1063–1159a); and the conclusion of the banquet, where the central figure is Wealhtheow, Hrothgar's queen (1159b–1250).

In the first part of the scene, two principal themes are developed. The first is the splendor of Danish civilization. This theme is of course strongly suggested in a material sense by the richness and beauty of the tapestry-hung hall itself (991–96) and in an ethical sense by the generous and magnanimous actions of Hrothgar. Danish splendor is also brought out by the very nature of the Danish comitatus:

> Ne gefrægen ic þa mægþe maran weorode
> ymb hyra sincgyfan sel gebæran.
> (1011–12)
>
> I've not heard of a nation then with a greater band
> of retainers bearing themselves better around their
> giver of treasure.

We may note that Hrothgar's troop is famous (because the poet has heard of it: the *ne gefrægen ic* formula is repeated again a few lines farther on, in line 1027); it is large in size; most important, it behaves properly. Furthermore, Danish greatness exists not only in the present but is carried back into the past by the selection of epithets throughout this passage.

Hrothgar is called *Healfdenes sunu* 1009, *bearn Healfdenes* 1020, *sunu Healfdenes* 1040; the Danes are *Þeodscyldingas* 1019 and *Healfdenes hildewisan* 1064.[2] While it is quite true that any one of these phrases might occur singly anywhere in the poem, here they seem to be rather noticeably bunched. Such formulas put particular stress on dynastic pride and order, and on the national community as a close-knit family.

The second theme emphasized is the harmonious relationship of the feasters at the banquet. Several traditional images serve to convey this idea: the sharing of food and drink together; the listening together to song and music; and the giving and receiving of gifts. By far the greatest amount of space is given to the last. Here, as usual, gifts stand for the establishment or reaffirmation of feudal relationships. Two aspects of the gift giving are particularly worthy of notice.

First, the gift giving is—must be—entirely public. Gifts must not only change hands but must be seen to change hands. Many watched, *manige gesawon* 1023, as the wargear was brought into the hall; Beowulf had no need to feel ashamed of these gifts in front of all the warriors (*for sceotendum* 1026); that public man, the poet himself, intrudes on the scene with his formulaic "I've never heard of," praising the gifts and the warmth of feeling in the giving, and after he has described the gifts, he voices approval of Hrothgar's manly generosity, remarking that no one can find fault with it (with the suggestion implicit that it is always open to public criticism).

Secondly, in the description of the weapons Hrothgar presents to Beowulf, we have what is in a way the converse of the famous "window" similes in the *Iliad,* where in the midst of the unceasing grind of battle Homer lets us have glimpses

2. To complete the record, the bare possibility might also be borne in mind that *hæleð Healfdena* 1069 is an error for *hæleð Healfdenes,* in the difficult passage at the beginning of the Finn Episode; this suggestion was first made by Grundtvig in 1820, and repeated in his edition of 1861.

of a pastoral world of peace. Here, in the peaceful and joyous setting of the hall, a miniature scene shows us the helmet's future use in protecting the hero against enemy swords (1030–34), and the saddle that we see was once Hrothgar's battle throne in the play of swords (1037b–42). There will be war in the future as there was war in the past; both future and past impinge on this brief present moment of peace. In the life that heroic poetry describes, war and peace are so close together as to seem inseparable.

The closeness of the two worlds is manifest in other ways.

> Bugon þa to bence blædagende,
> fylle gefægon; fægere geþægon
> medoful manig magas þara
> swiðhicgende on sele þam hean,
> Hroðgar ond Hroþulf. Heorot innan wæs
> freondum afylled; nalles facenstafas
> Þeodscyldingas þenden fremedon.
> (1013–19)

> In full possession of glory, they sat down on the benches then, and enjoyed the feast. Their bold kinsmen Hrothgar and Hrothulf courteously accepted many a mead-cup in that high hall. Heorot was filled inside with friends; at that time the mighty Scyldings practiced no criminal acts.

The introduction of the characters' names here would lack purpose if the audience did not know some story of later violence associated with Hrothulf.[3] But even though the poet's

3. So I myself believe, though it may well be an act of faith. The cautious reader should consult Kenneth Sisam (*The Structure of Beowulf* [Oxford, Clarendon Press, 1965], pp. 33–39) for a pertinent warning that *Beowulf* scholars may have created their own convenient legend on the basis of very little evidence in the poem or elsewhere.

reference to the amity between Hrothgar and Hrothulf is in this sense probably ironic, the irony of the scene is not merely heavy-handed. One condition does not cancel another. Both realities are there simultaneously: friendship and joy in the present world of peace, potential destruction in the future world of war.

The same closeness is brought out in the Finnsburg story which follows. There it is dramatized in two ways: first, by having the episode open as abruptly as it does, so that the fictional violence, the *fær* of the tale, seems to crash in on Heorot's own harp song and mead-bench with startling effect; and, secondly, by the events of the episode itself, where a sudden treacherous attack has disrupted what must have been (in the story) a similarly peaceful scene in Finn's hall.

The focus moves quickly to Hildeburh:

> Ne huru Hildeburh herian þorfte
> Eotena treowe; unsynnum wearð
> beloren leofum æt þam *lin*dplegan,
> bearnum ond broðrum; hie on gebyrd hruron,
> gare wunde. Þæt wæs geomuru ides!
> Nalles holinga Hoces dohtor
> meotodsceaft bemearn, syþðan morgen com,
> ða heo under swegle geseon meahte
> morþorbealo maga, þær he[o] mæste heold
> worolde wynne. (1071–80a)

In any case Hildeburh had no reason to praise the Jutes' good faith. Wholly innocent though she was, she was bereft of a dear son and a brother in that play of shields; they fell doomed, spear-wounded. Picture that woman's grief! Not without good cause did she lament fate's decree, when morning came and, as the sky brightened, she could see the evil murder of kinsmen, where before she had known the greatest joy in the world.

The night before, just such a scene as the happy feast in Heorot must have been before Hildeburh's eyes, and for her it was a family reunion, the greatest joy in the world. In the brutal light of morning, the two scenes—peace and slaughter—could only seem to blur with each other in an unreal nightmare. We think of the way the poet of *The Wanderer* superimposes a scene of joy in the mead-hall on the despairing desolation of the exile's seascape. Taking this view of the scene, we can perhaps better recognize the parallel so often noted between Hildeburh and Wealhtheow. For both women perceive clearly (one after the fact, one before) the terrible instability of the heroic world, where the change from order to chaos can be instantaneous.

Instability is indeed really the most striking feature of the makeshift treaty that Finn and Hengest manage to patch together. That they are constructing only a fragile pseudo-order is plain even in the details of the treaty's description.

> þæt ðær ænig mon
> wordum ne worcum wære ne bræce,
> ne þurh inwitsearo æfre gemænden
> ðeah hie hira beaggyfan banan folgedon
> ðeodenlease, þa him swa geþearfod wæs;
> gyf þonne Frysna hwylc frecn*an* spræce
> ðæs morþorhetes myndgiend wære,
> þonne hit sweordes ecg *seðan* scolde.[4]
> (1099b–1106)

so that there no [Frisian] man was to break the pact by word or deed, nor ever mention, with deliberate malice, that the lordless Danes were following the murderer of their ring-giver, as they were indeed

4. Retention of the MS *syððan* in 1106 is tempting ("then it would be sword's edge after that"), but such a construction would be extremely unusual.

> compelled to do; if, then, any Frisian were to reawaken deadly hate by his provocative talk, then sword's edge would decide it.

Words and phrases which point to the real situation and to the imminent violence which that situation must lead to are scattered all through this: *inwitsearo, hira beaggyfan banan, ðeodenlease, morþorhetes, sweordes ecg.* The tortured clauses of the treaty seem to struggle to keep control over these facts, but it will all come to sword's edge again sooner or later.

After the pact is concluded and the oath ratified by some kind of exchange of treasure (if we keep the MS reading *að* in line 1107),[5] we return to Hildeburh's point of view in the description of the funeral. Men can at least draw up treaties, they can act in some way, however foolishly, but women can only see and suffer. In heroic poetry, as we have seen, to be unable to act is in itself an acute form of suffering. We will see later in this chapter how this applies to Hengest. The funeral pyre that Hildeburh sees is a horrifying vision of indiscriminate death, the destruction of bodies, the waste of wealth. War is viewed as an insatiable fire that swallows everything and everyone:

> Lig ealle forswealg,
> gæsta gifrost, þara ðe þær guð fornam
> bega folces; wæs hira blæd scacen.
> (1122b–24)

> Fire, greediest of spirits, devoured all those of both nations who had been taken off by war; their glory had gone.

5. The usual emendation is to *ad* (pyre). But that the ceremonial sacrifice of treasure would play a part in this funeral as it plays a part in the great royal funerals of Scyld and Beowulf seems doubtful. Not only the circumstances of this funeral but its gloomy tone and disgusting details set it apart from the other two. On the other hand, it is crucially important that the oath be made binding.

The funeral seems an ironic wrenching of things from their proper uses:

> Æt þæm ade wæs eþgesyne
> swatfah syrce, swyn ealgylden,
> eofer irenheard, æþeling manig
> wundum awyrded; sume on wæle crungon.
> Het ða Hildeburh æt Hnæfes ade
> hire selfre sunu sweoloðe befæstan,
> banfatu bærnan ond on bæl don
> *ea*me on eaxle. (1110–17a)

> Easy to see on the pyre was a blood-bright mailshirt, a golden pig-figure, an iron-hard boar-image, many a nobleman ruined by wounds; a lot of men fell in that slaughter. Then, at Hnæf's pyre, Hildeburh gave orders that her own son be committed to the flame, that his bone-vessel be burned, that he be placed on the pyre beside his uncle.

An interesting series of objects: a mailshirt, a pig, a boar, a man, a son. All inanimate? All a series of now useless things flung into the fire? The armor and the boar-images were once of some use; they are objects exactly like those presented as gifts at Heorot. Hildeburh has her family reunion now: her son and her brother lie shoulder to shoulder on the pyre.

Here in this description, and in the Finn tale as a whole, the poet offers his audience the vision of a possible or indeed probable future for the inhabitants of Heorot, a future placed very close to them, a future where all may be changed and twisted to images of horror: guests treacherously attacked rather than honorably and merrily feasted; arms and weapons tossed on a pyre to burn and melt rather than being ceremoniously presented to the living; a hall reddened with blood rather than adorned with tapestries.

At the end of the Finn tale, the happy uproar of the feasters in Heorot is heard once again, and now Wealhtheow enters immediately after Hildeburh's exit. There can be no doubt that the two "peace-weavers" are to be thought of together, as most recent criticism has recognized. They are, to be sure, at different stages of their careers as peace-weavers: Hildeburh has failed in her efforts and can now only suffer, while Wealhtheow is still struggling to hold things together, even though it is plain that failure and suffering seem to be in store for her also. What was destroyed at Finnsburg and what Wealhtheow wishes to perpetuate in Heorot is *sib,* the peace founded on good relationships. The picture of harmony in the hall—entertainment by the minstrel, the happy hum of talk along the benches, the abundant and generous pouring of drink—is itself a picture of *sib.* It is juxtaposition that associates Wealhtheow with the woman-victim Hildeburh, and that makes Wealhtheow seem to walk through all this merriment in tragic isolation up to where Hrothgar and Hrothulf are sitting. Even the sudden shift to hypermetric verses (rarely used in *Beowulf*) in line 1163 may be used to direct the audience's attention to the ironic potentialities of her progress.

Hie on sælade
drihtlice wif to Denum feredon,
læddon to leodum. Leoð wæs asungen,
gleomannes gyd. Gamen eft astah,
beorhtode bencsweg; byrelas sealdon
win of wunderfatum. Þa cwom Wealhþeo forð
gan under gyldnum beage, þær þa godan twegen
sæton suhtergefæderan; þa gyt wæs hiera sib ætgædere,
æghwylc oðrum trywe. Swylce þær U*n*ferþ þyle
æt fotum sæt frean Scyldinga; gehwylc hiora his ferhþe treowde,
þæt he hæfde mod micel, þeah þe he his magum nære
arfæst æt ecga gelacum. (1157b–68a)

They carried the noble lady [Hildeburh] on a sea-voyage to Denmark, and brought her to her people.

> —The song, the minstrel's lay, was sung. Hilarity rose again, the noise on the benches brightened; cup-bearers poured wine from marvelous vessels. Then gold-crowned Wealhtheow came walking forward to where that great pair sat, uncle and nephew; their *sib* was then still together, each one true to the other. And Unferth the spokesman also sat there at the feet of the Scyldings' lord; each of them trusted his spirit, that he had a great heart, even though he had not been honorable to his kinsmen in the play of sword-edges.

It is relationship, *sib,* which is emphasized here in the picture of the uncle and nephew sitting together. And what creates this relationship between the two of them, and between them and Unferth, is faith, good will, trust, as the words *trywe* and *treowde* make clear in this passage.[6] Yet I think that even if we did not have some evidence from outside the poem that Hrothgar and Hrothulf were to come eventually into conflict we could sense that something is strange about this relationship as it is set forth here. The very closeness and intimacy of the juxtaposition of uncle and nephew seems to hint at potential violence.[7] The Finn story has shown us that the outward appearances of such a scene are not to be trusted: perhaps, for all we know, Hengest sat dutifully at Finn's feet a moment before the final massacre.

6. The use of etymologically related words elsewhere in the poem shows an interesting pattern. It seems easy for a man who was *trywe* to become a *treowloga,* a faith-breaker like the ten cowardly retainers (2847); it is easy for a peace treaty that was built on trust (*getruwedon* 1095), like the one at Finnsburg, to become suddenly worthless. On the other hand, Beowulf is not mentioned as placing trust in anything other than his own strength, and God's favor (669, 1533, 2540).

7. See Randolph Quirk's discussion of this passage in "Poetic Language and Old English Metre," in *Early English and Norse Studies Presented to Hugh Smith,* ed. Arthur Brown and Peter Foote (London, Methuen, 1963), p. 167.

Unferth too revolves in his own orbit at the feet of Hrothgar, and they include him in the scene by extending to him their trust and by praising his *mod micel. Mod micel* is certainly most often a complimentary phrase, but it might mean simply the capacity for violent action. Even if we leave aside as probably insoluble the question of whether or not Unferth was the "evil counselor" in the Hrothulf story or had anything to do with it at all, Unferth's fratricidal past is itself the very denial of relationship. His odd name, Unferth or Unfrith (Un-peace), could just as well have been Unsib.[8]

The only way that Wealhtheow knows to prevent the explosion which seems imminent in this tense grouping is to resort to what one must call incantation. Her speech, though long, deserves quotation in full.

Spræc ða ides Scyldinga:
"Onfoh þissum fulle, freodrihten min,
sinces bryttal Þu on sælum wes,
goldwine gumena, ond to Geatum spræc
mildum wordum, swa sceal man don.
Beo wið Geatas glæd, geofena gemyndig,
nean ond feorran þu nu hafast.
Me man sægde þæt þu ðe for sunu wolde
hereri[n]c habban. Heorot is gefælsod,
beahsele beorhta; bruc þenden þu mote
manigra medo, ond þinum magum læf
folc ond rice, þonne ðu forð scyle
metodsceaft seon. Ic minne can
glædne Hroþulf, þæt he þa geogoðe wile
arum healdan, gyf þu ær þonne he,
wine Scildinga, worold oflætest;
wene ic þæt he mid gode gyldan wille
uncran eaferan, gif he þæt eal gemon,
hwæt wit to willan ond to worðmyndum

8. See p. 69 n.

umborwesendum ær arna gefremedon."
(1168b–87)

Then the lady of the Scyldings spoke: "Take this cup, my noble lord, giver of treasure! Be happy, gold-friend of men, and speak in soft words to the Geats, as a man should do. Be gracious to the Geats and remember gifts; from near and far you now have [enough gifts?]. I have been told that you wished to have this warrior for your son. Heorot is cleansed, that bright ring-hall; enjoy the rewards of many men while you can, and leave people and kingdom to your kinsmen, when you must go forth to meet destiny. I know my gracious Hrothulf, and I know he wishes to treat the young men with respect, if you should leave the world before he does, lord of the Scyldings. I fully expect that he will wish to repay our sons liberally, if he bears in mind all we have done for him when he was a boy to please and honor him."

Wealhtheow insists on the performance of those rituals that assert and reinforce the traditional values, that bind men together in the acts of taking and giving: take this cup, speak to the foreigners, give them gifts. For it seems probable that these foreigners, these Geats, are seen by Wealhtheow in two lights: they are possible allies in the future on the side of her sons if trouble is to come; they are possible rivals in the present to her sons, at least if Beowulf is really to be "adopted" by Hrothgar.[9] Her process of thought might be rephrased as follows, using deliberately colloquial terms: they told me (you didn't tell me this, Hrothgar) that you wanted to have

9. I am not the first to think of this interpretation of her speech; see Levin L. Schücking, "Heldenstolz und Würde im Angelsächsischen, mit einem Anhang: Zur Charakterisierungstechnik im Beowulfepos," *Abhandlungen der Philologisch-historischen Klasse der sächsischen Akademie der Wissenschaften,* 42, No. 5, Leipzig, 1933, 41.

Beowulf for your son. How typically nice of you, but Heorot is all cleansed now, he's done his job. Why don't you enjoy your wealth while you're alive, and then leave it to your own relatives, not to strangers?

In either case, the Geats must be won over by Hrothgar's generosity, and it is generosity that is particularly stressed in all the phrases applied to Hrothgar and his hall in this speech: *sinces brytta, goldwine gumena, spræc mildum wordum, geofena gemyndig, beahsele beorhta, bruc . . . /manigra medo, læf/folc ond rice, arna gefremedon.* Generosity ought to affect Hrothulf too as well as the Geats; a secure future for Wealhtheow's children will be guaranteed if Hrothulf is impressed enough by his uncle's liberality to behave gratefully and properly in the future.

If he is. Incantation, the imposing of word patterns on the brute turbulence of reality, accounts for the pathos of Wealhtheow's words. I *know* my Hrothulf, I *know* what he will wish to do, I *expect* that he will wish to be good to our sons. Stated as if they were facts, these brave fragile hopes are cast out over the uncontrollable future, a future that will be wholly dependent on Hrothulf's will and good faith, on what he in reality will wish to do, and on his own conception of relationship and *sib*. A defeat of Wealhtheow's impassioned expectations seems inevitable.

Perhaps the gifts themselves are another form of incantation. In the following passage, which is focused on the great necklace that is presented to Beowulf, the poet is pointing both to the splendor and binding power of such material gifts and to their ultimate uselessness. For the necklace will be passed on by Beowulf to Hygelac, who will wear it on his fatal expedition to the continent, and the description that follows of Hygelac's death in that battle brings out very strongly some of the ironies surrounding the idea of possession.[10]

10. The preceding reference to Hama is omitted because I can make very little of it in view of the scanty evidence available. E. G.

Þone hring hæfde Higelac Geata,
nefa Swertinges, nyhstan siðe,
siðþan he under segne sinc ealgode,
wælreaf werede; hyne wyrd fornam,
syþðan he for wlenco wean ahsode,
fæhðe to Frysum. He þa frætwe wæg,
eorclanstanas ofer yða ful,
rice þeoden; he under rande gecranc.
Gehwearf þa in Francna fæþm feorh cyninges,
breostgewædu ond se beah somod;
wyrsan wigfrecan wæl reafedon
æfter guðsceare; Geata leode
hreawic heoldon. (1202–14a)

That was the neck-ring which Hygelac of the Geats, nephew of Swerting, had with him on his last raid, when beside his battle-standard he stood guard over treasure and booty. Fate took him off, when in his heroic pride he asked for trouble in the fight against the Frisians. He carried that necklace with its precious stones all the way over the cup of the waves, a powerful lord; he fell under his shield. Then the king's life passed into the possession of the Franks, and his armor and the necklace too. Inferior soldiers robbed the dead after the slaughter; the Geatish people held the field of the corpses.

The heavy rhetorical rhythms are characteristic, and hammer on the same old theme of sudden disastrous change. Hygelac

---

Stanley sees the Hama allusion as a warning against avarice, but this seems irrelevant here ("Hæthenra Hyht in *Beowulf*," in *Studies in Old English Literature in Honor of Arthur G. Brodeur*, ed. Stanley B. Greenfield [Eugene, Ore., University of Oregon Press, 1963], pp. 146–47). See R. E. Kaske, "The Sigemund-Heremod and Hama-Hygelac Passages in *Beowulf*," *PMLA*, 74 (1959), 489–94, for a far more plausible conjecture, namely, that Hama's prudent preservation of his own life and property is contrasted with Hygelac's foolhardy loss of both.

had the necklace, but only on his last journey; he defended it in his last stand, but no one can stand against his own death-fate; he wore it proudly in his voyage to the continent, but he fell dead under his shield. At the end the enemy Franks owned the neck-ring, while Hygelac and the Geats (as corpses) owned only the cold ground of the battlefield.

In terms simply of the order of presentation, a similar thematic sequence of "gifts" followed closely by "death" appeared earlier in the banquet scene: the description of Hrothgar's great gifts to Beowulf was followed immediately by the bloody Finn tale. Gifts are obvious symbols of human success and felicity, but they cannot govern the future, they cannot keep people alive or ensure that their expectations will always come true. Like the Finn tale, this account of Hygelac's death opens up a vista into the future, that future so close to the present of the poem. The Finn story, however, was really a situation in the past, relevant only by analogy to the presumed future of Heorot. Hygelac's death has a greater degree of reality and immediacy; it will happen, in the very course of this poem, and it will happen to the man closest to the hero of the poem.

Yet Wealhtheow's faith in the power of gifts is again strongly emphasized in her second speech. Unable to know the future, she can only fear it. And her fear takes the form of the anxious and urgent imperatives she showers on Beowulf.

> Bruc ðisses beages, Beowulf leofa,
> hyse, mid hæle, ond þisses hrægles neot,
> þeo[d]gestreona, ond geþeoh tela,
> cen þec mid cræfte ond þyssum cnyhtum wes
> lara liðe; ic þe þæs lean geman.
>
> * * *
>
> Ic þe an tela
> sincgestreona. Beo þu suna minum
> dædum gedefe, dreamhealdende.
>
> (1216–20, 1225b–27)

> Wear this neck-ring, my dear young Beowulf, in good fortune; enjoy this armor and mighty treasure; have great success in life, be resolute in your strength and be kindly in your advice to these boys; I will remember you for it with a reward. . . . I will give you much treasure. Act well toward my son and preserve this happy peace.

Take, take these gifts; I will pay you, I will pay you—and be good to my children. The last four lines of the speech become pure incantatory prayer:

> Her is æghwylc eorl   oþrum getrywe,
> modes milde,   mandrihtne hol[d];
> þegnas syndon geþwære,   þeod ealgearo,
> druncne dryhtguman   doð swa ic bidde.
> (1228–31)

> Here every warrior is true to the other, merciful in heart, loyal to his lord; these men are in harmony and this nation prepared; once entertained with drink at a feast like this, soldiers do as I ask them.

All relationships are *right*: trust, good faith, loyalty. And her burning will can be extended into the future, if these things are true. This is the peace-weaver laboring at her task: weaving harmony, tying the thread with double-secure knots, checking the possible weak places in the fabric.

But fate weaves patterns other than those men can know. As Wealhtheow secretly fears and as the audience doubtless knows, the harmonious peace in Heorot is indeed to be shattered in the distant future; but, more important, it is also about to be shattered in the next few minutes by the wholly unexpected *fær* of Grendel's mother, another female busy about the interests of her son. The Danes who reoccupy Heorot for the night are *ealgearo;* they prepare well as they set their arms carefully about them; they are truly ready, as ready as any men can be—ready for anything but what happens.

> Wyrd ne cuþon,
> geosceaft grimme, swa hit agangen wearð
> eorla manegum, syðþan æfen cwom.
> (1233b–35)

> They did not know fate, that grim ancient decree,
> how it had happened to many a man, after evening
> came.

And so Hnæf and Finn and Hygelac were all, whatever their state of readiness, taken by surprise. A desperate instability is always the chief characteristic of this heroic world, but none of the living can ever believe that evening comes.

Hrothgar's Sermon and Its Context

After his victory over Grendel's mother, Beowulf comes back to Heorot with his Geats and enters the hall, four of his men carrying Grendel's giant head. He also brings back as a trophy the hilt of the great giant-sword he found in the underwater dwelling; in a formal speech, he presents this hilt to Hrothgar.

Much seems to be made all through this passage of the change of ownership and shift in power that is symbolized by the hilt. Beowulf remarks in his presentation speech that he has taken it away from the enemy (*ic þæt hilt þanan / feondum ætferede* [1668b–69a]), after using the sword to avenge the Danish victims of Grendel's depredations.

> Ða wæs gylden hilt gamelum rince,
> harum hildfruman, on hand gyfen,
> enta ærgeweorc; hit on æht gehwearf

æfter deofla hryre Denigea frean,
wundorsmiþa geweorc, ond þa þas worold ofgeaf
gromheort guma, godes andsaca,
morðres scyldig, ond his modor eac,
on geweald gehwearf woroldcyninga
ðæm selestan be sæm tweonum
ðara þe on Scedenigge sceattas dælde.
(1677–86)

Then the golden hilt [Goldenhilt?], that ancient piece of giants' work, was given into the hand of the old warrior, white-haired leader in battle; that product of marvelous smiths came into the possession of the lord of the Danes after the fall of the devils, when that wolf-hearted man [Grendel], God's adversary, had given up this world, guilty of murder, and his mother also—it came into the control of the best of mighty kings between the seas, of those who share out wealth in Denmark.

The fact of transfer of ownership is insistently stressed in this long sentence, even to the point of awkwardness. The hilt that the young man Beowulf obtained from the Grendel race he passes on to the old man Hrothgar. In the dim past the hilt must have had other mysterious makers and owners (*enta ærgeweorc, wundorsmiþa geweorc*) about whom we will never be able to know very much; now it has somehow fallen into the possession of a new and different kind of owner, the mightiest and most generous of Northern kings. How strange it all is.

Hrothgar now examines the hilt before he replies to Beowulf. On it is inscribed the story of the drowning of the old race of giants in the Flood.

Hroðgar maðelode, hylt sceawode,
ealde lafe, on ðæm wæs or writen
fyrngewinnes, syðþan flod ofsloh,

gifen geotende, giganta cyn
(frecne geferdon); þæt wæs fremde þeod
ecean dryhtne; him þæs endelean
þurh wæteres wylm waldend sealde.
(1687–93)

Hrothgar spoke—he looked at the hilt, ancient heirloom, on which was carved the beginning of the long-ago struggle when the flood, surging ocean, slew the race of giants (they suffered terribly); they were a nation alienated from the eternal Lord; the Ruler gave them a final reward for that by means of the swelling power of water.

Doubtless the giants once enjoyed, as Grendel later enjoyed, a brief and illusory feeling of power in their very moment of rebellion and alienation from God; but *flod ofsloh,* the floodwaters struck, and they got their reward. *Edwenden,* reversal, change, the unexpected and sudden blow of fate—this is the form in which God's retributive order is imposed on the rebellious giants, and in this way Beowulf imposes his order on the Grendel race. Obviously both the dramatic role of the hilt itself, as it functions in the action of the poem as Beowulf's weapon and trophy, and the story depicted on it reinforce the theme of the opposition of good and evil. It is important to note as well the fact that the hilt story also emphasizes the theme of the sudden and extreme shift of power, a lesson implicit both in the frequency with which the hilt has changed hands and in the calamitously sudden overthrow of the arrogant giants.

To warn Beowulf now of such change is precisely the chief purpose of Hrothgar's sermon that follows this rather elaborate introduction. Indeed, the theme of change is made part of the very form of the sermon. For the sermon first offers us an ideal picture of Beowulf (1700–09a), wreathed in terms of praise; then, immediately afterward, it presents an anti-Beowulf, one who is everything that Beowulf is not, in the figure of Heremod. The two figures are so unlike that it would seem impossible even to imagine one becoming the other, but that is just the point: the main body of the sermon is devoted to a careful analysis of exactly how and why this kind of change may occur. And Hrothgar concludes his speech with a telling reminder of his own experience: how sudden grief came to him at the very peak of his fame and power:

> Hwæt, me þæs on eþle edwenden cwom,
> gyrn æfter gomene, seoþðan Grendel wearð,
> ealdgewinna, ingenga min. (1774–76)
>
> See how a reversal of all this came upon me in my country, and grief after joy, when that ancient adversary Grendel became my invader.

This process of change is associated with frequent images of organic growth in the case of both Beowulf and Heremod. After referring to Beowulf's birth, Hrothgar says:

> Blæd is aræred
> geond widwegas, wine min Beowulf,
> ðin ofer þeoda gehwylce. (1703b–05a)
>
> Your glory is raised up far out over the distant highways, my friend Beowulf, over every nation.

The image of Beowulf's vital fame rising up and spreading out so that it can be seen from far off is itself an image of growth.[11] And Hrothgar adds:

> Ðu scealt to frofre weorþan
> eal langtwidig leodum þinum,
> hæleðum to helpe. (1707b–09a)

11. One can entertain the possibility also of some semantic contamination between the two homonyms *blæd* (breath, life, fame), from *blawan* (blow), and *blæd* (plant-growth, fruit), from *blowan* (grow). The meanings of these words are so similar in some poetic contexts that it is not always easy to know which is being used.

> You are destined to become for a long time a comfort
> for your people and a help to men.

Beowulf will grow toward other men, to serve and help them, and to become what they wish him to be.[12]

Heremod is just the opposite, as a passage that we looked at earlier (pp. 3–5) shows:

> Ne wearð Heremod swa
> eaforum Ecgwelan, Arscyldingum;
> ne geweox he him to willan, ac to wælfealle
> ond to deaðcwalum Deniga leodum.
> (1709b–12)
>
> Heremod was not like that to the descendants of Ecgwela, the honorable Scyldings; he did not grow up to be what they wished—on the contrary he grew into the slaughter and violent death of the Danish people.

He does not grow, that is to say, into society but away from it; he kills men and moves out, out into the state of exile, *mondreamum from,* far from human joys. God had given him strength and power unmatched by other men, just as he had done with Beowulf. But Heremod's growth is misdirected:

> Hwæþere him on ferhþe greow
> breosthord blodreow. (1718b–19a)
>
> But in his heart grew a bloodthirsty breast-hoard.

The image of growth underlines Heremod's freedom of choice. There are many directions in which to grow; one chooses to grow toward good or evil.

12. The occurrence of three hypermetric lines (1705–07) at this point may in some obscure way underline the "expansive" nature of Beowulf's past and future development. One would like a plausible explanation of why hypermetric passages appear where they do in Old English poetry.

For Hrothgar sees God in this sermon as the generous king (quite unlike the stingy Heremod) who showers gifts on men out of his love for them. It seems an essential part of God's love for him to wish men to be wholly free to make use of this abundance as they please.

Wundor is to secganne
hu mihtig god manna cynne
þurh sidne sefan snyttru bryttað,
eard ond eorlscipe; he ah ealra geweald.
Hwilum he on lufan læteð hworfan
monnes modgeþonc mæran cynnes,
seleð him on eþle eorþan wynne
to healdanne, hleoburh wera,
gedeð him swa gewealdene worolde dælas,
side rice, þæt he his selfa ne mæg
for his unsnyttrum ende geþencean.
(1724b–34)

How wonderful it is to tell of how mighty vast-minded God allots to mankind wisdom, and land, and honored valor; He owns title to all things. In His love He sometimes lets roam the thoughts of a man of great race; He gives him joy of the earth to hold in his homeland, and a fortress to guard his men; and, when he owns all these, He gives him large shares of the world and a wide-stretching kingdom, so that in his folly he himself can no longer even imagine the end of it all.

The passage vividly and forcefully conveys the essential concept of freedom. First the miraculous nature of God's power and bounty is indicated, how, in his love, he permits a man's mind to *hworfan,* to move freely where it wishes. The act of giving on God's part is emphasized by the succession of verbs of bestowal—*læteð, seleð, gedeð*—which mount to a climax of generosity. Making the same point in another way, other phrases lay stress on the real ownership of all these gifts by the fortunate man (they are actually given and actually received): *to healdanne, hleoburh wera* (containing the idea of protecting property), *gewealdene*. Finally the images of physical spaciousness here—*eorþan wynne, worolde dælas, side rice*—are in fact (as they so often are in *Paradise Lost*) images of the full freedom of choice and of God's overwhelming abundance of love. The combination of all this is impressive: it is understandable that the man given such mighty gifts cannot imagine an end to them and cannot anticipate any sudden change, such as sickness, old age, malice, or violence.

The image of growth clearly remains in the poet's mind, as we can see in this passage:

Ac him eal worold
wendeð on willan (he þæt wyrse ne con),
oðþæt him on innan oferhygda dæl
weaxeð ond wridað. (1738b–41a)

No, for him all the world goes as he wishes (he does not know the worse side), until within him an enormous pride grows and puts forth shoots.

Growth toward good and evil, while it is made possible by God's gifts, depends wholly on the individual's will. The pride that develops in the hypothetical rich man of Hrothgar's sermon is essentially a shift in his attitude. That world which had once seemed to him too much now seems too little; he grows in arrogance and conceit and cares nothing for the *forðgesceaft*, the abundant world God had given him.[13]

Þinceð him to lytel þæt he lange heold,
gytsað gromhydig, nallas on gylp seleð
fædde beagas, ond he þa forðgesceaft

13. Here taking *forðgesceaft* in the sense of "created things, the world" rather than in the sense of "the future life." The former sense is the first listed in Bosworth-Toller and may be found in *The Order of the World* 3 and in *Riddle* 84: 9.

forgyteð ond forgymeð, þæs þe him ær god sealde,
wuldres waldend, weorðmynda dæl. (1748–52)

> What he has held for so long now seems to him too little; he covets fiercely—never any longer does he proudly bestow ornamented rings; and he then ignores and scorns the created world, the great share of honors which God, Ruler of glory, had given him.

His pride takes the form of stinginess; he no longer will give away the *fædde beagas* even though he must ignore God's own generosity in giving them to him.

Again addressing Beowulf directly, Hrothgar urges him to protect himself against evil and pride and to choose the better part, *þæt selre geceos* 1759.[14] The last phrase is almost certainly Christian and there is traditional Christian imagery in the sermon elsewhere (e.g. the arrows of the devil). But the point that Hrothgar's exemplum seems designed to make, if our discussion of it up to this point has any validity, is not at all the expected Christian exhortation to take heed of the future life and to avoid damnation. Indeed the future life may be irrelevant, or at least not essential, to the problem presented here: how to live a life that is to be ended finally by death. What seems to be crucially important is a man's consciousness or lack of consciousness of his own mortality.

Beowulf can make the right choice, Hrothgar seems to be saying, only if he knows first that his strength, his *mægnes blæd,* is only for a short time and that death can come in many forms and at any moment, and if he also knows the proper attitude to be taken toward the things of this world. God has provided a model of behavior here: things are to be distributed as generously by human rulers as God has distributed them among men. It might be noted that, elsewhere in Old English literature, the two poems known as *The Fates of Men* and

14. As many have pointed out, there is an apparent echo of Luke 10:42: *Maria optimam partem elegit, quae non auferetur ab ea.*

The Gifts of Men deal in their own way with precisely these two kinds of knowledge, essential both for the Christian and the hero.

While the secular and social dimensions of the sermon have been emphasized here, it is not implied that the sermon contains no familiar theological ideas as well. We call it a sermon traditionally because it is one; it has analogies with the Latin homiletic tradition. My point may be simply that it is a sermon appropriate for heroic poetry, as most Christian sermons would probably not be.[15] It deals with the use and abuse of power by the world's great men, with the sure certainty of the unexpected in this life, with royal niggardliness as the emblem of all sins, and finally with the compelling necessity for the epic hero to understand and be ready to live close to death. Of course Beowulf does not need this sermon, but the poet needs it, one may assume, as an explicit statement of values found implicitly everywhere in the poem.

The Scenes with Wiglaf

The two scenes we have examined bring out certain negative aspects of the heroic world. Both scenes are essentially monitory in nature. The Great Banquet dramatizes the precarious stability of human communities founded on *sib*, on trust and fidelity, and kept functioning by the constant exchange of gifts and duties. Hrothgar's sermon, in a much more didactic way, warns Beowulf of the difficulty of main-

15. Sisam (*The Structure of Beowulf*, pp. 78–79) finds "no characteristically Christian doctrine" in Hrothgar's speeches. R. E. Kaske ("*Sapientia et Fortitudo* as the Controlling Theme of *Beowulf*," *Studies in Philology*, 55 [1958], 433), although his interpretation of the sermon differs from mine, agrees that "Hrothgar's explicit aim is not eternal salvation, but wise kingship."

taining one's moral balance and integrity in a world of such catastrophic change. The scenes involving the young retainer Wiglaf, on the other hand, reassert very powerfully the positive values of the heroic world, and at a time when it is essential to have them reasserted.

Like Grendel's mother, Wiglaf is first sprung on us without warning (in lines 2599 ff.). It is possible that the original audience, if the story were familiar enough to them, waited eagerly for the introduction of both characters. But, even if the story were not so familiar, the more perceptive members of the audience should have been able to sense when the surprise was about to arrive in each instance. As we have seen, the concluding lines of the Great Banquet scene are full of almost saccharine phrases of peace, harmony, and triumph; one expects that only trouble is forthcoming, and what immediately follows is the savage irruption of Grendel's mother into Heorot. The situation is reversed in the case of Wiglaf. The beginning of Beowulf's fight with the dragon, a fight that gives every sign of imminent disaster for the hero, immediately precedes Wiglaf's entrance as rescuer. Not only does this passage (lines 2538–95) vividly describe events that are in themselves unusual and disturbing—a burning stream pours from the dragon's barrow and prevents Beowulf from closing with his enemy; Beowulf's iron shield does not protect him against the flames; his sword is incapable of wounding the dragon—but the narrator intersperses the description with his own gloomy comments and forebodings. At the close of the passage Beowulf stands alone and nearly helpless in the fire blast, while his retainers race off to safety in the nearby forest.

It seems inherent in the rhetorical rhythms and cyclic emotional patterns of this kind of poetry that so much horror will be followed by something good, just as the false security of Heorot at bedtime was followed by sudden slaughter. The noticeable rhetorical heightening in each instance could scarcely have any other purpose than to sharpen the edges of the contrast.[16]

What is presented as contrast in terms of temporal sequence—dark before (disaster), light after (rescue)—is also presented as a spatial chiaroscuro in the handling of the contrast between Wiglaf and the other retainers. The terror caused by the dragon is great enough to make the average *hæleð* run away; ten of them do, because they are frightened, not because they have been ordered by Beowulf to stay out of the fight. One critic has represented the retainers as being torn between obedience to Beowulf's order to stay out of the dragon fight (2529 ff.) and their natural wish as good retainers to come to his assistance.[17] If such internal conflict had existed, however, the poet would probably have called attention to it; all Anglo-Saxon poets were well equipped with language suitable for describing just such conflicts. But here I think we have inconsistency rather than a real conflict. The poet is intent on creating a nonce-effect of extreme contrast between what the retainers do and what Wiglaf does, in response to the same challenge of the dragon's terror. That the retainers' flight is somewhat inconsistent with what we are told of them elsewhere is not important.[18]

Indeed, Wiglaf and the retainers have only a dim existence as *characters,* in the usual modern sense of that word. We are not invited to think about the complexities of their inner lives. They exist together in this scene only to dramatize as vividly as possible through their actions the idea of choice: that some may freely choose to run away and that Wiglaf freely chooses to stay. Furthermore Wiglaf is really a part of the character of Beowulf rather than a fully developed

16. See also Adrien Bonjour, "The Use of Anticipation in *Beowulf,*" *Review of English Studies* (O.S.), *16* (1940), 290–99.

17. Alain Renoir, "The Heroic Oath in *Beowulf, the Chanson de Roland,* and the *Nibelungenlied,*" in *Studies in Old English Literature in Honor of Arthur G. Brodeur,* p. 244.

18. See Chapter Three, n. 15.

individual entity himself. He is an effect of Beowulf; he is what Beowulf ideally makes people do; he is love and loyalty outside of Beowulf but occasioned by Beowulf.

All this is perhaps merely to say that Wiglaf is primarily part of the heroic system, a system resoundingly evoked in the very words by which Wiglaf is first introduced:

> Wiglaf wæs haten Weoxstanes sunu,
> leoflic lindwiga, leod Scylfinga,
> mæg Ælfheres; geseah his mondryhten
> under heregriman hat þrowian.
> Gemunde ða ða are þe he him ær forgeaf,
> wicstede weligne Wægmundinga,
> folcrihta gehwylc, swa his fæder ahte.
> Ne mihte ða forhabban; hond rond gefeng,
> geolwe linde, gomel swyrd geteah,
> þæt wæs mid eldum Eanmundes laf,
> suna Ohtere[s]. (2602–12a)

> He was called Wiglaf, son of Weohstan and an admired shield-warrior, a nobleman of the Scylfings and a kinsman of Ælfhere; he saw his own lord helmeted and suffering pain from the heat. Then he thought back on the favors which his lord had given him, the wealthy estate of the Wægmundings and with it every customary privilege which his father had had. And he could not hold back: hand seized shield, the yellow linden-wood, and he drew out the ancient sword which men knew to be the legacy of Eanmund, Ohthere's son.

Wiglaf is here located in a public and aristocratic world. His identity is merely one intersection of coordinates in a web of relationships: son of Weohstan, lord of the Scylfings, kinsman of Ælfhere, bearer of Eanmund's sword, and retainer of Beowulf. In themselves all these relationships imply inescapable obligations; they present all we need know about his "character" and his past at this stage, although we are given the casual bonus of one adjective, *leoflic,* likeable, admired or valued by others, to describe him.

A part of the system, Wiglaf responds. In Wiglaf the system functions perfectly. He sees his lord in pain and danger; he remembers Beowulf's generosity; his conditioned hand cannot restrain itself from moving to his sword hilt. The passage that comes next, a rather long digression (in view of the tension of the moment) on the history of the sword that he draws, has as its chief function the further definition of the system by focusing in concrete terms on the sword.

What is this sword as it is presented here? A public object, first, well known among men, and therefore another way of giving Wiglaf identity; he is the man who owns that sword. It is a sword that receives particular attention here because Beowulf's own sword has just failed unexpectedly; we are eager to know what the history and virtues of this sword may be and how likely it is to do the job. But most important the sword is a *laf,* an heirloom, something left by father to son. This something that is left is indeed a material sword, but it is more: it is an example of conduct, a way of using a sword properly, as Wiglaf's father behaved properly (we are told) in killing Eanmund and in bringing the plunder (including this sword) to his lord Onela. Onela gives the wargear back to Weohstan, who keeps it for his son:

> He frætwe geheold fela missera,
> bill ond byrnan, oððæt his byre mihte
> eorlscipe efnan swa his ærfæder;
> geaf him ða mid Geatum guðgewæda,
> æghwæs unrim, þa he of ealdre gewat,
> frod on forðweg. (2620–25a)

He kept these treasures for many years, the sword

> and mailshirt, until his son could do deeds of valor as his father had done before him; then he gave the wargear to his son, living among the Geats now, and countless quantities of everything, when he went from life, old on that final road.

For Weohstan the sword was simply the hope that his own son could continue the tradition of *eorlscipe* and could thus carry the heroic past on into the future.

In the scenes we examined earlier, the same theme of the possible uses of material objects was approached from different directions. In the Great Banquet scene, when we observed Wealhtheow's anxious concern about the binding power of such gifts, we felt the poet's skepticism about their ability to determine men's future behavior. Hrothgar's sermon went even further in stressing the possibilities for complete moral corruption inherent in material wealth. But Wiglaf's sword represents the ideal functioning of a symbolic gift, where a *laf* succeeds in transmitting what it is intended to transmit.

It has been suggested that this sword has one other important meaning in the plot itself; it may by reason of its past history carry the assurance of doom for the Geats, for it was the weapon that once belonged to Eanmund before he was killed, the son of Eanmund's slayer now possesses it, and Eanmund's brother Eadgils now sits on the Swedish throne.[19] In such circumstances swords can cause trouble, as we can see in this poem in the Ingeld story. Yet we cannot

19. That the sword is mentioned here primarily because of its importance in the future stages of the long feud between Geats and Swedes was suggested by Adrien Bonjour, "Weohstan's Slaying of Eanmund," *English Studies,* 27 (1946), 14–19, and also in *The Digressions in Beowulf* (Oxford, Basil Blackwells, 1950), pp. 35–39. Another explanation of the meaning of the sword much closer to the one offered here is that of R. E. Kaske, "Weohstan's Sword," *Modern Language Notes,* 75 (1960), 465–68.

be certain that this dimension of meaning is present in this passage unless our attention is explicitly called to it (as it certainly is in the Ingeld story). Again it is the difficult problem of not knowing what memory span for details of this sort we can assume for the audience.

In any event, the poet makes clear that what is important now is the impending test for Wiglaf and the sword.

> Þa wæs forma sið
> geongan cempan, þæt he guðe ræs
> mid his freodryhtne fremman sceolde.
> Ne gemealt him se modsefa, ne his mæges laf
> gewac æt wige; *þæt* se wyrm onfand,
> syððan hie togædre gegan hæfdon. (2625b–30)
>
> For the young fighter, that was the first time he was obliged to enter combat beside his noble lord. His spirit did not melt, nor did his noble father's heirloom turn weak in the fight; the dragon found that out when they encountered each other.

Alliteration highlights certain words (*gemealt, modsefa, mæges laf*) that figure in a rhetorical parallel with a curious chiastic structure: one would expect spirit to weaken and sword to melt, but the actions are reversed. The effect is to entangle abstract and concrete in deeper identity. Wiglaf's courage *is* his *mæges laf,* his kinsman's heirloom; the sword is only a tangible sign of it. To state this another way: the sword is his obligation to behave in a heroic way. Hence it is not surprising that Wiglaf's speech, which comes next, is concerned with the decorum of heroic relationships almost exclusively as they are bodied forth in material objects.

Thus his first gesture as he turns to the cowardly retainers is to point to *ðas beagas,* these rings, which he wears and which they are now all wearing, and which constitute material tokens of obligation exactly like Wiglaf's sword.

Ic ðæt mæl geman, þær we medu þegun,
þonne we geheton ussum hlaforde
in biorsele, ðe us ðas beagas geaf,
þæt we him ða guðgetawa gyldan woldon
gif him þyslicu þearf gelumpe,
helmas ond heard sweord. (2633–38a)

I think of the time when we drank mead in the beer-hall, the time when we promised our lord, the man who gave us these rings, that we would pay him back for this wargear, these helmets and keen swords, if any need like this should ever arise for him.

Like its opening, Wiglaf's speech as a whole is entirely conventional. Its closest analogues in Old English poetry include the beots in the latter part of *The Battle of Maldon.* Among the conventions are the oath taken at a feast in the mead-hall in time of peace, the obligation to return the favor of having been singled out for special attention by the lord, and now the sudden emergency, the *þearf,* which puts it all to the test.

From the first, Wiglaf places himself solidly in the heroic community of the comitatus: it is all "we," "our lord," "he chose us." Wiglaf exhorts his comrades in this fellowship to come to Beowulf's aid, but he can do no more than appeal to them, for it is their decision to make as individuals. And in the end Wiglaf too must give voice to his own decision:

Nu is se dæg cumen
þæt ure mandryhten mægenes behofað,
godra guðrinca; wutun gongan to,
helpan hildfruman, þenden hyt sy,
gledegesa grim. God wat on mec
þæt me is micle leofre þæt minne lichaman
mid minne goldgyfan gled fæðmie.
(2645b–52)

> Now that day has come when our own lord needs our strength, needs brave fighters; let us advance and help our commander while there is heat (?) and fierce flame-terror. As for myself, God knows I would much rather have the flame seize my own body along with my gold-giver's.

Note the emphatic shift in the last three lines to the first person singular: *mec, me, minne, minne.* A liege man's standing obligation combines with the challenge of the emergency (*nu is se dæg cumen*) to lead to this moment of heroic choice. The response to the heroic demand is never merely conventional so long as it is free and unpredictable, the decision of each individual. Wiglaf commits himself to his choice; the retainers make theirs, apparently without responding to Wiglaf's eloquent appeal. As ordinary reasonable men, they run away; fighting fire-dragons was never an imaginable part of the contract. And in fleeing they serve, as we have seen, as the sullen ground for Wiglaf's bright virtues. The view of some that the retainers in their flight reveal that degeneracy of the Geatish nation which will soon lead to its downfall is a mistaken one; these men are not really any more degenerate than Hrothgar's Danes in the early part of the poem, even though Wiglaf condemns them. It is the absolute nature of the rhetoric of contrast that causes these exaggerations. We must be able to tell true heroes from ordinary men: the difference lies in the strength and dedication of their respective wills.

The emphasis on weapons and armor and treasure in Wiglaf's speech and throughout the scene as a whole reaches a significant climax at the end of his speech.

> Ic wat geare
> þæt næron ealdgewyrht, þæt he ana scyle
> Geata duguðe gnorn þrowian,
> gesigan æt sæcce; urum sceal sweord ond helm,

byrne ond b*ea*duscrud, bam gemæne.
(2656b–60)

> I know one thing: he has never deserved anything like this—to be the only one of the Geatish nobles to endure sorrow and sink down in battle. Sword and helm, byrnie and war shirt, will be common to both of us!

In these final lines, which state an unconditional commitment, there is no longer any giving or taking of treasure and weapons in symbolic, almost sacred, transfer. Ownership is obliterated now: lord and retainer become one.

The idea of the merging of identity is carried out in the action of the fight itself. Who kills the dragon? Readers often accuse the poet of being a little evasive on this point, since the real truth may be that Wiglaf actually kills the dragon but Beowulf must get credit for the victory. But the poet is anything but evasive. He says explicitly and carefully that they both kill him:

Feond gefyldan (ferh ellen wræc),
ond hi hyne þa begen abroten hæfdon,
sibæðelingas. Swylc sceolde secg wesan,
þegn æt ðearfe! Þæt ðam þeodne wæs
siðas[t] sigehwil*a* sylfes dædum,
worlde geweorces. (2706–11a)

> They felled the enemy (courage drove out his life), and they both then had succeeded in destroying him, those noble kinsmen. That is how a fighting-man should be, a retainer in time of need! For the lord that was his last hour of victory gained by his own deeds, the last act performed in the world.

In the first sentence, the honor of the victory is obviously divided evenly. Both share in the impersonal *ellen,* the courage that kills the dragon. The close relationship of the two victors as *sibæðelingas* is also stressed. The second sentence awards warm praise to Wiglaf for his dutiful behavior; the third obliquely gives credit to Beowulf for victory (*sylfes dædum*, by his own deeds, he has attained a *sigehwil*). The very structure of the passage, in other words, suggests an attempt by the poet to balance his allotment of praise.

But we may find stronger evidence than these statements in the complicated action of the fight itself. At the outset, Wiglaf is forced to take shelter behind Beowulf's shield when his own is burned by the dragon's fiery breath. Beowulf then strikes once more at the dragon and this time shatters his sword (an action showing at the same time his unbroken will and his actual helplessnes in the situation). After the dragon seizes Beowulf in his final rush, Wiglaf manages to stab the monster, wounding him severely enough to force him to release Beowulf but not severely enough to kill him. Recovering, Beowulf succeeds in finishing the monster off by cutting it in half.

In terms of physical action, the fight is characterized above all by teamwork in the way that each combatant helps the other. What kills the dragon? Neither one of the two heroes as individuals, but the relationship between these two *sibæðelingas* almost as a hypostatized entity in itself, the reality of heroic comradeship, affectionate loyalty, and self-sacrificing courage.[20]

We may find a terse summary of most of the themes we have been examining in one three-line passage:

> Ða ic æt þearfe [gefrægn]   þeodcyninges
> andlongne eorl   ellen cyðan,
> cræft ond cenðu,   swa him gecynde wæs.
> (2694–96)

20. In the ancient Sumerian epic *Gilgamesh,* the hero Gilgamesh and his beloved comrade Enkidu share credit, in much the same way, for the killing of the monster Humbaba. See *The Epic of Gilgamesh,* English version by N. K. Sanders (Baltimore, Penguin Books, 1960), p. 82.

> Then I heard that the warrior by the side of the people's king at the time of his great need made known his courage, his strength and boldness, as it had been bred into him.

Let us look closely at these lines. The *ða ic gefrægn* formula shows that the traditional quest for fame has indeed succeeded, for someone has heard the story and is reciting it to others. The phrase *æt þearfe* contains the idea of the time of testing and emergency. Alliteration, as usual, reinforces meaning: *þearfe* is defined by being linked with *þeodcyninges,* and *andlongne eorl* is linked with the essential virtue of *ellen*. At the same time, juxtaposition places *andlongne* quite literally beside *þeodcyninges*. Enjambed alliteration further binds *cyðan* to its objects *cræft* and *cenðu,* and also to *gecynde,* a word that suggests the reason for the eorl's heroic behavior. The passage as a whole then is a tightly woven super-formula of six verses, stating with intensity and economy the need in time of trial for making public show of physical strength and courage, because it is the traditional behavior of a hereditary warrior caste.

Wiglaf's second speech, made immediately after Beowulf's death, is a bitter reproach to the cowardly retainers, who now return to the scene from their hiding-places in the forest.

> Ða ne dorston ær dareðum lacan
> on hyra mandryhtnes miclan þearfe,
> ac hy scamiende scyldas bæran,
> guðgewædu, þær se gomela læg,
> wlitan on Wilaf. He gewergad sæt,
> feðecempa, frean eaxlum neah,
> wehte hyne wætre; him wiht ne speo*w*.
> (2848–54)

> Before, they had not dared to make play with spears in their lord's moment of great need; on the contrary, now they carried their shields and armor,

> ashamed, to where the old man lay, and they looked at Wiglaf. That fighter sat exhausted, near his lord's shoulders, trying to bring him to with water; but it was useless.[21]

Now the retainers bring shields and spears and mailshirts to Beowulf, as they failed to do when he needed their help. Intent on trying against all hope to revive Beowulf, Wiglaf at first ignores them. The contrast in activities—Wiglaf bending solicitously over his lord, the retainers looking guiltily at Wiglaf (rather than at Beowulf)—stresses their alienation from each other. Even though his lord is dead, Wiglaf is *frean eaxlum neah,* in the very place a man should occupy in battle, near his lord's shoulders or shoulder-to-shoulder with him (cf. the compound *eaxlgestealla* for comrade). When Wiglaf at last turns to address them, there is no longer any mention of "we," the pronoun used so often in his first speech: it is "ye" now, for they have lost their right to fellowship.

> Þæt, la, mæg secgan se ðe wyle soð specan
> þæt se mondryhten se eow ða maðmas geaf,
> eoredgeatwe þe ge þær on standað,
> þonne he on ealubence oft gesealde
> healsittendum helm ond byrnan,
> þeoden his þegnum, swylce he þrydlicost
> ower feor oððe neah findan meahte,
> þæt he genunga guðgewædu
> wraðe forwurpe, ða hyne wig beget.
> (2864–72)

> Anyone who wished to tell the truth could say this much: that the lord who gave you all those treasures, the equipment that you are standing in there, when he used to bestow helmets and mail-

21. See the earlier discussion of this passage in Chapter One, pp. 6–7.

> shirts (the best he could find anywhere, far or near) on the men sitting on the ale-benches in his hall, the way a lord gives to his men—that he completely and disastrously threw that armor away, when war came upon him.

Wiglaf's searing reprimand focuses instantly on the very symbols of their humiliation, the arms Beowulf had presented to them in the hall and which they now carry. These objects are the very trust and faith that their leader once placed in them and on them: once signs of pride, now signs of shame. The arms have been thrown away; they have become emptied of meaning now, and that world of loyalty and affection which Wiglaf's long first sentence evokes must now exclude these men. The time of trial found them unable to meet the test.[22]

A deeper appreciation of this scene between Wiglaf and the retainers requires now a brief look at the surrounding context. After Beowulf has made his dying speech, he passes on to Wiglaf the golden ring and the weapons (2809–20). The passage from lines 2821 to 2845a, which immediately precedes the return of the retainers, offers us a tableau of frozen action in which Wiglaf stares at the dead body of his lord, as the poet ranges over the meanings that may lie in this tableau and in this death. Here we should consider those meanings most closely related to Wiglaf.

The sight of one's dead lord would cause one immediate response above all others in any Germanic warrior: the instinct to seek vengeance. And so here the first image which follows that of Beowulf stretched on the earth is of the *bona*, the one responsible for the death:

22. The coming of this inevitable testing time is emphasized by three similar formulas, which have almost a refrainlike function in this speech: *ða hyne wig beget* 2872, *þa him wæs elnes þearf* 2876, *þa hyne sio þrag becwom* 2883.

Ða wæs gegongen guman unfrodum
earfoðlice, þæt he on eorðan geseah
þone leofestan lifes æt ende
bleate gebæran. Bona swylce læg,
egeslic eorðraca ealdre bereafod,
bealwe gebæded. (2821–26a)

It was painful for that man young in years to see on the earth the one he loved best having it so hard at the end of his life. The killer also lay dead, the terrifying earth-dragon, deprived of life, driven by destruction.

Perhaps the idea of requiring compensation for a death in the form of a wergild would have occurred to the Anglo-Saxon mind almost simultaneously with the idea of vengeance. This idea too is mentioned in lines 2842b–43: Beowulf's death was paid for by a great mass of treasure. The idea recurs in some of the ensuing meditations on the significance of the treasure.

In his role as survivor and avenger, Wiglaf can be seen as related in certain ways (mostly by contrast) to the anonymous protagonists of the well-known elegiac passages that appear in the latter part of the poem, the Old Father (2444 ff.) and the Last Survivor (2231 ff.). As we will see more fully in the next chapter when these passages are examined, the Old Father suffers and dies because he can neither take any revenge nor claim any payment that might ease the paralyzing grief of a kinsman's death. Wiglaf has both satisfactions, however great his grief may be and however ironical the satisfactions may sometimes seem: he has not only participated in the vengeful killing of the dragon but he sees it lying there dead; and he is in charge of inspecting and collecting the vast treasure which is at times viewed by the poet, not without tragic irony, as Beowulf's wergild.

The Last Survivor, suffering total defeat, turns his nation's wealth over to the earth and waits mournfully for death to take him. Wiglaf, last of the Wægmundings, *endelaf usses cynnes* (last remnant of our race), as Beowulf calls him, is in this sense a last survivor himself, but his survival is far more dynamic and positive. By his words and actions he provides the definitive statement of the heroic ethos, and he sets in motion the final great action of the poem, Beowulf's funeral. That the Old Father and the Last Survivor are anonymous while Wiglaf, as we have seen, is so meticulously furnished with pedigree and "name" has its own significance. In heroic poetry, only action can give a man a name.

The last lines of Wiglaf's reproachful speech seem to link the cowardly retainers with the Last Survivor.

> Nu sceal sincþego ond swyrdgifu,
> eall eðelwyn eowrum cynne,
> lufen alicgean; londrihtes mot
> þære mægburge monna æghwylc
> idel hweorfan, syððan æðelingas
> feorran gefricgean fleam eowerne,
> domleasan dæd. Deað bið sella
> eorla gehwylcum þonne edwitlif!
> (2884–91)

> Now all taking of treasure and giving of swords, all pleasure in your homes and all that you love, shall come to a stop for your race; every man of your nation shall wander destitute of the right to land, once distant noblemen hear of your flight and your shameful act. Death will be better for every man than a life of disgrace!

The use of treasure, that loving exchange of gifts that we have seen so consistently associated with the heroic life itself, will now come to an end for them. Like the Last Survivor, they will now be compelled to long for death. And they too will be essentially anonymous: their refusal to act has meant the obliteration of their heroic identity. Against such a background Wiglaf stands out and survives as an identifiable man in the clearest way imaginable.

The Feud: Hengest and Ingeld

The story of Finn, which Hrothgar's scop tells at the Great Banquet, and the story of Ingeld, Beowulf's prediction to his king Hygelac of ultimate trouble stemming from the marriage of Ingeld to Hrothgar's daughter Freawaru, have some curious similarities. Both scenes of course deal with feuds, but it is more interesting to note that both deal with the same rather special stage of a feud: the temporary suspension of violence through some kind of treaty or alliance. In each case, the woman who will suffer the most from the feud (through no fault of her own) is introduced at the outset of the story and given prominence. To the extent that such a device succeeds in eliciting our initial sympathy for the woman victim, our attitude toward the feud tends to be nonpartisan and disapproving and the events appear more tragic than glorious. In each case, furthermore, the second chief character is a man trapped in an almost insoluble conflict of loyalties who is finally nudged by someone else into taking action. Both tales, finally, use the same symbols to represent the conflict and its cause.

There is no need now to reemphasize the importance in the Finn story of Hildeburh; this was discussed earlier in the chapter. But we have not yet given our attention to Hengest, the other main character in the tale. It should be made plain at the outset that much of the interpretation of the events in this episode is bound to be quite conjectural, because the difficulties of the crabbed and condensed text are so great. For this reason, I will first quote in full the concluding lines of the Finn episode with the readings I consider best and then I will offer a provisional translation of it that puts me out on many limbs.

1125 Gewiton him ða wigend wica neosian,
freondum befeallen, Frysland geseon,
hamas ond heaburh. Hengest ða gyt
wælfagne winter wunode mid Finne
[ea]l unhlitme. Eard gemunde,
1130 þeah þe he [ne] meahte on mere drifan
hringedstefnan; holm storme weol,
won wið winde, winter yþe beleac
isgebinde, oþðæt oþer com
gear in geardas, swa nu gyt deð,
1135 þa ðe syngales sele bewitiað,
wuldortorhtan weder. Ða wæs winter scacen,
fæger foldan bearm. Fundode wrecca,
gist of geardum; he to gyrnwræce
swiðor þohte þonne to sælade,
1140 gif he torngemot þurhteon mihte
þaet he Eotena bearn inne gemunde.
Swa he ne forwyrnde woroldrædenne,
þonne him Hunlafing hildeleoman,
billa selest, on bearm dyde,
1145 þæs wæron mid Eotenum ecge cuðe.
Swylce ferhðfrecan Fin eft begeat
sweordbealo sliðen æt his selfes ham,
siþðan grimne gripe Guðlaf ond Oslaf
æfter sæsiðe, sorge mændon,
1150 ætwiton weana dæl; ne meahte wæfre mod
forhabban in hreþre. Ða wæs heal roden
feonda feorum, swilce Fin slægen,
cyning on corþre, ond seo cwen numen.
Sceotend Scyldinga to scypon feredon

1155 eal ingesteald eorðcyninges,
swylce hie æt Finnes ham findan meahton
sigla, searogimma; hie on sælade
drihtlice wif to Denum feredon,
læddon to leodum.[23] (1125–59a)

Then the warriors, who had lost friends in the fighting, went off to their dwellings, to visit Frisia with its estates and chief fortress. But Hengest went on living with Finn that bloodstained winter, for he had no choice at all. He kept thinking about his own country, even though he was not able to put any ring-prowed ship into motion in the sea; the ocean surged with storms, fought against the gale, and winter fettered the waves in an ice-bond, until spring came again into men's courts, as it still does now, that weather bright as glory always keeping its appointment. Then winter had passed, and the lap of earth was beautiful. Now the exile yearned to leave the courts where he was a guest; his mind was on vengeance for past injury more than on the sea-voyage, if he could manage to carry through the angry encounter in which he had in mind some of the Jutes. And so he did not refuse that obligation the world imposes, at the time when Hunlafing placed in his lap the battle-flame, best of swords, whose edges were well-known among the Jutes. That was just the way that cruel sword-evil in turn fell upon bold-hearted Finn in his own home, when Guthlaf and Oslaf had told of the fierce attack and

23. The text is basically Dobbie's, although I have made one or two minor changes in punctuation. His text is much to be preferred to Klaeber's overemended version of the passage. The only emendations here adopted are these:

1128–29: Finne / eal—MS finnel
1130: *ne* not in MS
1151: roden—MS hroden.

> the sorrow after that sea-voyage, and had reproached [Finn?] for their great troubles; the restless blazing heart could not be contained within the breast. Then the hall was stained red with the life-blood of their enemies, and Finn was killed, a king with his men all around him, and the queen taken. The bowmen of the Danes carried all the contents of that great king's hall to their ships, whatever they could find on Finn's manor of jewels and precious gems; they carried the noble lady [Hildeburh] on a sea-voyage to Denmark, brought her to her people.

Again we have the poet working in contrasts at the beginning of this passage. The Frisian warriors—Finn's real retainers—move freely out, away from the hall, toward their homes; yet Hengest, compelled by the treaty to pretend to be Finn's man, must stay with the one he hates, cooped up in the hall over a long winter that is described as *wælfagne,* haunted and stained by the memory of many killings. The Frisians visit their homes; Hengest thinks about his. They act, while he cannot (*ne meahte . . . drifan*)—and this is the most intolerable situation heroic poetry knows. Both the internal turmoil and the agonizing frustration of Hengest are objectified beautifully in the images of the stormy sea and the ice-locked waves. Then spring comes; winter vanishes; action is possible.

Much of what follows is told in such an elliptical way that it remains fairly obscure, but this much seems generally clear: Hengest burns to achieve the satisfaction, so long postponed, of avenging the death of his king, Hnæf. His eagerness is stressed in the usual ironic way by the statement that he did not refuse the obligation, when Hunlafing (?) put the sword in his lap. The compound that is used of the sword, *hildeleoman* 1143 (battle-blaze), may even be its name, as some have suggested, or else simply a descriptive term; in either case, its meaning is appropriate here, for the sword kindles the ensuing violence—indeed, it is the immediate cause of it. Although we have no evidence to support such a guess, we can at least surmise that the sword is probably Hnæf's own sword, and thus itself embodies and suggests (like Wiglaf's sword) a whole complex of obligations.

What is released now is literally *sweordbealo* (sword-evil), and it falls upon Finn in his own home. This final outburst of savagery is described in impersonal terms. Agents and participants are hardly mentioned (though what exactly we should make of Guthlaf and Oslaf remains something of a mystery). What takes over now is *wæfre mod:* the restless heart (like Hengest's restless heart, in his exile longing for seafaring), the fiery heart that now blazes up out its long confinement.[24] The rhetorical parallels in these last lines of the episode make interesting connections. The hall is reddened with blood, Finn is slain, the queen is taken: all three events become brutal acts of violence when put in such a series, even though Hildeburh is supposedly being rescued. And the word *feredon* (carried) is used twice: the Danes carried off all the valuables they could find at Finn's hall and they carried off the queen, another valuable item of loot presumably. Such an association reminds us of the funeral earlier in the episode, where people also put various things in the fire—pieces of armor, men. A latent image of fire runs through the final lines as well. It appears in *hildeleoman* and perhaps in *wæfre mod,* as well as generally in the way in which an impersonal force seems to take lives and consume things. To those who take part in this final action, the triumphant Danes, the feud doubtless seems to have a successful outcome: vengeance is taken and honor is upheld. But the last person the poet lets us see is Hildeburh once

24. It might be noted that, in the poem *Daniel,* line 240, the word *wæfre* is applied to flame: *wylm þæs wæfran liges.*

more. The feuders have already killed her son and her brother; now they kill her husband and take her home to her people.

The Ingeld story begins as Beowulf tells his interested uncle Hygelac of the *medudream,* the mead-joy, of Heorot. Much of this joy, in Beowulf's account, seems to be centered on the figures of the two royal women: Wealhtheow making her queenly progress around the hall, while her young daughter Freawaru serves mead to the feasting retainers. Beowulf tells Hygelac something about Freawaru.

> Sio gehaten [is],
> geong, goldhroden, gladum suna Frodan;
> [h]afað þæs geworden wine Scyldinga,
> rices hyrde, ond þæt ræd talað,
> þæt he mid þy wife wælfæhða dæl,
> sæcca gesette. Oft seldan hwær
> æfter leodhryre lytle hwile
> bongar bugeð, þeah seo bryd duge!
> (2024b–31)

> Young and gold-adorned, she is betrothed to the courteous son of Froda [i.e. Ingeld]; that [betrothal] has suited the lord of the Scyldings and guardian of the kingdom; he believes it to be a good plan to settle a great number of murderous feuds and conflicts by means of that women. But it is usually very rare that the killing spear lies still for even a short space of time after the fall of a prince, no matter how fine the bride may be!

In terms of the development of the hero's character, it is plain that one of the chief purposes of the Ingeld story is to show us Beowulf's political insight, for the time is fast approaching in the poem when he must assume kingship. He is intelligent enough to foresee that Hrothgar's attempt to use marriage to put an end to feud will be a failure, and he describes graphically just what is likely to happen. But now we are looking at the episode thematically rather than in terms of character, and we can see strong similarities to the Finn story.

The Ingeld story begins with a woman who is destined, like all women in the poem, to suffer as an innocent victim. Hrothgar intends to use his daughter as a thing, as an instrument—*mid ðy wife* 2028 is significantly in the instrumental case—in order to bring the feud to an end. Yet the alliteration in line 2031 underlines a significant and ironic contrast: *bongar bugeð . . . bryd.* In proportion as the bride becomes a thing, the inanimate spear becomes half-personified, becomes a *bona,* takes on its own spontaneous and ominous vitality.

For in the world of feud which is described in the following dramatic scene, things seem themselves to be actors and causes of action.[25] Danish warriors (or perhaps only one Danish warrior) make the mistake of wearing *gomelra lafe,* things which once belonged to the Heathobeards of a previous generation who had been killed by the Danes in an earlier stage of the feud. These objects awaken memories; they bring past into present. And the past is brought into the present in both the recollections and the very presence of the old warrior.

> Þonne cwið æt beore   se ðe beah gesyhð,
> eald æscwiga,   se ðe eall gem[an],
> garcwealm gumena   (him bið grim sefa),
> onginneð geomormod   geong[um] cempan
> þurh hreðra gehygd   higes cunnian,
> wigbealu weccean,   ond þæt word acwyð:
> "Meaht ðu, min wine,   mece gecnawan

25. The precise facts of the action in the Ingeld story are still obscure, even though the general emotional drift seems plain. Detailed discussion of the problems may be found in Dobbie's notes, as well as in many other places.

þone þin fæder to gefeohte bær
under heregriman hindeman siðe,
dyre iren, þær hyne Dene slogon,
weoldon wælstowe, syððan Wiðergyld læg,
æfter hæleþa hryre, hwate Scyldungas?
Nu her þara banena byre nathwylces
frætwum hremig on flet gæð,
morðres gylpeð, ond þone maðþum byreð,
þone þe ðu mid rihte rædan sceoldest."
(2041–56)

Then at the beer-drinking will speak an old spear-warrior, one who sees the *beah* [literally "ring"; here possibly "sword"], one who remembers all, the spear-death of men (his mind is full of bitterness), and in his grief he will begin to make trial of the heart of a young warrior, working his way deep into the thoughts of his mind, awakening there evil war; he will speak these words: "My friend, can you recognize the sword your father carried into battle for the last time, when he wore his helmet and carried the steel he loved, that time when Danes, bold Scyldings, killed him and held the field, after Withergyld had fallen after the fall of many men? Now—here—the son of one of those killers walks the floor of this hall showing off his adornments and boasting of killing; and he wears that same treasure which you should rightly own."

The old warrior's sight of the ring (or sword) is what begins the action. It carries him back to a death, a *garcwealm,* in the past, and then draws him forward into a future where the *garcwealm* can be repeated, where he will be able to awaken new *wigbealu.* In operating on the mind of the young man, he must first evoke a vivid scene in the past: the day the young man's father went off to battle for the last time, wearing this sword. *This* sword, the one I am pointing at. The sword in that past scene was then and there; the sword you see now is now and here: *nu her*. But they are the same. The sword is a *laf*, something left to posterity, and the feud is a *laf*: it can transcend time. Like Wiglaf in his first speech, the old warrior introduces the *nu* clause, which demands immediate commitment by the young man in the present.

> Manað swa ond myndgað mæla gehwylce
> sarum wordum, oððæt sæl cymeð
> þæt se fæmnan þegn fore fæder dædum
> æfter billes bite blodfag swefeð,
> ealdres scyldig; him se oðer þonan
> losað [li]figende, con him land geare.
> (2057–62)

> In this way he will remind and admonish him on every occasion with words of pain, until finally the time will come when the woman's retainer will sleep bloodstained from the sword's bite, forfeiting life for his father's deeds; the other man [the killer] will get away from there alive, knowing the land well.

As the old man repeats his speech over and over, the young listener feels the pain more acutely. At last the future comes and the feud flares up again out of the past: the Danish retainer who accompanies Freawaru is killed for his father's deeds, not his own. If the scene is actually a wedding feast, as seems likely, we see once again the lightning change from peace to war, from heaven to hell.

> Þonne bioð [ab]rocene on ba healfe
> aðsweor*d* eorla; [syð]ðan Ingelde
> weallað wælniðas, ond him wiflufan
> æfter cearwælmum colran weorðað.
> (2063–66)

> Then the oath-swearing of men will be broken on both sides; after that, murderous emotions will surge

up in Ingeld, and love for his wife will grow cooler
after such wellings of misery.

The alliterating words *wælniðas* and *wiflufan* stand in sharp ironic contrast; the very closeness of their juxtaposition dramatizes the sudden change. Violence is here symbolized by the familiar image of the *wylm,* the swelling, surging wave of emotion that shatters the restraints of the peace treaty, just as the symbolic waves in the story of Hengest finally freed themselves from their ice-bonds. The waves of hatred quench Ingeld's warm feelings for his Danish wife; those feelings now grow cooler. In his conclusion to this story, Beowulf remarks that it is his opinion that the professed friendship of the Heathobeards for the Danes is not *fæst,* not stable. But what can remain *fæst* against these elemental surges of human emotion, against blazing fire and stormy sea?

Fundamentally both Hengest and the young man in the Ingeld story (as well as Ingeld himself) are like Wiglaf. All three move into action in response to reminders of their heroic obligations, which take the form of material objects carrying memories highly charged with emotion. But Wiglaf has a more immediate and more urgent stimulus than the others, since he actually sees his beloved lord in mortal danger before him, and his response is not shadowed by the moral ambiguities that necessarily surround Hengest and Ingeld, perhaps because his enemy is not human. Their actions can never have the same purity, for they are caught in the headlong blind drive of the vendetta. What they do—and it is what they must do—merely adds to the death toll and shatters that pathetic hope of peace which the poet evokes from the figures of innocent and suffering women. In Wiglaf the heroic code appears, isolated, a pure ideal. We must understand his behavior in order to understand and sympathize with the behavior of Hengest and Ingeld. But in the feud the heroic code is turned against itself: the virtues of fidelity and courage lead to the destruction rather than the preservation of society.

The Feud: Ravenswood

It is not necessarily over-ingenious to see a progression in the poem from the story of Finn to the Ingeld scene and then to the battle of Ravenswood, which is described by the Messenger near the end of the poem. The poem does seem to have something of a Yang-Yin structure to it, after all: as the kind of heroic achievement that Beowulf represents nears its end in Beowulf's own death, the kind of self-destructiveness the feuds represent—the negative side of the heroic ideal—comes into clearer and clearer focus.

The story of Finnsburg, told as an integral part of the celebration of Beowulf's defeat of Grendel, is offered to us ostensibly as a rousing minstrel's tale intended to entertain the feasters. It has no direct and explicit relevance to the audience that hears it, other than in the fact that Danes of a previous generation were involved in the story, although, as we have seen, it is certainly true that there is an important implicit or analogical relevance to the situation of Wealhtheow and the Danish court. Again, the Finn tale, for all its intensity, is not presented in specifically dramatic terms by the poet but rather in the form of narrative summary; the episode, for example, contains no speeches.

The Ingeld story, on the other hand, has somewhat more immediacy. In form, what makes it particularly memorable is the direct presentation of the old warrior's speech. It is more immediate also because we have more interest in the characters. We have come to know Hrothgar well, and this is the story of what will probably happen to Hrothgar's daughter, in a feud that will lead to the destruction of Heorot itself. Yet in spite of this, the Ingeld story is still somewhat removed from a full degree of reality by the very fact that it is presented not as historical fact but as Beowulf's prediction of the future, and it is told not to the Danish participants themselves but to the detached though curious Geatish king Hygelac.

Ravenswood is quite another matter. Here we have what Klaeber calls "the only detailed account of a real battle in *Beowulf*." [26] It is very detailed, and very real; it is presented in the form of a masterly scenic narrative full of suspense. To be sure, this battle took place in the past, but it was a past accessible to the human imagination, two generations back, not in the half-legendary past of the fight at Finnsburg or of the story of Sigemund's killing of the dragon. It is a past, moreover, that has the greatest importance for the Messenger's Geatish audience, not only because their own grandfathers and fathers were in the battle but because the battle was an early stage of the same long-lived feud that is certain to break out again in the very near future after the news of Beowulf's death has spread north to the Swedes. Indeed no story could have more harsh relevance.

Because the Ravenswood battle is presented as a scene, it differs from the numerous other references in Part II of the poem to the Geatish-Swedish wars. These references are typically condensed summaries of the ups and downs of the hostility, often describing in rather abstract terms a rapid series of events. The following passage is a fair example:

> Þa wæs synn ond sacu   Sweona ond Geata
> ofer *w*id wæter,   wroht gemæne,
> herenið hearda,   syððan Hreðel swealt,
> oððe him Ongenðeowes   eaferan wæran
> frome, fyrdhwate,   freode ne woldon
> ofer heafo healdan,   ac ymb Hreosnabeorh

26. Fr. Klaeber, *Beowulf and the Fight at Finnsburg* (3d ed. Boston, D. C. Heath, 1950), p. 223.

eatolne inwitscear oft gefremedon.
(2472–78)

> Then there was hatred and conflict of Swedes and Geats over the wide water, and fighting on both sides, and sharp battle, after Hrethel died; Ongentheow's sons were bold and aggressive, with no intention of keeping the peace across the sea. Instead, again and again, they carried out atrocious and vindictive raids near Hreosnabeorh.

Lines like these suggest very effectively the unending *heard ceap,* the rugged economics, of the vendetta: exile, rebellion, pursuit, revenge, conspiracy, the precarious peace, counterplot, massacre. We should note here that this passage follows a description of the death of King Hrethel; it is typically a king's death that releases such anarchic savagery. The frequency with which such passages as these occur in Part II serves to make us more and more conscious of the world of feud, and to prepare us for the climactic scene at Ravenswood.

The Messenger begins his report to the waiting Geats, a report that immediately follows Wiglaf's reprimand to the cowardly retainers, by offering for their contemplation a compact picture, almost an icon, composed of three figures: Beowulf dead, the dragon dead beside him, and Wiglaf sitting motionless over both.

Nu is wilgeofa Wedra leoda,
dryhten Geata, deaðbedde fæst,
wunað wælræste wyrmes dædum.
Him on efn ligeð ealdorgewinna
sexbennum seoc; sweorde ne meahte
on ðam aglæcan ænige þinga
wunde gewyrcean. Wiglaf siteð
ofer Biowulfe, byre Wihstanes,
eorl ofer oðrum unlifigendum,

healdeð higemæðum heafodwearde
leofes ond laðes. (2900–10a)

> Now the bountiful lord of the Geats is fast in the bed of death, lies in his slaughter-couch, victim of the dragon's deeds. Beside him lies his deadly opponent, brought down by dagger-wounds; with his sword Beowulf was never able to make any wound at all in the monster. Wiglaf son of Weohstan sits over Beowulf, one good man sitting over another no longer alive; in his exhaustion he keeps guard over the head of friend and foe.

The dominant impressions we receive from this heroic Pietà are those of immobility and helplessness. The verbs in these lines fall into the same pattern of meaning: *is deaðbedde fæst, wunað wælræste, ligeð, siteð, healdeð*. The scene is composed as a static picture: nothing moves. But even though he is motionless in this tableau of grief, Wiglaf has an intense vitality. He has just ended his vehement speech of reproach to the retainers, and the echo of it is still in our ears. In his role here as "guardian" he suggests a surviving spirit of heroic dedication and loving responsibility; by his own attitude he dramatizes concretely the love and loyalty Beowulf has inspired, and he further dramatizes the possibility of their survival after Beowulf's death.

The relevance of this tableau to the main theme of the Messenger's speech is made plain in the references in the quoted passage to the *wilgeofa Wedra leoda, / dryhten Geata*. Dominating the entire speech by the Messenger is the master-image of the *fyll cyninges,* the King's Fall. Beowulf's death is national disaster. The audience must see the death scene clearly before the Messenger moves on to interpret the political meanings of the picture in terms of its predictable effects on others: on the Franks and Frisians, the Hugas and the Hetware, on the Swedes, and finally on the Geats themselves. The strong pattern of cause and effect is emphasized at the outset by the correlative rhetorical pattern. The *nu is* of the opening lines is to be taken together with the lines that follow:

> Nu ys leodum wen
> orleghwile, syððan under[ne]
> Froncum ond Frysum fyll cyninges
> wide weorðeð. (2910b–13a)

[Now that the king is lying dead . . .] now the people may expect a time of troubles, after the fall of the king becomes widely known among the Franks and Frisians.

As the Messenger goes on to predict the reaction of neighboring nations to the news of Beowulf's death, the image of the King's Fall is expanded greatly in importance. As the shock waves of the event radiate outward, the Geats come to realize more fully that only the strength of Beowulf's heroic reputation has protected them for decades. But now, as the other nations, enraged by Geatish attacks in the past, in their turn come to "read" the picture that was held up for contemplation, the ring will begin to close.

The mention of Hygelac's death at this point further expands the range of meaning of the master-image.

> Wæs sio wroht scepen
> heard wið Hugas, syððan Higelac cwom
> faran flotherge on Fresna land,
> þær hyne Hetware hilde ge*n*ægdon,
> elne geeodon mid ofermægene,
> þæt se byrnwiga bugan sceolde,
> feoll on feðan, nalles frætwe geaf
> ealdor dugoðe. Us wæs a syððan
> Merewioingas milts ungyfeðe.
> (2913b–21)

That fierce quarrel with the Hugas was started when Hygelac sailed with an armed fleet to the lands of the Frisians, and there the Hetware attacked him in

> battle and, since they outnumbered him, quickly succeeded in making the armed warrior give way; he fell among his men—that lord gave no treasure to his loyal retainers. Ever since then, the favor of the Merovingian [king] has not been granted us.

Since the importance of Hygelac as a central and unifying figure in the poem as a whole has been recognized and well described by Professor Brodeur, there is no need to discuss it at length here.[27] But we should recognize that this particular passage is a climax to the story of Hygelac as it has been slowly developed throughout the poem. Here we have the fourth and final mention of Hygelac's disastrous expedition to the continent, and here, for the first time, the political rather than the personal implications of the raid are made clear.

We are certain that Hygelac's raid, in the early years of the sixth century, is historical fact.[28] Perhaps we might guess that it was, even in the absence of knowledge from outside the poem, for it has something of the puzzling intractability of history in the context of *Beowulf*. This attempt at political aggrandizement may have been Geatland's proudest and most ambitious moment, but it may also have sealed its doom. But it is too easy, and perhaps misleading, to cast this event into the black-and-white patterns of moral lessons to be drawn from history. When the raid is first mentioned, at the time of the Great Banquet, it is true that the poet seems to blame Hygelac for his arrogance in seeking out trouble (*syððan he for wlenco wean ahsode* 1206). But it might be a little nearer the truth to say that Hygelac could not have loved his people so much loved he not glory more. From one point of view, Hygelac's adventurous raid is the fine excess of a truly heroic

27. *The Art of Beowulf* (Berkeley and Los Angeles, University of California Press, 1959), pp. 71–87.

28. The relevant excerpts from Gregory of Tours may be found in Klaeber's Appendix, pp. 267–68.

character. If the poet reproves Hygelac for his action, it is in much the same tone that a later poet reproves Earl Byrhtnoth of Essex for allowing the Viking invaders to come ashore and fight in the battle of Maldon.

But the poet's attitude toward the raid is still ambivalent. Perhaps this ambivalence finds expression in the very role he assigns Beowulf in this expedition. Nothing anywhere in the poem suggests that Beowulf's devotion to Hygelac is ever anything but absolute and unqualified. He accompanies his king on this raid and later avenges his death on the Franks. Yet we are never told that Beowulf was involved in the planning of the raid or in the looting and fighting that took place in its early stages; he is somehow kept disengaged from all aspects of it except the simple obligations to follow his lord and to avenge him when he falls in battle. Moreover we are not told elsewhere in the poem that Beowulf himself engages in aggressive warfare of this kind when he becomes king.[29]

In the context of the Messenger's speech, in any event, we are probably to see the raid as an instance of Geatish arrogance, if only because here the account of the raid forms one half of a rhetorical parallel, when it is taken together with the Geatish attack on the Swedes, which the Messenger mentions next.

> Ne ic to Sweoðeode sibbe oððe treowe
> wihte ne wene, ac wæs wide cuð
> þætte Ongenðio ealdre besnyðede
> Hæðcen Hreþling wið Hrefnawudu,
> þa for onmedlan ærest gesohton
> Geata leode Guðscilfingas. (2922–27)

Nor do I expect any peace or faith on the part of the Swedish people; on the contrary, it was common knowledge that Ongentheow took life away from

29. Unless one considers him very deeply involved in Eadgils' expedition of revenge against his uncle Onela, which he may be, but the text is not very clear on this point (lines 2391–96).

> Hæthcyn son of Hrethel at Ravenswood, that time the Geatish people, in their arrogance, first went to meet the warlike Swedes.

Here the symmetrical pattern (attacks from both north and south in reaction against past Geatish aggression) seems to be established at the expense of consistency. We were told earlier (2475 ff.) that this particular series of wars was originally launched by the Swedes and that the Geatish expedition to Ravenswood was actually a countermeasure of revenge, almost an act of self-defense.

The Messenger has told us that King Beowulf has fallen, and King Hygelac; now we hear also of the fall of King Hæthcyn. The master-image has been expanded to include incidents of the past and portents of the future. But the presentation up to this point has been essentially static. The development and restatement of the theme of the King's Fall into terms of real dramatic power await the juxtaposition of this static form of presentation with the explosive scene of violence that follows.

For it is just at this point in the speech that the word *sona* introduces abruptly a series of sudden actions, bursting upon us after all the slow and mournful building up of somber expectation:

> Sona him se froda fæder Ohtheres,
> eald ond egesfull, *o*ndslyht ageaf,
> abreot brimwisan, bryd ah*red*de,
> gomela[n] iomeowlan golde berofene,
> Onelan modor ond Ohtheres,
> ond ða folgode feorhgeniðlan,
> oððæt hi oðeodon earfoðlice
> in Hrefnesholt hlafordlease.
>
> (2928–35)

> Instantly the aged father of Ohthere, old and terrible, struck a counter-blow, felled the sea-king

> [Hæthcyn]; the old man rescued his wife, that old woman of a former day, mother of Onela and Ohthere, now bereft of gold; and then pursued his mortal enemies until they got away painfully into Ravenswood, lordless.[30]

Here is a series of events almost too rapid for the hearer to take in. The invading Geats, momentarily triumphant, run head-on against the fury of Ongentheow—a fury given expression here by the hammering consecutive verb phrases—and are sent reeling back into a desperate position in Ravenswood. The action begins in fury and continues without pause. Cowering in the shelter of the wood, the beaten Geats face certain extinction at the hands of this grim old devil who howls his threats of hanging and massacre at them all through the long night. For there is certainly no moral ambiguity in Ongentheow's motivation at this point. That he is rescuing his wife and protecting his land from invaders adds to the very force of his onslaught: it is the uncomplicated release of righteous indignation.

What the poet shows us here is Ongentheow playing the role of the strong king, vigorously defending his beloved people against foreign attack. His very presence underlines the fact that the Geats are (temporarily at least) *hlafordlease,* a defenseless people without a king. They are saved from their dangerous situation by the sudden arrival of Hygelac:

> Frofor eft gelamp
> sarigmodum somod ærdæge,
> syððan hie Hygelaces horn ond byman,
> gealdor ongeaton, þa se goda com
> leoda dugoðe on last faran. (2941b–45)

30. The reading *gomela[n] iomeowlan* (2931) and its translation here follow the interpretation suggested by John C. Pope, "*Beowulf* 3150–3151. Queen Hygd and the Word 'Geomeowle,'" *Modern Language Notes,* 70 (1955), 77–87.

> Comfort came once more to the sadhearted men together with early dawn, after they recognized the sound of Hygelac's horn and trumpet, when the brave one followed after the track of the picked body of retainers.

Their emotional response to Hygelac's arrival is dramatized by the very word order. Comfort, security, relief flood back with the light of dawn after that night of horror and with the welcome daylight of Hygelac's name, then the sound of his trumpets, and finally the sight of him hurrying to their rescue.

The rest of the battle is presented in the same terms of swirling and tumultuous action. The poet immerses us in the desperate seesaw action of the fighting. Now it is Ongentheow's turn to place his back grimly against the wall. He is pursued by the Geats with the same headlong violence with which he pursued them and is at last brought to bay like a trapped animal. He goes down fighting savagely and gallantly in an unequal battle against two young Geatish warriors, Wulf and Eofor. In this fight we may believe that he would have had the audience's sympathy. Patriotic or nationalistic feeling is usually ignored by the poet of *Beowulf,* although not always by the characters themselves.

It is of vital importance to our experience of the poem that we live through the action of this battle and feel all its emotions. The gripping narrative ensures that we do. We perceive that these are men released from any burden of rational choice or self-discipline by the animal necessity of survival. Brought to bay, they fight like animals. Is the poet not inviting us to think of the story in just those terms? Two men named Wolf and Boar drag down the mighty Ongentheow in the Wood of the Ravens, and the Messenger's speech ends with a dialogue between Raven and Eagle.[31]

31. See Hans Weyhe, "König Ongentheows Fall," *Englische Studien,* 39 (1908), 14–39, especially pp. 35–36.

To share this experience is to know at the same moment why it is that men fight—beyond any question there is tremendous excitement and exhilaration in this scene—and what it is that Beowulf has resisted all his life. Perhaps not resisted consciously, except insofar as he has tried to keep the peace with his neighbors as best he could, but resisted by the force of his own massive and silent example. The Ravenswood battle is pure heroic poetry, for all its ferocity. It ends traditionally with Hygelac showing his emphatic approval of the actions of Wulf and Eofor by giving them munificent rewards. Yet here, as everywhere in the poem, we can perceive the central tragic fact about the society that heroic poetry reflects: that in its very strength and beauty, in its cohesive loyalties and allegiances, lie inevitable forces of destruction and anarchy. Hygelac's action in honoring the slayers of Ongentheow is impeccable heroic etiquette, yet it plants the seed of disaster; the greater the Geatish triumph, the more violent the predictable vengeful reaction on the part of the Swedes. Like the story of Finnsburg, the account of the battle of Ravenswood has an ostensibly happy ending, but both stories are fundamentally tragic prophecies in their contexts. The Geatish audience's temporary euphoria would have been shattered by the implications of the Messenger's comment:

> Þæt ys sio fæhðo ond se feondscipe,
> wælnið wera, ðæs ðe ic [wen] hafo,
> þe us seceað to Sweona leoda,
> syððan hie gefricgeað frean userne
> ealdorleasne, þone ðe ær geheold
> wið hettendum hord ond rice.
> (2999–3004)

That [i.e. what I have just shown you in the violence of Ravenswood] is the feud and hostility, the murderous hatred of men, with which I fully expect the Swedish people will come looking for us when

they hear our lord is dead, the lord who once guarded
wealth and kingdom against enemies.

Ravenswood is only the ultimate development of the world of feud. As such, it is the greatest of all the many negative images in the poem: it is placed opposite the figure of the hero. We have not seen Beowulf involved in this world of feud; the poet has never placed him in the distressing situations of Hengest or Ingeld. Consistently Beowulf's energies are directed outward and away from the world of human violence and warfare, directed outward with the purpose of preserving human community by fending off threats from the outside. All through the poem Beowulf's is the embodiment of a moral discipline so perfect as to seem instinctive and effortless. His tremendous strength, both physical and spiritual, is applied to precise objectives for the good of other men: it is never wasted, never turned on itself, never beyond the control of his calm heroic will.

Ravenswood is Beowulf's absence. It is what the world is like without him and without the almost superhuman values he asserts. It is ironic that for the Geats the story of the battle is superficially one of rescue and salvation. Their experience of being helpless and lordless during the battle is acute and frightening, but brief: Hygelac rides melodramatically over the hill to save them. But they were saved then only by the arrival of Hygelac, and saved later from the dragon's attacks only by the courage of Beowulf. But the Messenger's speech was prefaced by an elaborate reminder of the deaths of these two kings. That was the last rescue; there will never be another.

Ravenswood, as a vision of the perpetual violence which is man's lot, moves out of history into a timeless world. That battle of the far past is now, and it is the future for the Geatish nation. The scene suddenly and vividly fuses *wen,* the expectation of the probable future, with *geo,* the distant but inescapable past, and both with the insistent verbs of driving action in the present. The startling sense of life and reality in the narrative of the battle, its greater vividness and concreteness of detail in a poem where so much is half-veiled in misty hints, its exposure of basic universals of human experience in a scene that is both specific and half-allegorical—all these go far to give the Messenger's later prophecy of unending warfare and ultimate extinction for Beowulf's people the solid impact of fact, not fantasy. We know that it was, and if it was it will be.

CHAPTER FIVE

The Hero Departs

While talk of the lack of unity in *Beowulf* is no longer as fashionable as it once was, we should remind ourselves, before we look at Part II of the poem (roughly the last thousand lines from 2200 on), that many good readers have found the poem defective in structure. In his *Epic and Romance,* W. P. Ker made some brief comments on the poem that were often quoted by critics in the early years of this century:

> The later adventure of Beowulf has the character of a sequel, which extends the poem, to the detriment of its proportions, but without adding any new element of complexity to the epic form. . . . The adventure with the dragon is separate from the earlier adventures. It is only connected with them because the same person is involved in both.[1]

Over the past thirty years, most of the critical writing on *Beowulf* has been directed toward a defense of the poem's unity, and many unifying factors have been pointed out. But it is still a fact that the poem falls into two distinct parts,

1. *Epic and Romance* (2d ed., London, Macmillan, 1908; reprinted New York, Dover Publications, 1957). The first quotation is from p. 89, the second from p. 160. Multiple authorship has recently been proposed again by Francis P. Magoun, Jr., "*Béowulf B:* a Folk-Poem on Béowulf's Death," in *Early English and Norse Studies Presented to Hugh Smith,* ed. Arthur Brown and Peter Foote (London, Methuen, 1963), pp. 127–40.

each with its own locale and cast of minor characters. I myself believe in the poem's unity, but it is an emotional unity hard to analyze and describe in the usual terms of criticism: it is a unity based on the very fact of diversity.

There are two principal ways of viewing the relationship between the two parts of the poem. One can emphasize the continuity between them and speak of a "bridge," a progressive transition in action and theme from the first part of the poem into the second, and in general make much of the similarities between the two parts. On the other hand, it is perhaps even more rewarding to focus our attention on the dissimilarities and on the lack of continuity. There is no intention here of being paradoxical: contrast itself is a relationship, as every student of poetry knows, and as every reader of this poem in particular should be ready to admit. Oppositions and differences in theme and subject can be used positively in defense of the poem's unity. But it is wrong to present this in terms of a compulsory choice; the poem shows both kinds of relationship.

What are some of the elements in the poem that contribute to our sense of its continuity and development? In his excellent discussion of the structure and unity of *Beowulf*, Arthur G. Brodeur has called attention to the hero's consistency of character in both parts (certainly an important element of unity) and has also illuminated in particular the strongly unifying structural role played in the poem by the character of Hygelac.[2] From the introduction of Beowulf in the poem as *Higelaces þegn* 194 to the Messenger's account of Hygelac's part in the battle of Ravenswood, the central position of Hygelac as a key or pivotal character is beyond question.[3] The entire story of Beowulf's achievements in Den-

2. Chapter III of *The Art of Beowulf* (Berkeley and Los Angeles, 1959), published in an earlier form in *PMLA, 68* (1953), 1183–95.

3. We need not even include in such an argument Brodeur's own belief that Hygelac's death in the raid on the Frisians affected the

mark becomes something brought in love and pride as a gift by Beowulf, Hygelac's most loyal retainer, to his king. All through the first part we look forward, with Beowulf, to returning home to Hygelac; through much of the second part we look back across the long years to the glories of Hygelac's reign.

Another thematic development that serves to connect the two parts, while still preserving their necessary distinctness, is the increasing concern in the latter scenes of Part I with the problems of kingship. It is true that at the very outset of the poem the Scyld proem offers us a brief paradigm of the qualities of the *god cyning* and it is also true that Hrothgar is presented to us as a model of Germanic royal dignity; but this general theme seems at first quite remote from young Beowulf and his mission as monster killer and heroic exorciser of the hall. The Breca episode, with its flashback to the hero's boyhood, adds even more to our impression that Beowulf is much too young to be worrying yet about kingship, or the political world generally. Only in the Great Banquet, after the immediate threat of Grendel has been removed, do we see Queen Wealhtheow trying to bring Beowulf into the political world as protector of her vulnerable sons. Beowulf, however, takes no active role in this scene. Later, after he has returned from killing Grendel's mother, Beowulf is the object of Hrothgar's sermon, which is specifically concerned with the problems and temptations of men in authority. Hrothgar later predicts (1845 ff.) that the Geats will one day choose Beowulf for their king. Finally, the Ingeld story, which is told by Beowulf to Hygelac after he returns home, climaxes this trend in the poem: there we see Beowulf no longer passively

---

politics of Denmark as well as of Geatland. He maintains that Hygelac's death led to the fall of Hrothgar's son Hrethric in his struggle against the usurping Hrothulf for the Danish throne, but there is little evidence to support this hypothesis.

receiving political advice but giving it and thereby revealing himself as an acute political analyst.

In the Ingeld story as Beowulf tells it, there is a very significant shift in the attitude taken toward the world of Heorot. It is no longer merely a brightly lit arena for the hero's exciting victories; it becomes a locus of political realities. The lurking threat of violence which Danish decorum concealed and which even Wealhtheow could only hint at now comes to the surface and is named. Indeed here, for the first time, we see the potential tragedy of Heorot's world (perhaps it is the world of youth) in somewhat the same way that we see the devastating feuds between Swedes and Geats in Part II. Denmark is no longer simply the Good King's Court of fairy tales or Arthurian legends: it is an actual country, in danger not from trolls but from its own leaders.

There are other connections of this kind that might be noted; so brief a summary hardly does justice to the subtle variety of tonal shifts accompanying this transition from the first part to the second. But, important as the transition is, it is much less important poetically than the elaborate set of contrasts that are made between the two parts of the poem.

The dominant tone of Part I is unquestionably a tone of accomplishment and triumph. It is certainly true that powerful and mysterious evil exists in the world the Danes know, but Hrothgar can be helped, and Heorot and the evil mere are finally cleansed, even though it may not be in Beowulf's power to take command of Denmark's uneasy political future. At the beginning of Part I, Hrothgar and his men are in a state of helpless anguish in the face of a struggle that is demonstrably *to strang, lað ond longsum* for then to have any chance of winning. At the end of Part I, the threat has been removed. The progress of Beowulf through Part I, as we have seen, is a long, unbroken, upward curve of achievement, as he surmounts challenge after challenge, from the Danish coastguard's first questions to the chilling horrors of the mere. What Part I dramatizes unforgettably is what man, at his finest, *can do*. Beowulf is above all the *sigoreadig secg,* the man blessed with victory.

In sharpest contrast to this, one main theme of Part II is what man *cannot do,* his absolute limitations. Images of death and loss dominate the poem's conclusion. The famous elegiac passages of Part II, which we will examine later in the chapter, are only focal points of a general conviction of man's helplessness: they represent, above all, situations where nothing can be done.

The very words *ne meahte* (could not) and their equivalents echo through Part II like a heavy refrain. The byrnie buried by the Last Survivor cannot travel any longer by the side of its master: *Ne mæg byrnan hring / æfter wigfruman wide feran, / hæleðum be healfe* 2260b–62a. The Old Father can do nothing to help his son on the gallows: *ond he him helpe ne mæg, / eald ond infrod, ænige gefremman* 2448b–49. Old Hrethel's dilemma is phrased in the same negative terms:

Wihte ne meahte
on ðam feorhbonan fæghðe gebetan;
no ðy ær he þone heaðorinc hatian ne meahte
laðum dædum, þeah him leof ne wæs.
(2464b–67)

He was wholly unable to force the murderer to settle the feud, and none the sooner could he make plain by his actions his enmity toward that warrior, even though Hrethel no longer had any love for him.

Weapons are rendered powerless. Beowulf realizes that a wooden shield cannot help him from dragon-fire (2339b–41a), and Wiglaf's byrnie cannot give him any assistance in the flames (2673b–74). Twice we are told that swords are unable to give Beowulf any aid (2682b–84a; 2904b–06a). Beowulf cannot survive unburned near the hoard because of the dragon's fire (2547b–49) and must finally concede that he is unable to stay any longer in the land of the living: *ne mæg ic her leng wesan* (2801). Wiglaf laments his inability to preserve his king's life (2877–78a) and cannot keep him alive for all his efforts:

> Ne meahte he on eorðan, ðeah he uðe wel,
> on ðam frumgare feorh gehealdan,
> ne ðæs wealdendes wiht oncirran.
> (2855–57)

> Not on this earth could he keep life in that captain of spearmen, however much he longed to, nor divert from its course anything decreed by the world's Ruler.

The "cannot" phrase occurs for the last time in the poem in the following passage:

> Wundur hwar þonne
> eorl ellenrof ende gefere
> lifgesceafta, þonne leng ne mæg
> mon mid his [ma]gum meduseld buan.
> (3062b–65)

> It is a mystery just when it will be that a courageous man journeys to the end of the life decreed him, when he can no longer go on living in the mead-hall with his kinsmen.

The last two passages make plain that it is death which is the absolute limit placed on human powers, the end of all our journeys, and the ultimate cause of this mournful and despairing refrain.

The difference in setting between the two parts is also significant. Part I takes place almost entirely indoors, in that warm noisy world of the great hall where to go outside for a morning's excursion to look at the haunted mere is an adventure. Most of its scenes are public scenes, marked by considerable pomp and formality, and it is crowded with characters. There are seven speaking roles in Part I, two prominent pantomimists (Grendel and his mother), and a half-dozen other characters who are named as being present in the scenes (such as Hrothulf), besides large numbers of spear-carrying Danes and Geats. This is not even to count such memorable figures as Hengest, Heremod, or the old warrior in the Ingeld tale—those who are described only in song or story—but they too add to our impression of a large cast.

Part II takes place outdoors. The only hall even mentioned is Beowulf's royal hall, and it is mentioned only because the dragon burns it to the ground at the outset. Consequently the characters seem as lonely and exposed as the men on the heath in *King Lear*. Only three Geats are given speeches—Beowulf, Wiglaf, and the Messenger—and their speeches often seem to have the peculiar candor and inwardness of the soliloquy: even when not actually alone, they sound like men speaking alone. Indeed, the typical character of Part II may be the anonymous voice, like the Messenger or the Last Survivor or the Geatish woman who wails her lament beside Beowulf's funeral pyre, the same anonymous voice we find in the "timeless-nameless" figures of the Old English elegies —a wanderer, a seafarer, an exiled woman.

The change of setting reflects general movements of the poem: from a world of many meetings and youthful comradeship in adventure to a world of the loneliness of old age when the hero has outlived all those he loved; from a world seen as an arena for heroic or political action to a world where the characters become more abstractly representative of Man, seen against a dark and hopeless background of mutability.

The same contrast can be seen in the treatment of time in the two parts. By and large, Part I takes place in the present, that clear bright present of youth. There is strenuous action alternating with conversation; there is suspense and even, in the arrival of Grendel's mother, a certain amount of surprise for the audience. Past and future are not much talked about. When the past does appear, as it does in the stories of Finn or Sigemund or Heremod, it usually comes at least ostensibly in the guise of pleasurable song, artistically distanced and used to make an esthetically pleasing contrast or to point a convenient moral in a present tale. It comes, that is to say, as an integral part of Danish civilization and is not allowed to disturb the *dream* of Heorot's inhabitants. It is also a past, as we saw earlier, that is usually far back in time and thus without much direct effect on the Denmark of the present. Nor does the veiled menace of the future disturb the Danes (with the important exception of the apprehensive Queen Wealhtheow), for they live in an absorbing present. Only after we have left Denmark behind us and hear Beowulf prophesying the failure of Freawaru's marriage to Ingeld do we find this future presented in a way that approaches the vividness of the present. But by then we are in another country, in more than one sense.

The quite different treatment of time in Part II is remarkable in several ways. While it is true that there is a strong foreground narrative in the present—the dragon fight and Beowulf's death and funeral—about a third of the 973 lines are given over to description of events in the past, and there are also several glimpses of the future.[4] But it is not the relative amount of space devoted to past and future that is important so much as the impression we receive that different moments in time are being presented almost simultaneously with great stress being laid on their intimate relation to each

4. An objectively accurate count is probably impossible, since readers will not agree on how to classify certain passages, especially transitional ones, under such vague headings as "past," "present," or "future." My own count (actually the average of several varying counts) finds slightly over 300 lines of Part II devoted to "past" and a little over 600 lines to "present," while perhaps some 40 are devoted to "future."

other: present, past, and future impinge so pressingly on each other that our normal sense of time sequence is threatened. To discuss the implications of this complex point of view is to discuss the meaning of Part II and, to some extent, of the entire poem.

We can make a start at understanding the treatment of time in Part II by looking at the long and remarkable sentence with which the second part opens:

> Eft þæt geiode ufaran dogrum
> hildehlæmmum, syððan Hygelac læg
> ond Hear[dr]ede hildemeceas
> under bordhreoðan to bonan wurdon,
> ða hyne gesohtan on sigeþeode
> hearde hil*d*frecan, Heaðoscilfingas,
> niða genægdan nefan Hererices,
> syððan Beowulfe brade rice
> on hand gehwearf; he geheold tela
> fiftig wintra (wæs ða frod cyning,
> eald eþelweard), oððæt an ongan
> deorcum nihtum draca rics[i]an,
> se ðe on heaum hofe hord beweotode,
> stanbeorh steapne. (2200–13a)

Afterwards in later days it came about through clashes of battle, after Hygelac had fallen, and swords had put an end to Heardred despite his shield's defense at that time when the warlike Swedes, fierce battle-wolves, found him and attacked him, Hereric's nephew, with violence among the victorious people—after all that, the broad realm came into the hands of Beowulf; he ruled it well for fifty years (and by then he was an old king, an aged guardian of his nation), until a certain one in the dark nights began to rule, a dragon who guarded treasure in a great house, in a steep stone-barrow.

Up to this point in the poem we have never moved in time in this way. The scene-by-scene narrative we have been accustomed to—a moment before in the poem, Hygelac was ceremoniously presenting gifts to Beowulf in the Geatish hall—is here jettisoned altogether as a great forward leap along the time scale puts "future" events far back into the past. Hygelac is now long dead, and his son and heir dead. The fifty-year period of Beowulf's peaceful reign flashes by so fast that it is almost lost in the midst of this sentence. Time's movement here is punctuated by explosive and violent acts; things seem literally to come about by clashes of battle. After his predecessors on the throne meet sudden deaths, Beowulf becomes king and simultaneously an aged king faced with a final threat to his rule in the person of the dragon, who appears here ironically as only the next in line in the rapid series of rulers: Hygelac, Heardred, Beowulf, dragon.

What is important is the way we are suddenly and firmly placed at a moment in time where the point of view is shifted to looking back at the past. It is this point of view that is characteristic of Part II. The foreground action takes place on Beowulf's *endedæg,* the last day of his long life. All the intermediate events of Beowulf's reign and the Swedish-Geatish wars that have been omitted in this opening sentence are later to be introduced gradually, and always retrospectively, as a past to be meditated upon long afterward rather than as a present that demands decisions now. Typically, the characters in Part II reminisce: they reflect on their past and search it for meanings. History is made in Part I. In Part II it is studied, with an austere seriousness about the real place of man in the endless stream of time. As the poem moves back and forth across these great dark spaces in time, our impression inevitably grows stronger that Hrothgar's court and Beowulf's own beneficent reign are tiny islands of intense light in a world of drifting darkness.

The effect of this preoccupation with time is often complex, as we can see in the description of the dragon's first attack:

> Hordweard onbad
> earfoðlice oððæt æfen cwom;
> wæs ða gebolgen beorges hyrde,
> wolde se laða lige forgyldan
> drincfæt dyre. Þa wæs dæg sceacen
> wyrme on willan; no on wealle læg,
> bidan wolde, ac mid bæle for,
> fyre gefysed. Wæs se fruma egeslic
> leodum on lande, swa hyt lungre wearð
> on hyra sincgifan sare geendod.
> (2302b–11)

> The guardian of the hoard waited in impatient misery until evening came. The barrow's protector was angry; the enemy intended to pay with fire for the theft of that precious drinking-cup. And then day passed by as the dragon wished. He did not lie on the wall or intend to wait, but shot forth impelled by fire, moving in flame. That beginning was terrible to the people in the land, as terrible as the painful end soon turned out to be for their treasure-giver.

Like Grendel, the dragon must wait for evening to satisfy his vengeful fury, and we must wait with him until the day is over. The dragon endures this misery of waiting, as the poet stresses his malevolent will. The moment darkness falls, the dragon lunges out like a striking snake and blasts the countryside with flame. To the degree that we experience the delay and suspense here, we respond to time in one sense, to the feeling, that is, of being in the present. But this sudden impact of the dragon as he strikes the countryside is followed by another kind of impact as we flash in one sentence from *se fruma,* the beginning, to the tragic ending, *wearð / . . . sare geendod.* We realize that Beowulf will die—*has died*—

because of this dragon. At which moment of time does the dragon strike with greater impact, in the narrative present or in the future we are told of here?

In another instance, alliteration points to a similar effect of "double time" in a statement like this one:

Frea sceawode
fira fyrngeweorc forman siðe.
(2285b–86)

> The lord looked at the ancient artifact of men for the first time.

Here the collocation of *fyrn-* (long ago) and *forman siðe* (now for the first time) creates the same effect of a lightning-flash across expanses of time. Again, we have something like the same effect in this sentence:

Sceolde *læn*daga
æþeling ærgod ende gebidan,
worulde lifes, ond se wyrm somod,
þeah ðe hordwelan heolde lange.
(2341b–44)

> The nobleman good from his earliest years was compelled to experience the end of his borrowed days of life in the world—and the dragon as well, though he had held hoarded wealth for a long time.

Here the word *ærgod* takes us far back into Beowulf's past, while the next word, *ende,* refers to the imminent termination of his life; as a result we have a brief and intense impression of the speed with which a man's *lændagas* vanish. Mention of the dragon is also accompanied by a reference to the long years stretching far back before this moment, during which the dragon had been guarding its hoard.

To inquire at any length into the interesting problem of the sources of this retrospective attitude in the poem would be outside the bounds of this study, but a few remarks might be ventured. It is possible that this part of the poem once had an independent existence as a shorter lay on Beowulf's death.[5] We can conjecture that funeral elegies generally (if indeed they existed in Old English) would probably have been characterized by such a retrospective approach. Perhaps the style is typical of written epic poetry, at least as it is characterized by Jan de Vries, who writes:

> When the epic tradition is dying out, at the last moment a poet appears who gives it its great and lasting form. The epic testifies to a nostalgia, a longing for a time that is gone irrevocably. Thus, out of a misty, remote, distant past the heroic figure seems to rise up once more, to be fixed forever by the poet's words.[6]

We should also bear in mind that this same point of view is one of the chief characteristics of that puzzling genre, the Old English elegy, which is often a retrospective meditation on certain objects regarded as especially meaningful. The best example for our purposes here is of course *The Ruin,* for that entire poem is an exploration of the meaning of the past and of human existence generally, as this meaning is suggested by the sight of Roman ruins.[7] But the other elegies contain similar passages. These well-known lines from *The Wanderer* could be taken as a classic instance:

> Eala beorht bune! Eala byrnwiga!
> Eala þeodnes þrym! Hu seo þrag gewat,
> genap under nihthelm, swa heo no wære.[8]

5. See Magoun, "*Béowulf B:* a Folk-Poem on Béowulf's Death," p. 130.

6. *Heroic Song and Heroic Legend,* trans. B. J. Timmer (London, Oxford University Press, 1963), p. 137.

7. See the remarks by R. F. Leslie in his edition of *Three Old English Elegies* (Manchester, Manchester University Press, 1961), pp. 28–30; and my article, "Image and Meaning in the Elegies," in *Old English Poetry: Fifteen Essays,* ed. Robert P. Creed (Providence, Brown University Press, 1967), pp. 153–66.

8. *The Wanderer,* lines 94–96, quoted from *The Exeter Book,*

> Ah, the bright cup! Ah, the mailed warrior! Ah, the prince's splendor! How that time has gone, darkened under night's cover as if it had never been.

The bright gleam of polished metal, an image of hall-joy, is set in visually effective contrast to the extinguishing darkness of lost time.

Passages of this kind, as we have recently come to realize, are properly included in the universal *ubi sunt* tradition of the Middle Ages. Investigations have shown how widespread the topos is in medieval literature generally, especially in Latin homiletic literature.[9] Latin homilies may well be the ultimate sources of such passages, yet every reader must feel that it is a long way from the tone of the typical Latin homily to the tone of the elegies or of *Beowulf*. Perhaps the Latin tradition coalesced with an already existing interest by Anglo-Saxon poets in similar emotional themes in the pre-Christian heroic tradition. This particular tone of grief and loss is probably inherent in epic poetry itself. In the way they have of picturing from the cruel perspective of long time, if not of eternity, the loss of "name," of fame and heroic identity, such passages furnish what may be the necessary and inevitable complement to the achievement of glory that is the epic's chief concern. Part I of *Beowulf,* as we have seen, shows the establishment of heroic identity, whereas much of Part II deals with the slow erosion of identity by time.

Whatever their origin may be, the Old English elegies are likely to come sooner or later to reflections on mutability and mortality, occasioned by looking at ruins, bodies of the slain, empty halls, gold, unpolished armor, the cups and dishes of great feasts—all the symbols of human life in war and peace.

---

ed. G. P. Krapp and E. V. K. Dobbie, Anglo-Saxon Poetic Records, 3 (New York, Columbia University Press, 1936), p. 136.

9. See, for example, J. E. Cross, "'Ubi Sunt' Passages in Old English—Sources and Relationships," *Vetenskaps-Societetens i Lund Arsbok,* 1956, pp. 26–44.

In this sense, the second part of *Beowulf* is thoroughly elegiac.

To begin with, the image of looking is itself given great emphasis. The Last Survivor broods over the gold and armor he is committing to the earth, examining each item with such intensity of vision that it acquires a kind of luminous personification (2247–66). The lord to whom the stolen cup is brought looks at it in apparent awe (2281b–86). The wounded Beowulf has his eyes fixed on the barrow as he makes his dying speech (2717), orders young Wiglaf to go examine the treasure (2743 ff.)—which he subsequently does examine in detail—and in his last moments looks at the gold that Wiglaf has brought out of the dragon's barrow. Later the Geats are repeatedly urged to look at the tableau of Beowulf lying dead beside the dragon. Beowulf's funeral is presented in graphic visual terms as something to be looked at, and the poem ends with the compelling image of Beowulf's barrow, set on a cliff as a beacon for seafarers to see, *wide gesiene,* visible at a great distance.

The characteristic hovering style of Old English verse, with its appositives like the successively glinting facets of an object held to the light and turned slowly, serves to bring out this kind of passive and meditative vision with particular clarity and power. The vision is a passive one both because it is usually a vision of the inanimate and motionless and because no action is usually even possible for the one who looks. As we saw earlier, it was a different matter in Part I, where looking at a sword or at a haunted mere was usually the motive for immediate action. But so different is the emotional atmosphere in Part II that Beowulf's adventures in Denmark themselves become part of a past that is both fixed and fading, which the audience looks on as it looks at the other objects. Part II devotes much space to following the aged Beowulf in his attempts to reassess and reevaluate his life from this new standpoint.

Yet it is equally important to see clearly that this way of

looking does not entirely dominate the latter part of the poem. In fact, it acquires most of its peculiar distinctness by standing in contrast with a vivid and action-demanding present, just as in Part I Beowulf's heroic dynamism took form against the passivity of the Danes. The story of the dragon fight is skillfully interwoven through all these meditative passages and has its own unmistakable urgency; a man finds it difficult to meditate on live dragons. In addition to the insistent reality of this present, there is a real future as well, suggested by the large-scale figure of young Wiglaf, by Beowulf's expressions of hope for his people's future, and by the predictions of the Messenger. The poet's increasing concern with universal aspects of human existence does not lead him to lose his grip on history.

When we return to the elegiac portions of the poem, we find that much of the looking done by characters and narrator in Part II is directed toward a few especially significant objects. The hoard of treasure, for example, is the center of many meanings. It would be as well to admit that we cannot recapture all these meanings now. For it seems likely that even the pre-Christian attitude toward treasure must have contained its own inherent complexities; when a Christian point of view (and which Christian point of view?) is superimposed on it without entirely replacing it, we have rich possibilities for ambiguity, if not for genuine confusion. Part of the confusion on the part of modern readers may stem from the unlucky fact that two key passages which might have helped to clarify the poet's ideas about treasure are themselves rather obscure.[10] We can only sketch out some of the things treasure seems to represent in this poem without worrying about exhaustiveness or consistency.

10. Lines 2764b–66, where the meaning of *oferhigian* is not securely established and where the word *hyde* might mean either "hide" or "heed," so that the meaning of the sentence varies radically depending on the choice made; and lines 3074–75, the notorious *goldhwæte* passage, where no scholarly consensus seems even on the horizon.

First of all, and most important to remember, in the normal frame of reference of Germanic heroic society, gold is a good. It is persistently associated, as we have seen again and again, with those links of loyalty between men which create and uphold that society; we see it most often in the ceremonial giving and receiving of gifts, which are public pledges of that loyalty. In this poem gold is particularly associated with Heorot, the gold-hall, the center of Danish splendor. The dying Beowulf thanks God (2794–98) for the treasure that he can now give to his people; he believes that wealth will help them maintain themselves as a free and independent nation after he has gone. That anything remotely resembling "greed" should be attributed to him for expressing this sentiment shows a misunderstanding of some of the fundamental concepts of the poem.[11] To express the very highest ideals of fidelity and sacrifice in terms of material things is more than frequent in Germanic heroic poetry, it is inevitable: there is no other means available for expressing them. We saw in Chapter Four how Wiglaf's two classic speeches revolve wholly around such symbols. Wiglaf's final "curse" on the cowardly retainers is framed in the same terms, when he predicts that exchanging of treasure will come to a stop and everyone will be empty-handed. It is not Wiglaf's intention to help the Geats by freeing them from the temptations of avarice: this is simply his way of picturing the complete breakdown of society.

That gold has primarily this social meaning might also be

11. An opinion expressed by Margaret E. Goldsmith in several articles; see "The Christian Theme of *Beowulf*," *Medium Ævum*, 29 (1960), 81–101, and "The Choice in *Beowulf*," *Neophilologus*, 18 (1964), 60–72. Representative of the allegorical approach in general is Lewis E. Nicholson, "The Literal Meaning and Symbolic Structure of *Beowulf*," *Classica et Mediaevelia*, 25 (1964), 151–201. For one recent sharp attack on its application to *Beowulf* see John Halverson, "*Beowulf* and the Pitfalls of Piety," *University of Toronto Quarterly*, 35 (1966), 260–78; see also Charles Moorman, "The Essential Paganism of *Beowulf*," *Modern Language Quarterly*, 28 (1967), 3–18.

guessed from studying the relationship of the dragon to his treasure. Just as Grendel sometimes functions as a mock retainer, the dragon is a little like a mock king. As we saw earlier, he exists in something like a dynastic line; he sits in a *hof,* a castle, and devotes himself to guarding his immense treasure. He is of course an extremely stingy king, like the old Danish king Heremod, and therefore a model of a bad king. His chief purpose indeed seems to transcend ordinary stinginess: he does not even use the treasure himself but exerts every effort to keep it from being put to any use whatever. In the poem's terms, Heorot is where treasure is used to the fullest extent; the dragon's mound is where it must be wholly unused. Thus the dragon is infuriated when even a small item from his vast hoard is made functional again by being put to use as a peace offering by the man who robs him. Heorot is the center of social vitality; we remember that the dragon's castle is after all a grave.

We can see this important contrast illustrated in a passage that occurs just before Beowulf's long speech.

> Weard unhiore,
> gearo guðfreca, goldmaðmas heold,
> eald under eorðan. Næs þæt yðe ceap
> to gegangenne gumena ænigum!
> Gesæt ða on næsse niðheard cyning,
> þenden hælo abead heorðgeneatum,
> goldwine Geata. (2413b–19a)

> The repulsive guardian, the ready war-wolf old under the earth, guarded gold-treasures. No easy bargain for any man to get hold of them! The war-tough king [Beowulf] took his seat on the cliff, while he, gold-friend of the Geats, spoke greetings [farewells?] to his hearth-companions.

The scene sets two kings in contrast to each other. The dragon is assigned certain attributes conventionally associated with royalty: he is old and warlike in his earth-hall; he protects golden treasures from enemies. Beowulf is also old and warlike and guards treasure, but he is here significantly called a *goldwine*, a "gold-friend." The relationship of a *goldwine* to his men and to his treasure is illustrated for us here by the affectionate conversation Beowulf is having with his intimate companions. He is lord of the gold and lord of the Geats, and their friend; the gold he guards is used for the Geats. The phrases *goldmaðmas heold* and *goldwine Geata* epitomize the negative and positive uses of treasure.

With some of these ideas in mind, we can now approach the lament of the Last Survivor, which is the first of the two elegiac set pieces in the poem, with some better understanding of how it fits into a larger pattern of meaning. The speech itself is introduced by an important passage:

Þær wæs swylcra fela
in ðam eorð[hu]se ærgestreona,
swa hy on geardagum gumena nathwylc,
eormenlafe æþelan cynnes,
þanchycgende þær gehydde,
deore maðmas. Ealle hie deað fornam
ærran mælum, ond *se* an ða gen
leoda duguðe, se ðær lengest hwearf,
weard winegeomor, wende þæs ylcan,
þæt he lytel fæc longgestreona
brucan moste. Beorh eallgearo
wunode on wonge wæteryðum neah,
niwe be næsse, nearocræftum fæst.
Þær on innan bær eorlgestreona
hringa hyrde hordwyrðne dæl,
fættan goldes, fea worda cwæð: . . .
(2231b–46)

There in that earth-house were many such [valuable objects], treasure hoarded from long ago, just as

> some unknown man in deep thought had hidden them there in days long past, beloved treasures and vast legacy of some noble race. Death had carried off all of them long before, and that one man who still wandered longest as a guardian grieving for his lost friends expected the same fate—that he too would be allowed to enjoy those long-amassed treasures for only a little time. Already prepared, a barrow stood in a field near the sea's waves, newly made beside the cliff, made secure by the builder's skill. Into it the protector of rings carried a great mass worth hoarding of the warriors' treasure, plated gold, and spoke these few words. . . .

The speaker is anonymous and unknown, *gumena nathwylc.* Himself barely visible back in the far mists of time, his identity has been reduced to the carrying out of a single function: to survive long enough to place, with his last impulse of energy, the treasure in the earth from which it came, and to pronounce the requiem for his nation. The surrounding sense of the past is very heavy in this passage (*ærgestreona, on geardagum, ærran mælum, longgestreona*). The unimaginable length of time that such phrases suggest—the whole life span of a society—is deliberately set beside the tiny length of time, the *lytel fæc,* which is granted to this individual, or to any individual. The newly built barrow, evidence of human action, stands beside the ageless cliff: *niwe be næsse.* Yet the speaker survives to tell the story; if only for the *lytel fæc,* he is a *weard,* a *hyrde,* a protector and conserver of value. And value may reside not so much in the rings he buries as in the words he speaks.

> Heald þu nu, hruse, nu hæleð ne moston,
> eorla æhte! Hwæt, hyt ær on ðe
> gode begeaton. Guðdeað fornam,
> feorhbealo frecne, fyr*a* gehwylcne

leoda minra, þa*r*a ðe þis [lif] ofgeaf,
gesawon seledream. [Ic] nah hwa sweord wege
oððe fe[ormie] fæted wæge,
dryncfæt deore; dug[uð] ellor s[c]eoc.
Sceal se hearda helm [hyr]sted golde
fætum befeallen; feormynd swefað,
þa ðe beadogriman bywan sceoldon,
ge swylce seo herepad, sio æt hilde gebad
ofer borda gebræc bite irena,
brosnað æfter beorne. Ne mæg byrnan hring
æfter wigfruman wide feran,
hæleðum be healfe. Næs hearpan wyn,
gomen gleobeames, ne god hafoc
geond sæl swingeð, ne se swifta mearh
burhstede beateð. Bealocwealm hafað
fela feorhcynna forð onsended! (2247–66)

Hold now, earth, what men can hold no longer—the possessions of heroes. Good men got these things from you once; now death and terrible evil have taken away every man of my people who has given up this life. They have seen hall-joy. I have no one now to lift the sword or polish the plated cup or the precious goblet. That host went elsewhere. Bright gold will fall from the iron helmet: those sleep who should mend the battle-mask. And the mailshirt which often endured the bite of iron over the breaking of shields now crumbles after its owner, no more to march out to battle beside the fighting-man. No joy of harp, no pleasure of song; no fine hawk swoops through the hall, no swift horse stamps in the courtyard. Evil death has sent many a living race on its way!

Again we should remind ourselves that this treasure consists largely of functional objects. Modern readers tend unconsciously to think of treasure in terms of coins, ingots, jewelry, but Anglo-Saxon treasure is more practical. These are things to be carried, worn, drunk out of, fought with, eaten from, as well as exchanged. Hence the very mention of these things serves to recreate in the imagination the movement of a functioning society, but only momentarily; for the Last Survivor is committing to the grave both the treasure and the living society for which it stands.

A remarkable thing about this passage is its steady movement toward a state of total rest. The treasure is heavy: earth must now hold it, since men no longer have the strength. There is no one to lift a sword, no one to polish a cup or helmet. Things fall and crumble. The images combine to create a vivid impression, kinesthetic in nature, of sheer weight. The men slump down into sleep and, as they vanish, the objects they once possessed themselves take on a spectral flicker of existence. The mailshirt used to stand up to the bite of swords in battle; it once traveled beside its owner. But even these ghostlike actions subside too into the same trance of powerlessness. At the end, flashes of energy and mobility appear in the images of harp-playing, a hawk in flight, a stamping horse; but all these actions are enclosed in a heavy series of emphatic negatives in such a way that the actions are simultaneously evoked and terminated. The only action at the end is that of Death itself, which took them away (*fornam*) and sent them elsewhere (*hafað . . . forð onsended*).

Associated with the treasure, with the earth in which it lies, and with death itself, both in this context and in other contexts in Part II, is the strange figure of the dragon. If we approach the dragon with due consideration of these persistent associations, it is difficult not to see him as distinctly a death figure, both a grave-guardian and an agent of death. The burial barrow in which the Last Survivor deposits the treasure eventually becomes the dragon's home; he issues forth from it only to kill.

We should bear this aspect in mind as we begin a discussion of the dragon as symbol, for much that has been said about the possible symbolic meaning of the dragon in recent years has little support in the poem itself. Some who try to read the poem as pure Christian allegory claim to recognize the monster's infernal features: *et apprehendit draconem, serpentem antiquum, qui est diabolus, et Satanas.*[12] In ordinary Christian allegory the dragon is the devil. The trouble is that there is little indication that this particular dragon stands for the explicitly theological form of evil that Grendel and his mother stand for. To begin with, the Grendel race is named repeatedly as Cain's descendants and God's enemies; nothing of the sort is ever said about the dragon. In certain ways, to be sure, the dragon may be considered to be evil. His hatred for mankind and his destructiveness are plain and unambiguous. Yet, though he may be evil, he is not Evil. There is an amoral aspect to him, alien and remote. In some sense, there is nothing personal about what he does.

It is just this impersonality that distinguishes him most sharply from the Grendel family. If Grendel is mankind's enemy, it is largely because he is still the nightmare semblance of a human being himself, as we saw in Chapter Three, and because he is that wistful "hall-thane" who haunts the places where his honor died. But the dragon would scorn to live in a hall. His rage is directed unselectively against *aht cwices,* whatever lives. He obliterates men, halls and all. Even his mode of attack is significantly different. Whereas Grendel eats men and his mother wrestles strenuously with them, the dragon wipes them out with a more aloof blast of flame.

The Grendel race, furthermore, is to be thought of as damned, because once (in the person of its ancestor Cain) it made a free choice and has perhaps chosen again and again thereafter to abide by that choice. But we find it hard to think

12. *Revelations* (*Apocalypsis*) 12:9.

of the dragon as being damned in this particular way. "A dragon, ancient and exulting in treasure, is obliged by nature to live in a grave-mound," we are told elsewhere in a sequence of gnomic statements that goes on to point out that it is the nature of forests to bloom and of fish to multiply in the water.[13] Forests are not damned to bloom nor fish to multiply, because they have had no moral choice to make that would entail damnation. A dragon merely obedient to the biological law of his own strange nature might more appropriately be labeled doomed, a term relevant also to his function as the agent of Beowulf's doom. One gnomic-sounding statement in the poem itself reflects this general view of the dragon:

> He gesecean sceall
> [ho]r[d on] hrusan, þær he hæðen gold
> warað wintrum frod, ne byð him wihte ðy sel.
> (2275b–77)
>
> He is obliged to seek out a hoard in the earth, where, ancient in years, he guards heathen gold; it does him no good whatever.

The last phrase seems to be a commentary on the pointlessness of the dragon's blind and instinctive drive to guard treasure.

As we saw earlier, a great deal of space in the poem is devoted to exploring Grendel's thoughts, but very little is given to explaining the dragon's motives or feelings. We look at the dragon's external behavior rather than at his thoughts, because the dragon has no thoughts: he is an animal. In one description at least, he seems very much an animal, when he wakes to find the thief's footprints:

13. *Maxims II* (the so-called "Cotton Gnomes"), lines 26b–27a: *Draca sceal on hlæwe, / frod, frætwum wlanc.* Quoted from *The Anglo-Saxon Minor Poems*, ed. E. V. K. Dobbie, Anglo-Saxon Poetic Records, 6 (New York, 1942), Columbia Press, 56.

Hordweard sohte
georne æfter grunde, wolde guman findan,
þone þe him on sweofote sare geteode,
hat ond hreohmod hlæ*w* oft ymbehwearf
ealne utanweardne, ne ðær ænig mon
on þære westenne; hwæðre *wiges* gefeh,
bea[duwe] weorces, hwilum on beorh æthwearf,
sincfæt sohte. (2293b–2300a)

> The guardian of the hoard searched eagerly along the ground, wishing to find the man who had harmed it in its sleep. Hot and furious, it kept ranging around the outside of the mound. Even though there was no man there in the wasteland, still it exulted in fighting and the work of battle. Now and then it rushed back into the barrow, searching for the precious vessel.

The poet here seems fascinated simply by what the dragon does, by its restless furious movements, rather than by what it thinks or what it may symbolically represent.

If pressed finally to make a definite statement on what the dragon in *Beowulf* stands for, we would have to go back and call attention once again to the importance of its association with death, with graves, and with treasure that is itself "dead" because it is unused and because it is the relic of dead civilizations. For the hero himself, the dragon is fate or *Wyrd,* a force always closely associated with death in this poem and often indistinguishable from it, as an interesting recent study has pointed out.[14] Then too the dragon's chief weapon and its most memorable attribute is fire, and fire, as we saw in the case of the funeral at Finnsburg, has only destructive and deadly connotations in this poem. Fire is never associated with heroic energy as it is in the *Iliad,* for example.

14. Alan H. Roper, "Boethius and the Three Fates of *Beowulf,*" *Philological Quarterly, 41* (1962), 386–400.

During the fight with the dragon, the main focus of attention is another symbolic object, the iron shield that Beowulf has had specially constructed for this encounter. The very fact that a defensive weapon is singled out for attention is significant: the whole tone of Part II is suggested by this. The conclusion of the poem, after all, is an account of a long rearguard action, a warding off, a holding of ground rather than the capture of new ground. And we should recall the progression in emphasis from Beowulf's naked and invincible hand, which is all that is needed to force Grendel into total collapse, to the mailshirt he must wear to ward off tusks and daggers during his descent into the mere, and from the giant-sword hastily borrowed to kill Grendel's mother to such an unusual and elaborate artifact as this iron shield. Heroic existence is a series of increasingly difficult skirmishes in the one long battle.

The meaning of the symbol of the shield expands slowly in the course of the poem, in the process of becoming associated with other images and themes. Many of the traditional terms for king, for instance, such as *hleo, hyrde,* or *helm,* represent the king as shelter, shepherd, protecting helmet of his nation. It is true that Beowulf himself is not actually called a "shield," but there is one king in the poem who is—the Danish king Scyld, who figures in the introductory passage of the poem. "It is clear," writes Kemp Malone, "that Scyld lived up to his name; he served most effectively as the shield of his people. . . . The ideal king was given an ideal name. The word *scyld* 'shield' may have the abstract sense 'protection' and the personalized sense 'protector' (see the dictionaries). In giving the name Scyld to their creation, the poets took an epithet proper to royalty and made of it a royal name." [15] The story of Scyld's coming to rescue and protect the lordless Danes prefigures Beowulf's own role as savior-king. The defensive, shieldlike

15. "Royal Names in Old English Poetry," *Studies in Heroic Legend and Current Speech,* ed. Stefán Einarsson and Norman E. Eliason (Copenhagen, Rosenkilde and Bagger, 1959), pp. 181–82.

stance assumed by Beowulf toward the end of the poem is evident in a passage like this one, from one of the hero's speeches:

> Ic ðas leode heold
> fiftig wintra; næs se folccyning,
> ymbesittendra ænig ðara,
> þe mec guðwinum gretan dorste,
> egesan ðeon. Ic on earde bad
> mælgesceafta, heold min tela,
> ne sohte searoniðas. (2732b–38a)

> I have held these people for fifty years; there was no king of any neighboring country who dared attack me with troops or threaten me with terror. I have waited in my land for what has been decreed, when it came; I have held my own well; I have sought no scheming quarrels.

The verbs here—*heold, bad, heold, ne sohte*—all suggest the rocklike immobility of the shield-king, who guards, waits, frightens off attackers without attacking.

Yet, since critics must unfortunately take things up one at a time, we are again in danger of overemphasizing these passive and meditative tones of feeling in the latter part of the poem. Certainly Beowulf does not behave like a shield when he goes out to fight the dragon; not even iron shields can kill dragons. Here, as always in the poem, the figure of the hero as above all man of positive action looms largest. Not only do we see him in action in the dragon fight, but we are presented with a long review of his active career, offered to us both in the words of the poet and in Beowulf's long speech just before the fight begins.

Beowulf is reintroduced into the poem in line 2324, after an absence of over a hundred lines (a long time away from the hero in this poem). The passage in which he reappears bears comparison to the first description of the hero in Part I. Is it the same hero, or has something changed? There is one similarity: after he hears the news that his hall has been burned, he acts instantly, just as he acted when he first heard of Grendel's attacks. Then he ordered a ship prepared for his voyage to Denmark; now he orders a new kind of iron shield prepared for his fight against the fire-dragon. But the later passage differs in one respect: between the announcement of danger and the response there now falls a new shadow.

> Þa wæs Biowulfe broga gecyðed
> snude to soðe, þæt his sylfes h*a*m,
> bolda selest, brynewylmum mealt,
> gifstol Geata. Þæt ðam godan wæs
> hreow on hreðre, hygesorga mæst;
> wende se wisa þæt he wealdende
> ofer ealde riht, ecean dryhtne,
> bitre gebulge. Breost innan weoll
> þeostrum geþoncum, swa him geþywe ne wæs.
> Hæfde ligdraca leoda fæsten,
> ealond utan, eorðweard ðone
> gledum forgrunden; him ðæs guðkyning,
> Wedera þioden, wræce leornode.
> Heht him þa gewyrcean wigendra hleo
> eallirenne, eorla dryhten,
> wigbord wrætlic. (2324–39a)

Then a terror was quickly and truthfully made known to Beowulf: his own hall, best of buildings, throne of the Geats, had melted in waves of fire. That was distress for the heart, greatest of sorrows for that good man, [for] the wise one supposed that he had bitterly angered the Ruler and eternal Lord, contrary to old law. His breast surged with dark thoughts in a way unusual for him. The fire-dragon had destroyed with flames the fortress of the people, the stronghold and the coastland around it. The war-king and prince of the Geats planned vengeance on

> him for that. The protector and lord of warriors then ordered made for him a marvelous shield entirely of iron.

Although one might possibly connect the "dark thoughts" of Beowulf with the sentence that follows, thus understanding them as reactions of dismay or rage to the destruction caused by the dragon, it is much more likely that they are feelings of guilt at his having in some way brought this wrath on his people by offending God. To say that Beowulf feels guilty is not the same as to say that he is guilty, of course; his feeling of guilt may simply be one expression of his piety and conscientious responsibility. Guilt is not apparent in any of Beowulf's later words and actions, however (quite the contrary), and this passage seems curiously isolated in the poem, like the passage about the Danes' reversion to idol worship or the passage describing Beowulf's sluggish youth (2183b–89). What may really be most important here is simply that action is delayed while Beowulf feels emotion, and "dark" emotion at that. Such a reaction on his part would have been inconceivable in Part I.

However gloomy the past may seem in the larger perspective of this poem, to the hero himself the past is a source of strength and reassurance. The poet goes on to tell us that Beowulf scorns to approach the dragon with an array of his men, and the reason given for his confident attitude lies in the past.

> No he him þ*a* sæcce ondred,
> ne him þæs wyrmes wig for wiht dyde,
> eafoð ond ellen, forðon he ær fela
> nearo neðende niða gedigde,
> hildehlemma, syððan he Hroðgares,
> sigoreadig secg, sele fælsode
> ond æt guðe forgrap Grendeles mægum
> laðan cynnes. (2347b–54a)

He had no fear of the combat himself, and he

> considered the dragon's fighting skill, strength, and courage worth nothing, because he had survived many battles and clashes in the past, fighting his way out of tight places, since that time when, a triumphant warrior, he had cleansed Hrothgar's hall and had wrestled to their deaths in battle the Grendel family of hated race.

The last clause of the sentence sounds the note of triumph for those days in the past when the young Beowulf was *sigoreadig,* blessed with victory; and the two verbs *fælsode* and *forgrap* combine to suggest total achievement through strenuous action.

In this passage, and elsewhere in Part II, the idea of survival is of great importance.[16] Beowulf survived those fights with the Grendel race, and many later fights. Three of the *niðas* that he has come through safely are specified in the ensuing lines. First was the famous battle on the continent, in which Hygelac was killed.

> Þonan Biowulf com
> sylfes cræfte, sundnytte dreah.
> (2359b–60)

> Beowulf came away from that place by his own strength, exercising his power of swimming.

Beowulf's survival in this instance is stressed by contrast with what happened to those Hetware apparently responsible for Hygelac's death:

> Lyt eft becwom
> fram þam hildfrecan hames niosan.
> (2365b–66)

16. This is also pointed out by Stanley B. Greenfield, "Geatish History: Poetic Art and Epic Quality in *Beowulf,*" *Neophilologus,* 47 (1963), 211–17, where he makes a useful comparison of the three attitudes toward historical events represented in 2349b–99a, 2425–2515, and 2910b–3000.

> Few came back from that ferocious fighter to visit their homes again.

Hygelac's raid has other meanings in other contexts, but here the focus is on the image of Beowulf as survivor, the swimmer returning to his homeland, the *earm anhaga,* the man who is overcome with loneliness and grief for his dead lord.

Heardred grows up to become king of the Geats under Beowulf's protection and then is killed as a result of his involvement in the feud between the two Swedish brothers, Eanmund and Eadgils, and their uncle Onela. Beowulf survives this battle too and outlives this king, finally to become king himself. One more campaign is mentioned, the expedition to Sweden in support of Eadgils' bid for the throne, before the final summarizing statement about Beowulf's past is made:

> Swa he niða gehwane genesen hæfde,
> sliðra geslyhta, sunu Ecgðiowes,
> ellenweorca, oð ðone anne dæg
> þe he wið þam wyrme gewegan sceolde.
> (2397–2400)

> In this way he had survived every battle, violent conflict, act of courage, until that one day when he was obliged to fight against the dragon.

Some of the detail in this review of the past may fairly be described as exposition, introduced to satisfy the audience's curiosity (or refresh the audience's memory) about what had happened to Beowulf in the latter years of his life. But plain-Jane exposition is never enough in poetry, as any play of Shakespeare will show: it must be used for other artistic purposes as well. The description of past events here, by its very density of detail, creates an impression of crowded history, of a turbulent sea of disaster and violence, and of Beowulf somehow both being *in* that sea as active participant and yet never sinking in it, always being carried onward by strength and luck and the pressure of history to this present moment, this last of the "untils" of his life.

One way then of approaching Beowulf's long speech is to take it as continuing and exploring these same themes of survival and the past, as well as going on to state an important contrast between suffering and action that we have seen stated before in the somewhat different terms of Part I. His speech is delivered against a dark background of danger and foreboding, with "fate immeasurably near." Beowulf is described as being sad, and his spirit is said to be restless and on the verge of death. The apparent closeness of the end seems to drive his memory far back into the past, to reminiscences about his earliest childhood, as his whole life begins to take form now as a single entity. It is from this past that he must draw strength for the present emergency.

> Biowulf maþelade, bearn Ecgðeowes:
> "Fela ic on giogoðe guðræsa genæs,
> orleghwila; ic þæt eall gemon.
> Ic wæs syfanwintre, þa mec sinca baldor,
> freawine folca, æt minum fæder genam;
> heold mec ond hæfde Hreðel cyning,
> geaf me sinc ond symbel, sibbe gemunde.
> Næs ic him to life laðra owihte,
> beorn in burgum, þonne his bearna hwylc,
> Herebeald ond Hæðcyn oððe Hygelac min."
> (2425–34)

Beowulf son of Ecgtheow spoke: "I have survived many onslaughts and difficult times in my youth. I remember it all. I was seven years old when the prince of treasure, the friend and lord of nations, took me away from my father. King Hrethel owned me and protected me, giving me treasure and excellent food; he bore in mind our relationship. As a

> youth living in his halls, I was no more hated by him while he lived than was any of his own sons, Herebeald or Hæthcyn or my Hygelac."

Even though the first sentence of this speech carries on the idea of the surviving of dangers in war, Beowulf's first memories are really memories of love: of Hrethel's loving and generous treatment of his young grandson and of Beowulf's affectionate response to it, as well as his love for his uncles, especially for *Hygelac min*. It is Beowulf's own love and pity for Hrethel that give tragic depth to his memory of the suffering of the helpless old king when one of his sons accidentally kills another, and to the illustrative analogy of the Old Father's lament that follows, the second of the famous elegiac passages in the poem. Even love, in this heroic society, must be expressed in terms of action, and here, as Dorothy Whitelock has pointed out, no action is possible since no vengeance can be taken and no wergild can be exacted for the son's death.[17] The same is true of the imagined example of the father whose son has been hanged.

> Swa bið geomorlic gomelum ceorle
> to gebidanne, þæt his byre ride
> giong on galgan, þonne he gyd wrece,
> sarigne sang, þonne his sunu hangað
> hrefne to hroðre, ond he him helpe ne mæg,
> eald ond infrod, ænige gefremman.
> Symble bið gemyndgad morna gehwylce
> eaforan ellorsið; oðres ne gymeð
> to gebidanne burgum in innan
> yrfeweardas, þonne se an hafað
> þurh deaðes nyd dæda gefondad.
> Gesyhð sorhcearig on his suna bure

17. "*Beowulf*, 11. 2444–2471," *Medium Ævum*, 8 (1939), 198–204, and *The Audience of Beowulf* (Oxford, Clarendon Press, 1951), p. 18.

winsele westne, windge reste
reote berofene. Ridend swefað,
hæleð in hoðman; nis þær hearpan sweg,
gomen in geardum, swylce ðær iu wæron.
Gewiteð þonne on sealman, sorhleoð gæleð
an æfter anum; þuhte him eall to rum,
wongas ond wicstede. (2444–62a)

In just this way it is a great grief for an old man to have to go through, to have his boy swinging young on the gallows; then he will make up a chant, some painful song, when his boy hangs for the raven's delight and he, though old and wise, cannot help him at all. Always, each morning, the going away of his son will come back to his mind, and he will not be concerned with living on to see another heir in his fortress, when the one reached the end of his deeds by death's compulsion. Sorrowing, he will look at his son's bedchamber, the deserted wine-hall, the windswept resting-places robbed of joy. Riders and heroes sleep in the grave; there is no sound of the harp, no merriment there in the courts, as there once was. Then he will go to his bed and sing in his loneliness a lament for the one dead; all of it, the fields and buildings, seemed too big for him.

This is an acutely realized world of pain, and it is pain largely because action has been paralyzed. The verbs in this passage suggest either passivity or endurance (*to gebidanne* [twice], *ride, hangað, swefað*) or a very limited kind of action (*gyd wrece, gesyhð, gewiteð on sealman, gæleð*) that is almost another kind of thought. There is the ironic motion of the hanged son "riding" on the gallows, but at the end of this lament all riders are sleeping; wind and the pecking raven can still impart motion to the son, but his father cannot. As in the elegy of the Last Survivor, we see here the negative of the heroic world. This is the world of no action, and a world where time is arrested. The mornings, recurring time-marking events, have no purpose here but to remind the father of the same vacancy in his experience. He cannot think of a future or of another heir. Is it his own tormented vision that turns his son's empty bedchamber into a ruined windswept hall, shifting to a perspective beyond any single man's experience of time? In the world of no action, time present can blur with future or past; time no longer matters, because it is wholly unredeemable. This passage may be as close as anything in the poem to the "epic simile" of Homer and his imitators, and it gives something of the same effect of time arrested.

In its context, this anecdote of the Old Father is a long simile that serves to define Hrethel's feelings. Beowulf goes on to describe Hrethel's impotent suffering and his ultimate death from sorrow. But the urgent world of time and action floods back in on us abruptly in the next lines, already quoted above (pp. 180–81), where wild violence between Swedes and Geats is precipitated by King Hrethel's death. The same kind of ceaseless action continues as Beowulf goes on to tell of the fighting at Ravenswood and the death of Hæthcyn. Then he speaks of his relationship with Hygelac:

> Ic him þa maðmas, þe he me sealde,
> geald æt guðe, swa me gifeðe wæs,
> leohtan sweorde; he me lond forgeaf,
> eard, eðelwyn. Næs him ænig þearf
> þæt he to Gifðum oððe to Gardenum
> oððe in Swiorice secean þurfe
> wyrsan wigfrecan, weorðe gecypan.
> Symle ic him on feðan beforan wolde,
> ana on orde, ond swa to aldre sceall
> sæcce fremman, þenden þis sweord þolað,
> þæt mec ær ond sið oft gelæste.
> (2490–2500)

I repaid him in battle for the treasures he gave me,

> as I had the luck to do so, with my flashing sword; he granted me land, a home to enjoy. There was no need for him to recruit and pay inferior fighting-men from among the Gifthas or the Danes or Swedes. I always insisted on marching before him among the troops, alone in the vanguard, and that is how I must always do battle, as long as this sword lasts which has often done me service early and late.

Here is the ideal pattern of loving generosity on one side and loving service on the other. Beowulf fought strenuously for his lord Hygelac then; he goes on to recall that he later avenged Hygelac's death by killing the Frankish champion Dæghrefn; he will always go on fighting as long as he lives, whatever else in the world may change. Hygelac may die, but Beowulf's stance in relationship to his ideal of a lord will never falter. The last few verses imply that his dedication to this ideal is as bright and hard and long-lasting as his sword.

Such an expression of dynamic heroism might seem merely conventional if it did not follow so closely on the tragic study of Hrethel and the grieving father. The sharp contrast is unmistakable. The will to act must be defined by its opposite, the world without action. Yet by representing his hero as capable of comprehending both worlds, the poet gives him greater stature than at any time earlier in the poem, greater range of feeling. As a young man Beowulf could not have felt that sense of *lacrimae rerum* which he shows here. This is heroism by a new standard: to understand and sympathize with life's desperate sadness without losing the capacity to act in total dedication.

Beowulf's long life, which was relived in this speech, is, like the speech, close to its end.

> Beowulf maðelode, beotwordum spræc,
> niehstan siðe: "Ic geneðde fela

guðа on geogoðe; gyt ic wylle,
frod folces weard, fæhðe secan,
mærð*u* fremman, gif mec se mansceaða
of eorðsele ut geseceð."
Gegrette ða gumena gehwylcne,
hwate helmberend, hindeman siðe,
swæse gesiðas. (2510–18a)

Beowulf spoke, gave voice to his pledge for the last time: "I have risked myself in many battles in my youth; still I am willing to seek a fight, old guardian of the people though I am, and to do something worthy of fame, if that evil destroyer comes out of his earth-hall and finds me." Then for the last time he greeted each man of those bold helmet-wearers and dear companions.

The repetitive phrases *niehstan siðe* and *hindeman siðe* make plain that this is the hero's last vow and last farewell to his men. Death has been a constant theme in Beowulf's speech. There was a long roster of the dead: Herebeald, Hrethel, the hanged son, Hæthcyn, Ongentheow, Hygelac, Dæghrefn. As, in the course of the speech, they appear briefly and then fall away into darkness, the hero's form seems to become more clearly outlined and his voice more clearly heard. Even though the inexorable series of deaths in itself implies that he will soon become a part of the series—as Beowulf himself says later, *ic him æfter sceal* 2816—he is still at the moment a survivor, the last survivor of an entire generation.

Not only does Beowulf stand as living figure against the dark background of the dead but in the present scene he is set in contrast as an active figure with the passive characters who surround him, his retainers. These men are barely described. They listen to his speech, in which they are ordered to wait and are told that this adventure is not for them. Their armor is mentioned, but not their offensive weapons. After the fight begins all but Wiglaf run away into the forest.

Simply by giving them such minimal attention, the poet does in fact create the impression of characters almost wholly lacking in the substance of will power or the capacity to act, even more shadowlike than the procession of the named dead.

Beowulf's will, we should note, is particularly emphasized in the final lines of his speech. Several verbs contain the idea of will: *gyt ic wylle* 2512, *nolde ic* 2518, *nelle ic* 2524. The heroic will, that hard and flashing sword, survives to the last instant. As always with Beowulf, this will takes the form of a clear-eyed kind of resolution, anything but blind: as the "if" clauses in lines 2514–15 and 2519–21 suggest, he recognizes that the dragon cannot be fought in the same way that he fought Grendel and that the chances of his death in this fight are great.

The contrast I am trying to define here can be seen in the conclusion of his speech:

> "Gebide ge on beorge byrnum werede,
> secgas on searwum, hwæðer sel mæge
> æfter wælræse wunde gedygan
> uncer twega. Nis þæt eower sið
> ne gemet mannes, nefn[e] min anes,
> *þæt* he wið aglæcean eofoðo dæle,
> eorlscype efne. Ic mid elne sceall
> gold gegangan, oððe guð nimeð,
> feorhbealu frecne, frean eowerne!"
> Aras ða bi ronde rof oretta,
> heard under helme, hiorosercean bær
> under stancleofu, strengo getruwode
> anes mannes. Ne bið swylc earges sið!
> (2529–41)

"Wait on the mound, you warriors in armor protected by your mailshirts, to see which of the two of us will be better able to survive his wounds after the shock of battle. This is not your undertaking,

> nor is it in any man's measure [of strength] but mine alone to deal out punishment to the monster and do a hero's deed. I shall by my courage gain possession of the gold—or else war, that appalling deadly evil, will take your lord!" And with this the brave soldier stood up, holding his shield, and walked, resolute in helmet and armor, to the foot of the stony cliff; he put his faith in the strength of one man. No coward would dare try anything like that!

The Geatish retainers, in the relative security of their armor and their safe position on the hill, wait silent and motionless for the event to reveal itself, as Beowulf rises and walks toward the dragon's stronghold. It is not their *sið*, as Beowulf knows, because it is beyond their measure. Their role is sharply and explicitly distinguished from his own, which is the role of the unique and individual hero (*nefne min anes, anes mannes*), the man who is *eacen,* beyond the measure of ordinary man.

Since Wiglaf's speeches and the action of the dragon fight have already been discussed in Chapter Four, let us move ahead to examine the speech Beowulf makes after he has been mortally wounded by the dragon. The theme of heroic will dominates this scene and the rest of the poem, beyond the actual moment of his death. For will can be projected even beyond death in the form of the *laf*, an Old English word convenient to use because no modern word has quite the same range of suggestion: *what is left*—a legacy, an heirloom (material or spiritual), whatever of the spirit of the dead remains for the survivors. Beowulf's death scene (2709b–2820 approximately) is focused almost wholly on the idea of the *laf*.

Poisoned by the dragon's bite and suffering great pain, the dying king makes his way to a sitting place from which he can look at the dragon's barrow and see "how the eternal earth-hall held within it stone arches, fast on their foundations." For Beowulf, the barrow seems to have three not entirely separable meanings: it is the dragon's home, now standing open to the looter, and thus a sign of the hero's victory; it contains a vast treasure, a *laf* of enormous value that can be transmitted to the Geatish people; it is finally a grave, the only truly eternal kind of hall, and thus the locus of death. All three meanings appear in what Beowulf says as he looks, in that singular way of looking so typical of the latter part of the poem, first at the barrow and later at the treasure Wiglaf brings out of it for him to see.

The first of Beowulf's three speeches during this death scene is prefaced by mention of the hero's recognition of the fact that his number of days has run out and that death is "immeasurably near." This is then a dying man's speech, and it seems to revolve around three points of time. It begins with the pathetic remark that he would have presented his arms now to his son, if fate had allowed him to have a natural son to be his heir in the future. At the center of the speech are three sentences linked together by rhythmically parallel openings (*ic ðas leode heold; ic on earde bad, ic ðæs ealles mæg*), which state briefly his satisfaction in his past accomplishments as protecting king and impeccable hero. And the last nine lines are a command in the present to Wiglaf to go into the barrow and bring out the treasure for Beowulf to see before he dies. Seen this way, the speech consists of a disappointed hope about the future, a statement of past achievement, and a last dying act in the present.

The treasure is continuity that can transcend one man's time. It has lasted many years and will last many more; its life is much longer than a man's. Hence it can extend a man's power for good beyond his own death, if it is used wisely, and that is why Beowulf wishes to turn the treasure over to his people. But this speech hints at deeper truths: the treasure that Beowulf has guarded safe for fifty years is his nation, and what he leaves behind as his greatest *laf* is the history of his stewardship and the example of his selfless devotion.

Obediently Wiglaf enters the barrow, a marvelous world of gleaming gold and rusting armor. What seems to be most stressed about the treasure in this description is that it is unprotected: the ancient owners and polishers have gone, the dragon has just been killed. Treasure has no power to protect itself, it is vulnerable; its vulnerability hints at some fundamental ambiguity in its actual power. Yet the image of decay and impotence in the helmet that is *eald ond omig* 2763, old and rusty, is balanced by the image of the most prominent object in the barrow:

> Swlyce he siomian geseah segn eallgylden
> heah ofer horde, hondwundra mæst,
> gelocen leoðocræftum; of ðam leom*a* stod,
> þæt he þone grundwong ongitan meahte,
> wræ*t*e giondwlian. (2767–71a)

> He also saw a standard of pure gold hanging high over the hoard, greatest of marvels made and woven with all the skill of men's hands; light shone out from it so that he could see the floor clearly and look around at the things of value.

This golden *segn,* the ancient royal standard that Wiglaf brings out of the barrow to show Beowulf, seems more than half symbolic, suggesting the very principle of kingship which survives the rust and corrosion of time and which gives light to men. The royal *segn* that looms high over Scyld's head on the funeral ship (47 ff.), set in contrast as it is to the unknowable sea on which the ship is launched, is a similar image.

Beowulf's next speeches seem to continue this half-submerged theme of the *laf*. As he looks at the treasures Wiglaf has brought him, he says:

Ic ðara frætwa frean ealles ðanc,
wuldurcyninge, wordum secge,
ecum dryhtne, þe ic her on starie,
þæs ðe ic moste minum leodum
ær swyltdæge swylc gestrynan.
Nu ic on maðma hord mi*ne* bebohte
frode feorhlege, fremmað gena
leoda þearfe; ne mæg ic her leng wesan.
(2794–2801)

I say thanks in words to the Lord of all, King of glory and eternal God, for all these treasures which I now see before me, because I am allowed to make my people rich with them before the day of my death. Now that I have sold my old life for the hoard of treasures, keep on attending to the needs of the people. I cannot be here any longer.

Beowulf has gladly sacrificed his life for these treasures, which he believes will be a *laf* welcomed by his people. The metaphor of exchange here, a life for a treasure, contains the suggestion that the treasure is in some sense a measure of Beowulf's immeasurable value: immense, uncountable, a hero's wergild. Yet treasure itself has no moral will. The actual legacy that Beowulf leaves to Wiglaf is not material wealth, but responsibility for the nation, a responsibility that, always in the poem, is the right way of using wealth: *fremmað gena / leoda þearfe*. The imperative, itself frail and vulnerable, hangs in the darkening air. Yet this imperative is given further substance by Beowulf's final command to Wiglaf to build a memorial barrow.

Hatað heaðomære hlæw gewyrcean
beorhtne æfter bæle æt brimes nosan;
se scel to gemyndum minum leodum
heah hlifian on Hronesnæsse,
þæt hit sæliþend syððan hatan

Biowulfes biorh, ða ðe brentingas
ofer floda genipu feorran drifað.
(2802–08)

Order those famous in war to build a shining mound after my burning on the headland by the sea; high on Whale Cliff it is to rise as a reminder for my people, and sailors will one day call it Beowulf's Barrow, those seamen who drive their high ships from far off over the darkness of the waters.

The barrow is the objectification of memory and admonition. It is typical of this hero's practical altruism that he intends his grave to be a landmark and an aid to navigation. But it is to be an aid to moral navigation as well, an example that

firme is fixt, and sendeth light from farre
To all, that in the wide deepe wandring arre.[18]

The Geatish sailors on the dark sea of the world are more than halfway along toward becoming Spenser's frankly allegorical voyagers: they will orient themselves by the name and story of Beowulf.

At the end Beowulf turns his neck-ring and armor over to Wiglaf, voicing the all-important hope that Wiglaf will use them well. Both this symbolic act and the tone of Beowulf's last words bring out his quiet acceptance of the fact of death.

Þu eart endelaf usses cynnes,
Wægmundinga. Ealle wyrd fors*weop*
mine magas to metodsceafte,
eorlas on elne; ic him æfter sceal.
(2813–16)

You are the last survivor of our clan, the Wægmundings. Fate has swept away all my kinsmen to their destiny, those brave warriors; I must now follow after them.

18. *Faerie Queene,* I.2.1.

Not only the armor and the neck-ring are passed on to Wiglaf but also Beowulf's role as "last survivor" of so many years and battles. The old king at last turns to fall in line behind that great file of figures of the dead which he vividly sketched in his long speech before the fight.

The passage that immediately follows Beowulf's death is of a type conventional enough in Germanic poetry: the gloat over a fallen enemy (for a somewhat egregious example the reader may consult the poem on the Battle of Brunanburh). In this charged context, however, the convention has more complex functions.

> Bona swylce læg,
> egeslic eorðdraca ealdre bereafod,
> bealwe gebæded. Beahhordum leng
> wyrm wohbogen wealdan ne moste,
> ac hine irenna ecga fornamon,
> hearde, heaðoscearde homera lafe,
> þæt se widfloga wundum stille
> hreas on hrusan hordærne neah.
> Nalles æfter lyfte lacende hwearf
> middelnihtum, maðmæhta wlonc
> ansyn ywde, ac he eorðan gefeoll
> for ðæs hildfruman hondgeweorce.
> (2824b–35)

> The killer also lay dead, the terrifying earth-dragon, deprived of life, driven by destruction. The coiled dragon was no longer allowed to lord it over the ring-hoard; no, edges of steel swords, forged by hammers, hard and battle-notched, had taken his life, so that the far flyer sank to earth near his treasure-house, stilled by wounds. No longer in his play did he launch out into the air at midnight and show himself in all the arrogance of his wealth; no, he fell to the earth because of that act of the prince's hand.

For all its apparent gloating this passage contains a faint and surprising suggestion of sadness. It is not that we are really made to feel grief at the dragon's death, it is just that we are reminded again and again that it was once a living creature of fierce energies, a *widfloga* which once exulted in unrestrained movement in the free air, and that now it lies still, very still on the earth. The sharpened contrast here (note the two adversative constructions in the passage) between living activity and the immobility of death makes its own point.

Possibly a subtle transfer of feelings is going on here. The passage ends with an oddly objective phrase:

Biowulfe wearð
dryhtmaðma dæl deaðe forgolden;
hæfde æghwæð*er* ende gefered
lænan lifes. (2842b–45a)

> A great mass of noble treasure had been bought by Beowulf through his death; each of the two had traveled to the end of transitory life.

Again we have the image of the exchange, the bargain: Beowulf's death weighed against the dragon's death, and the loss of Beowulf weighed against the gain of the treasure. Ostensibly these are the consoling phrases of satisfied justice, but the objective statement in the second sentence that both hero and dragon are fellow victims of sad mortality blocks such easy consolations. Perhaps the reason the poet describes the dragon's stillness at such length is because his eyes are averted from the figure that lies just as still beside the dragon. The parallel between the two is hard to face, but the final sentence draws it. It is not justice or vengeance or triumph that dominates this scene, but the quiet fact of death the leveler, and death in the particular aspect of immobility, the ceasing of all action.

Immobility is further stressed by devices of contrast in the description (3030b–50) following the Messenger's speech, when the Geats obey the Messenger's invitation to go and look at Beowulf and the dragon. Often before Beowulf had given rings to the Geats; now he lies still in his *hlimbed,* his bed of rest. After all his joy in flying by night, the dragon has come back to his den and is now fast in death, fifty feet long as he lies inert, stretched out on the ground. Beside the two motionless bodies lie the objects of the hoard, themselves heavy with the weight of a thousand years of burial, pressed down into the ground by the binding force of an ancient spell.

Indeed the dominant image for these last 150 lines of the poem, as it was the dominant image in the lament of the Last Survivor, is one of dead weight, inertia, heaviness. Wiglaf tells the Geats of how, with his hands, he lifted the heavy weight, the *mægenbyrðenne* (3091) of the treasure, and carried it out for his king to see. At the end of his speech he orders the Geats to carry their dear lord to where he may lie long in God's protection:

> Ond þonne geferian frean userne,
> leofne mannan, þær he longe sceal
> on ðæs waldendes wære geþolian.
> (3107–09)

Men carry wood to the pyre. The detachment chosen by Wiglaf enters the barrow, bearing torches, to see the great treasure lying on the earth; they carry it quickly out and load it on a wagon. The dragon's body is pushed off the cliff, its immense weight to be borne by the sea. Beowulf's body is carried to the pyre and, in accordance with his instructions, laid tenderly in the midst of the ceremonial weapons that have been placed on it. Finally they commit the entire treasure to the funeral barrow and let the earth hold it.

This noticeable accumulation of kinesthetic images of lifting and carrying and laying down suggests the sheer weight of death, the way in which the earth pulls everything down toward it and holds all things in the end. This pattern is the climax of the many images of helplessness and inaction that we have seen in the poem: it is the final and permanent negation of all heroic action.

Yet the emotional associations surrounding Beowulf's funeral are not those of simple and black despair. In contrast to the images of weight there is a counterpattern of images of rising. Indeed many of the images of lifting and carrying themselves contribute something to this pattern. But we see the pattern also in the description of the funeral fire.

> Ongunnon þa on beorge bælfyra mæst
> wigend weccan; wud[u]rec astah,
> sweart ofer swi*o*ðole, swogende leg
> wope bewunden (windblond gelæg),
> oðþæt he ða banhus gebrocen hæfde,
> hat on hreðre. (3143–48a)
>
> * * *
>
> Heofon rece swe[a]lg.
>
> Geworhton ða Wedra leode
> hleo on hoe, se wæs heah ond brad,
> wægliðendum wide gesyne,
> ond beti[m]bredon on tyn dagum
> beadurofes becn, bronda lafe
> wealle beworhton, swa hyt weorðlicost
> foresnotre men findan mihton.[19] (3155b–62)

Then on the mound the warriors began to awaken the greatest of funeral fires. The wood-smoke rose up, black above the flame, a roaring blaze mingled with weeping rose up (the wind's tumult had died down) until in its hot heart it had destroyed the

19. The text of this much-damaged portion of the manuscript cannot be finally established; Dobbie's readings are adopted for convenience here.

> bone-house. . . . Heaven swallowed the smoke. Then the Geatish people built a shelter (?) on the promontory which was high and broad and visible to sailors a great way off, and in ten days they completed the brave man's monument, building around what the fire had left a wall which was the finest that the wisest men could design.

The fire is kindled in the pyre on its high hill; it rises higher and higher, unimpeded in its ascent even by the wind. That "heaven" swallows the smoke of the burning seems more likely in this context to be a reference to the great height attained by the column of flame and smoke than to any supernatural reaction. After the fire has died down, the Geats erect their great memorial barrow, a structure conspicuous for its height.

These physical images of falling and rising are an externalization of the meaning of the funeral scene. The sense of mingled loss and triumph they contain has its closest emotional analogue in the poem in the description of Scyld's funeral in the opening lines. We may find it easier to come to some definition of this emotion if we go back to look again at the Scyld proem.

We scarcely know enough about Germanic religious beliefs (especially at a time when in England such beliefs were already fast receding into oblivion) to do more than guess at the emotions felt by the original audience as they listened to the brilliant account of Scyld's funeral. But surely some profound and ancient myth of man's sacramental relationship to his environment is hinted at here, and the sea seems to stand for the mystery of that environment. In the beginning, *æt frumsceafte* 45, Scyld had come alone as a child from over the sea to save the Danes; now he is sent back to his place of origin by his people. We are invited to participate in the stately ritual, where emotions flow without strain into the affectionate and obedient acts of carrying and laying down the body, loading the ship with treasures, and sending it out to sea. The scene suggests most strongly a deliberate and conscious sacrificial act, not in propitiation of any defined and formalized supernatural power so much as in simple gratitude for the gifts (unaccountable) that life may send, gratitude that outweighs the natural and deep sorrow felt at the loss of Scyld, gratitude that at last finds its best expression in the free "giving" of Scyld back to his original source (unknowable).

> Þa gyt hie him asetton   segen ge[l]denne
> heah ofer heafod,   leton holm beran,
> geafon on garsecg;   him wæs geomor sefa,
> murnende mod.   Men ne cunnon
> secgan to soðe,   selerædende,
> hæleð under heofenum,   hwa þæm hlæste onfeng.
> (47–52)

> And then they placed a golden royal standard high over his head, let the sea carry him, gave him to ocean; their hearts grieved and mourned. Men are not able to tell truly—not counselors in hall, not any heroes under heaven—who received that cargo.

The first sentence dramatizes the dual act of honoring and releasing. Men place the royal standard high over his head in token of *lof*, his fame, which is the essence of his heroic identity; but they must let him go. He is committed to ultimate mystery, gently entrusted to the sea, *given* (to draw on the range of possible senses of the word in Old English) like a woman to marriage or a sacrificial offering to the altar. Men can never finally know the mystery of human achievement and human mortality; they can only guide their complex feelings into the forms of ritual.

Scyld's funeral is a way of seeing death as an almost exultant mystery. Beowulf's funeral is less exultant and much more painful (we know Beowulf much better than we know Scyld), but the mystery inherent in death, and in human experience generally, is often mentioned in the closing lines.[20] The Geats who see Beowulf and the dragon lying side by side have gone to look at a marvel (*wundur sceawian* 3032). Beowulf has died a marvelous death (*wundordeaðe swealt* 3037). The fifty-foot dragon is an amazing creature (*syllicran wiht* 3038). The great dragon hoard is *eacencræftig* (extraordinarily powerful), a word perhaps suggesting the supernatural, and *galdre bewunden,* with a spell cast on it (3051–52).

Mystery, immobility, finality: all these aspects of death seem to be combined in this one passage:

> Wundur hwar þonne
> eorl ellenrof ende gefere
> lifgesceafta, þonne leng ne mæg
> mon mid his [ma]gum meduseld buan.
> Swa wæs Biowulfe, þa he biorges weard
> sohte searoniðas; seolfa ne cuðe,
> þurh hwæt his worulde gedal weorðan sceolde.
> (3062b–68)

> It is a mystery just when it will be that a courageous man makes the journey to the end of the life decreed him, when he can no longer go on living in the mead-hall with his kinsmen. It was so with Beowulf, when he went to find the barrow's guardian in the treacherous fight; he himself did not know in what way his separation from the world of the living was fated to come about.

No matter how well we understand mortality in the abstract —and this was a major theme in Hrothgar's sermon—death always must take the individual by surprise. Man both understands death all too well and cannot understand it all, ever.

20. In his stimulating essay on the characteristics of the epic genre, Thomas Greene reminds us that Tasso and other critics have postulated epic awe, *maraviglia,* as the basic response man has to epic poetry. See "The Norms of Epic," p. 198.

In this passage the words in the first sentence recall those simple themes we have been examining: *wundur . . . ende . . . leng ne mæg*. The very image of life here is the clustering of the clan family in the lighted mead-hall, *mon mid his magum*. The wise counselor of King Edwin of Northumbria saw human life in the terms of the same metaphor in his famous parable of the sparrow who flies briefly through the warm hall on his way from winter into winter.[21] Death is then exile, separation from that world of men. As both killer and hall-burner, the dragon stands for death in two forms.

Such is one meaning of death for the individual, but the death of a king has wide-ranging effects on his people as well, as the Messenger's speech makes very clear. The closing lines of his speech are the third great elegiac passage of the poem. There he turns from prophecies of political calamity for the lordless nation to the question of what they can and must do now.

> *Nu* is ofost betost
> þæt we þeodcyning þær sceawian
> ond þone gebringan, þe us beagas geaf,
> on adfære. Ne scel anes hwæt
> meltan mid þam modigan, ac þær is maðma hord,
> gold unrime grimme gecea[po]d,
> ond nu æt siðestan sylfes feore
> beagas [geboh]te. (3007b–14a)

> Now it is best that we go quickly to look at the mighty king there, and escort on his way to the pyre the one who gave us rings. Not a part only should melt with that great man, but there is a whole hoard of treasures there, uncounted gold bargained for grimly and now, at the end, the rings purchased at the price of his own life.

21. Bede, *Historia Ecclesiastica* II, xiii.

Why is it necessary for the Geats to look at their dead king? What is it they will learn from looking? And what leads the Messenger to assume that they will commit the entire treasure won from the dragon to the funeral pyre, as indeed they later do? One fact that the Geats will come to understand by looking at their dead king is the fact of their own death, eventual and inevitable national death, for the kingdom that loses its protecting shield is doomed. Their recognition now of the value to them of Beowulf's life seems to lead them to commit the treasure to the flames as a measurement, however inadequate, of his worth and heroic power, possibly as a sacrifice in repayment for the life he enabled them to lead. Because of their quickening realization of the horror of their own future, they must now look at him so that they will be able to understand and share his calm courage, the *laf* which he has left them in the hope that they can use it. King and people are intimately identified: his pyre is their own.

Þa sceall brond fretan
æled þeccean, nalles eorl wegan
maððum to gemyndum, ne mægð scyne
habban on healse hringweorðunge,
ac sceal geomormod, golde bereafod,
oft nalles æne elland tredan,
nu se herewisa hleahtor alegde,
gamen ond gleodream. Forðon sceall gar wesan
monig, morgenceald, mundum bewunden,
hæfen on handa, nalles hearpan sweg
wigend weccean, ac se wonna hrefn
fus ofer fægum fela reordian,
earne secgan hu him æt æte speow,
þenden he wið wulf wæl reafode. (3014b–27)

Fire shall devour those [treasures], flame enfold them; no warrior shall wear an ornament in his memory, no beautiful girl shall have a precious ring

> around her neck—on the contrary, grieving and stripped of gold, she shall tread a foreign land often, not merely once, now that the leader of our army has laid down laughter, mirth, and joy. As a result many a spear will be grasped, cold to the touch in the morning, and raised in the hand, and no sound of harp will wake the warrior, but the dark raven, eager over the doomed, will say many things, will tell the eagle how much he got to eat, when he disputed with the wolf over the corpses.

What begins as an account of the sacrificial destruction of precious objects becomes, in a sudden and illogical shift of direction not unknown elsewhere in Old English lyric poetry, a lament for those who lose the objects, lose them not by surrendering them to the funeral pyre but by being stripped of them in national military defeat. Reminders of social existence, of a living world of human relationships—the memento and the heirloom, the girl's necklace, the *hleahtor* and *gleodream* of the hall with its harp song—all vanish as the passage moves on, the image of the walking girl subtly underlining the inevitable movement: the treasure to the fire, the Geats and their world to dissolution and annihilation. As one thing is laid down, another is taken up. The dying have laid aside laughter and the harp: now the enslaved woman walks and the hand reaches for the spear. The passage is constructed almost entirely of those negatives and adversatives we saw in the first chapter: massed in this way, they seem relentless, they crush out every flicker of human hope and memory. New images appear to replace the old: now it is the lonely woman separated from her people, sentenced to slavery in exile; it is the spear icy to the weary hand as life becomes an endless chaos of warfare. At the end the music of the harp, always the symbol of harmony and joyous order, is drowned out by the raucous cries of raven and eagle, hungrily welcoming man's death in this world and sounding a desolate parody, as they boast of their exploits and booty, of the competitive heroic society they both imitate and supersede.

In this strange processional elegy of a future now seen as the past and in the ceremonies of the funeral itself, the march into exile and death and the ritual of the funeral are triumphantly mingled: the dirge that the Geats sing is both for their king and for themselves. As many have observed, the funeral of Hector at the end of the *Iliad* has a similar emotional tone and shares many of the same images: mourning women who envision slavery for themselves; the sacrifice of treasure; the raging and all-consuming fire; the building of a mighty barrow. One underlying similarity is our awareness in each case that we are really watching the funeral of an entire nation.

Yet in the final lines of the Old English poem this realization of annihilation, overwhelming as it is, must remain subordinate to the intense and unswerving focus of attention on Beowulf. The twelve warriors ride around his barrow chanting of a king and of a man who saw death and who lived bravely. Treasure and future alike lie buried in the earth, but his men repay Beowulf in the only way they can, by acting now as heroes should, *swa hit gedefe bið,* in praising and loving a great man when he dies.

> Eahtodan eorlscipe ond his ellenweorc
> duguðum demdon, swa hit ged[efe] bið
> þæt mon his winedryhten wordum herge,
> ferhðum freoge, þonne he forð scile
> of lichaman [læded] weorðan.
> Swa begnornodon Geata leode
> hlafordes [hry]re, heorðgeneatas,
> cwædon þæt he wære wyruldcyning[a]
> manna mildust ond mon[ðw]ærust,
> leodum liðost ond lofgeornost. (3173–82)

They praised his heroism and nobly passed judgment on his brave accomplishments, as it is proper

> for a man to honor his dear lord in his words and to love him in his heart, when he must be taken away from the body. And that is how the people of the Geats, his old companions by the hearth, lamented their lord's fall, saying that he was of all great kings the most merciful of men and the gentlest, the kindest to his people and the most eager for fame.

The Geats mourn the passing of their king, but in words that rise to something close to triumph, in praises out of the heart of love that point to Beowulf's own affectionate and kind nature. To the extent to which they can courageously face their own destruction, they will draw their courage and their dignity from their love for their dead king, the incarnation of the heroic spirit and the radiant center of the poem.

WORKS CITED

Alfred, William, translation of *Beowulf,* in *Medieval Epics,* New York, Modern Library, 1963.

Blomfield, Joan, "The Style and Structure of *Beowulf,*" *Review of English Studies* (o.s.), *14* (1938), 396–403.

Bloomfield, Morton W., "Beowulf and Christian Allegory: An Interpretation of Unferth," *Traditio,* 7 (1949–51), 410–15.

Bonjour, Adrien, "The Use of Anticipation in *Beowulf,*" *Review of English Studies* (o.s.), *16* (1940), 290–99.

———, "Weohstan's Slaying of Eanmund," *English Studies,* 27 (1946), 14–19; reprinted in *The Digressions in Beowulf,* Medium Ævum Monographs, 5 (Oxford, Basil Blackwell, 1950), pp. 35–39.

Brodeur, Arthur G., *The Art of Beowulf,* Berkeley and Los Angeles, University of California Press, 1959.

———, "The Structure and the Unity of *Beowulf,*" *PMLA, 68* (1953), 1183–95.

Brook, G. L., *A History of the English Language,* London, Andre Deutsch, 1958.

———, *Selections from Laȝamon's Brut,* Clarendon Medieval and Tudor Series, Oxford, Clarendon Press, 1963.

———, and R. F. Leslie, ed., *Laȝamon: Brut,* Vol. I, Early English Text Society, No. 250, London, Oxford University Press, 1963.

Chambers, R. W., *Beowulf: An Introduction,* 3d ed. with a supplement by C. L. Wrenn, Cambridge, The University Press, 1959.

Clark, George, "Beowulf's Armor," *ELH,* 32 (1965), 409–41.

Clark Hall, John R., translation of *Beowulf and the Finnesburg Fragment,* 2d ed. revised by C. L. Wrenn, London, Allen and Unwin, 1940.

Cross, J. E., " 'Ubi Sunt' Passages in Old English—Sources and

Relationships," *Vetenskaps-Societetens i Lund Årsbok,* 1956, pp. 26–44.

De Vries, Jan, *Heroic Song and Heroic Legend,* trans. B. J. Timmer, London, Oxford University Press, 1963.

Diamond, Robert E., "Theme as Ornament in Anglo-Saxon Poetry," *PMLA, 76* (1961), 461–68.

Dixon, W. Macneile, *Tragedy,* 2d ed. London, C. Arnold & Co., 1925.

Dobbie, E. V. K., *Beowulf and Judith,* Anglo-Saxon Poetic Records, 4, New York, Columbia University Press, 1953.

———, *The Anglo-Saxon Minor Poems,* Anglo-Saxon Poetic Records, 6, New York, Columbia University Press, 1942.

Donahue, Charles, "*Beowulf* and Christian Tradition: A Reconstruction from a Celtic Stance," *Traditio, 21* (1965), 55–116.

Eliade, Mircea, *Images and Symbols,* trans. Philip Mairet, London, Harvill Press, and New York, Sheed and Ward, 1961. First published as *Images et symboles: essais sur le symbolisme magico-religieux,* Paris, Gallimard, 1952.

———, *Patterns in Comparative Religion,* trans. Rosemary Sheed, London and New York, Sheed and Ward, 1958. First published as *Traité d'histoire des Religions,* Paris, Payot, 1949.

Eliason, Norman E., "The Þyle and Scop in *Beowulf,*" *Speculum,* 38 (1963), 267–84.

Fisher, Peter F., "The Trials of the Epic Hero in *Beowulf,*" *PMLA,* 73 (1958), 171–83.

Fontenrose, Joseph, *Python: A Study of Delphic Myth and Its Origins,* Berkeley, University of California Press, 1959.

Goldsmith, Margaret E., "The Choice in *Beowulf,*" *Neophilologus, 18* (1964), 60–72.

———, "The Christian Perspective in *Beowulf,*" in *Studies in Old English Literature in Honor of Arthur G. Brodeur,* ed. Stanley B. Greenfield (Eugene, Ore., University of Oregon Press, 1963), pp. 71–90.

———, "The Christian Theme of *Beowulf,*" *Medium Ævum,* 29 (1960), 81–101.

Greene, Thomas, "The Norms of Epic," *Comparative Literature, 13* (1961), 193–207; in slightly different form this essay appears as the first chapter of *The Descent from Heaven: A*

Study in Epic Continuity, New Haven, Yale University Press, 1963.

Greenfield, Stanley B., *A Critical History of Old English Literature,* New York, New York University Press, 1965.

———, "Geatish History: Poetic Art and Epic Quality in *Beowulf,*" *Neophilologus,* 47 (1963), 211–17.

Grundtvig, N. F. S., *Beowulfes Beorh eller Bjovulfs-Drapen,* Copenhagen, 1861.

Halverson, John, "*Beowulf* and the Pitfalls of Piety," *University of Toronto Quarterly,* 35 (1966), 260–78.

Homer, *The Odyssey,* trans. E. V. Rieu, Baltimore, Penguin Books, 1946.

Irving, Edward B., Jr., "*Ealuscerwen:* Wild Party at Heorot," *Tennessee Studies in Literature, 11* (1966), 161–68.

———, "Image and Meaning in the Elegies," in *Old English Poetry: Fifteen Essays,* ed. Robert P. Creed (Providence, Brown University Press, 1967), pp. 153–66.

———, "The Heroic Style in *The Battle of Maldon,*" *Studies in Philology,* 58 (1961), 457–67.

Kaske, R. E., "*Sapientia et Fortitudo* as the Controlling Theme of *Beowulf,*" *Studies in Philology,* 55 (1958), 423–56.

———, "The Sigemund-Heremod and Hama-Hygelac Passages in *Beowulf,*" *PMLA,* 74 (1959), 489–94.

———, "Weohstan's Sword," *Modern Language Notes,* 75 (1960), 465–68.

Ker, W. P., *Epic and Romance,* 2d ed. London, Macmillan, 1908; reprinted New York, Dover Publications, 1957.

Klaeber, Fr., *Beowulf and the Fight at Finnsburg,* 3d ed. Boston, D. C. Heath, 1950.

Krapp, G. P., and E. V. K. Dobbie, *The Exeter Book,* Anglo-Saxon Poetic Records, 3, New York, Columbia University Press, 1936.

Leslie, R. F., *Three Old English Elegies,* Manchester, Manchester University Press, 1961.

Lord, Albert Bates, "Beowulf and Odysseus," in *Franciplegius: Medieval and Linguistic Studies in Honor of Francis Peabody Magoun, Jr.,* ed. Jess B. Bessinger, Jr., and Robert P. Creed, (New York, New York University Press, 1965), pp. 86–91.

Magoun, Francis P., Jr., "*Béowulf B:* a Folk-Poem on Béowulf's Death," in *Early English and Norse Studies Presented to Hugh Smith,* ed. Arthur Brown and Peter Foote (London, Methuen, 1963), pp. 127–40.

Malone, Kemp, "Coming Back from the Mere," *PMLA, 69* (1954), 1292–99.

———, "Royal Names in Old English Poetry," *Studies in Heroic Legend and Current Speech,* ed. Stefán Einarsson and Norman E. Eliason, Copenhagen, Rosenkilde and Bagger, 1959.

Moorman, Charles, "The Essential Paganism of *Beowulf,*" *Modern Language Quarterly,* 28 (1967), 3–18.

Nicholson, Lewis E., "The Literal Meaning and Symbolic Structure of *Beowulf,*" *Classica et Mediaevelia,* 25 (1964), 151–201.

Pepperdene, M. W., "Beowulf and the Coast-Guard," *English Studies, 41* (1966), 409–19.

Pirkhofer, Anton, *Figurengestaltung im Beowulf-Epos,* Heidelberg, C. Winter, 1940.

Pope, John C., "*Beowulf* 3150–3151. Queen Hygd and the Word 'Geomeowle,' " *Modern Language Notes,* 70 (1955), 77–87.

———, review of Arthur G. Brodeur's *The Art of Beowulf, Speculum,* 37 (1962), 411–17.

Quirk, Randolph, "Poetic Language and Old English Metre," in *Early English and Norse Studies Presented to Hugh Smith,* ed. Arthur Brown and Peter Foote (London, Methuen, 1963), pp. 150–71.

———, *The Concessive Relation in Old English Poetry,* New Haven, Yale University Press, 1954.

Renoir, Alain, "The Heroic Oath in *Beowulf,* the *Chanson de Roland,* and the *Nibelungenlied,*" in *Studies in Old English Literature in Honor of Arthur G. Brodeur,* ed. Stanley B. Greenfield (Eugene, Ore., University of Oregon Press, 1963), pp. 237–66.

Ringler, Richard N., "*Him Seo Wen Geleah:* The Design for Irony in Grendel's Last Visit to Heorot," *Speculum, 41* (1966), 49–67.

Roper, Alan H., "Boethius and the Three Fates of *Beowulf,*" *Philological Quarterly, 41* (1962), 286–400.

Rosier, James L., "Design for Treachery: the Unferth Intrigue," *PMLA,* 77 (1962), 1–7.

———, "The Uses of Association: Hands and Feasts in *Beowulf,*" *PMLA,* 78 (1963), 8–14.

Schücking, Levin L., "Heldenstolz und Würde im Angelsächsischen, mit einem Anhang: Zur Charakterisierungstechnik im Beowulfepos," *Abhandlungen der Philologisch-historischen Klasse der sächsischen Akademie der Wissenschaften,* 42, No. 5, Leipzig, 1933.

Sisam, Kenneth, *The Structure of Beowulf,* Oxford, Clarendon Press, 1965.

Stanley, E. G., "*Beowulf,*" in *Continuations and Beginnings: Studies in Old English Literature* (London, Nelson, 1966), pp. 104–41.

———, "Hæthenra Hyht in *Beowulf,*" in *Studies in Old English Literature in Honor of Arthur G. Brodeur,* ed. Stanley B. Greenfield (Eugene, Ore., University of Oregon Press, 1963), pp. 136–51.

Taylor, Paul Beekman, "Heorot, Earth, and Asgard: Christian Poetry and Pagan Myth," *Tennessee Studies in Literature, 11* (1966), 119–30.

The Epic of Gilgamesh, English version by N. K. Sandars, Baltimore, Penguin Books, 1960.

Tolkien, J. R. R., "*Beowulf:* the Monsters and the Critics," *Proceedings of the British Academy,* 22 (1936), 245–95.

Watts, Harold H., "Myth and Drama," in *Tragedy: Modern Essays in Criticism,* ed. Laurence Michel and Richard B. Sewall (Englewood Cliffs, N. J., Prentice-Hall, 1963), pp. 83–105.

Weyhe, Hans, "König Ongentheows Fall," *Englische Studien,* 39 (1908), 14–39.

Whitelock, Dorothy, "*Beowulf,* 11. 2444–2471," *Medium Ævum,* 8 (1939), 198–204.

———, *The Audience of Beowulf,* Oxford, Clarendon Press, 1951.

Wright, Herbert W., "Good and Evil; Light and Darkness; Joy and Sorrow in *Beowulf,*" *Review of English Studies* (n.s.), 8 (1957), 1–11.

INDEX OF PASSAGES QUOTED FROM *BEOWULF*

Where only a brief phrase is quoted or where the passage is merely paraphrased or alluded to, the page number is given in parentheses.